Rarotonga
& the Cook Islands

Nancy Keller
Tony Wheeler

D0104792

Rarotonga & the Cook Islands

4th edition

Published by
> **Lonely Planet Publications**
> Head Office: PO Box 617, Hawthorn, Vic 3122, Australia
> Branches: 155 Filbert St, Suite 251, Oakland, CA 94607, USA
> 10a Spring Place, London NW5 3BH, UK
> 71 bis rue du Cardinal Lemoine, 75005 Paris, France

Printed by
> SNP Printing Pte Ltd, Singapore

Photographs by
> Nancy Keller & Tony Wheeler

> Front cover: Palm trees on beach, Aitutaki (Stefand Scata – The Image Bank)

First Published
> December 1986

This Edition
> June 1998

Although the authors and publisher have tried to make the information as accurate as possible, they accept no responsibility for any loss, injury or inconvenience sustained by any person using this book.

National Library of Australia Cataloguing in Publication Data

> Keller, Nancy J.
> Rarotonga & the Cook Islands

> 4th ed.
> Includes index.
> ISBN 0 86442 553 8.

> 1. Cook Islands - Guidebooks.
> I. Title
> II: Rarotonga and the Cook Islands

919.62304

Nancy Keller

Born and raised in northern California, Nancy worked in the alternative press for several years, doing every aspect of newspaper work from editorial and reporting to delivering the papers. She returned to university to earn a master's degree in journalism, finally graduating in 1986. She's been travelling and writing ever since. Nancy has been author or co-author of several Lonely Planet books including guidebooks to Tonga, New Zealand, California & Nevada, Mexico and Central America.

Tony Wheeler

Tony was born in England but grew up in Pakistan, the Bahamas and the USA. He returned to England to do a degree in engineering at Warwick University, worked as an automotive design engineer, returned to London Business School to complete an MBA, then set out on an Asian overland trip with his wife Maureen. That trip led to Tony and Maureen founding Lonely Planet Publications in Australia in 1973, and they've been travelling, writing and publishing guidebooks ever since.

From Nancy Keller

I would like to dedicate this book to Kia Raina Mataiapo.

I owe great thanks to many people throughout the Cook Islands for their help while researching and writing this edition.

On Rarotonga, thanks to Io Tuakeu-Lindsay (Director) and Papatua Papatua of the Cook Islands Tourist Authority, and to Ewan Smith and Teariki ('Bubs') Numanga of Air Rarotonga. Thanks to Gerald McCormack of the Cook Islands Natural Heritage Project, and to Judith Kunzlé. Thanks also to Papa Tuti Taringa, Emil Cowan, Piri & Ricky Puruto and Moe, to the Baha'is, and to Titikaveka CICC. Thanks also, as always, to Papa Tangaroa Kainuku.

On Aitutaki, thanks to Tom & Mimau, Mr and Mrs Tunui Tereu, Josie, Robert Imagire, Nane Herman and Tuanu Tukoutu (Joshua) Ka.

On Atiu, thanks to Andrea and Juergen Manske-Eimke, and to Roger and Kura Malcolm. On Mauke, thanks to Nan Greenwood, Tapu and Disney, and to CAO Tautara Purea. On Mitiaro, thanks once again to Nane Pokoati.

On Mangaia, thanks to tourism director Poko Otheniel, CAO Otheniel Tangianau, Liz and Tuaine Papatua, Nga Teaio, Babe Pokino and Atingakau Tangatakino ('the GR').

On Manihiki, greetings to Kauraka Kauraka – rest in peace.

Thanks to Francis Mortimer of Air New Zealand's Auckland office for help with gathering details on Air New Zealand's services.

This Book
Tony Wheeler wrote the 1st edition of *Rarotonga & the Cook Islands*; Nancy Keller has updated all subsequent editions.

From the Publisher
This book was edited and proofed in Lonely Planet's Melbourne office by Rowan McKinnon with help from Steve Womersley, Sarah Mathers and Liz Filleul. Mark Griffiths and Helen Rowley drew the maps, and Mark also prepared the colour pages. The layout of the book was done by Jane Hart. Mark and Jane were both responsible for the book's design, and Jane and Judith Kunzlé did the illustrations. Mic Looby drew the cartoon for the No Dancing in Hurricane Season aside, Margaret Jung designed the front cover and Paul Clifton drew the back-cover map. Thanks to Quentin Frayne for his work on the language section and for the macron mirth.

Thanks
Many thanks to the travellers who used the last edition and wrote to us with helpful hints, useful advice and interesting anecdotes:

Ruth Prosser & Bruce Allan, Sven Armbrust, Belinda Beattie, Elizabeth Bullen, J Burkhardt, Dr John Cameron, Frederick D Coquelin, Elizabeth Crockett, Ulf Ellervik, Andre & Ursula Fischbach, B van Gaalen, Peter Gappmaier, D & R Godfrey, Diane & Roger Godfrey, Gary Graham, Birgit Heldmann, Jim Hendrickson, T Hill, Karen Hong, Norma Jenkin, Ben & Jennie, Anne-Christine Kahrs, Andreas Krueger, C & L Lee, Josvan Loo, Nancy Maguire, Simon McKinney, Urs Meier, Chris Kelly & Rudy Moberg, Linda Moore, Andrew Mortimer, Wolfgang Muhlbauer, Tim Searle, Peter Taylor and Martin Williams

Warning & Request
Things change – prices go up, schedules change, good places go bad and bad places go bankrupt – nothing stays the same. So, if you find things better or worse, recently opened or long since closed, please tell us and help make the next edition even more accurate and useful.

We value all of the feedback we receive from travellers. Julie Young coordinates a small team that reads and acknowledges every letter, postcard and email, and ensures that every morsel of information finds its way to the appropriate authors, editors and publishers.

Everyone who writes to us will find their name in the next edition of the appropriate guide and will also receive a free subscription to our quarterly newsletter, *Planet Talk*. The very best contributions will be rewarded with a free Lonely Planet guide.

Excerpts from your correspondence may appear in new editions of this guide; in our newsletter, *Planet Talk*; or in updates on our Web site – so please let us know if you don't want your letter published or your name acknowledged.

Contents

Boxed Asides

The 'Great Migration' 12	Tairi Terangi Meets his End
Cannibalism.. 14	at Tokongarangi 136
Strange Names....................................... 27	Aitutaki Gets a Mountain 137
Island Houses.. 30	Tapuaetai (One Foot Island) 138
Land Ownership 30	The Coral Route 141
Shooting Video 48	Bush Beer Schools 149
The International Date Line 49	Tutaka & Tivaevae 154
Aviation History..................................... 70	No Dancing in Hurricane
Air Travel Glossary 74	Season 155
Flying in the Cooks 80	The Wreck of the *Edna*....................... 156
Cook Islands' Interisland	The People of Mauke 158
Shipping Services............................ 82	The Divided Church............................. 159
Why the Shipping Services Don't	Kovitoa Ariki & Marae O Rongo.......... 160
Run to Schedule 81	Kea's Grave... 161
Matu Rori 114	Sweet Peat 164
Dogs & Pigs... 132	Terevai 164

Map Legend

BOUNDARIES

━ ·━ ·━ ·━ ·	...............International Boundary
━ ··━ ··━ ··━ ··	...................Provincial Boundary

ROUTES

════════════	.... Major Road
════════════	.... Minor Road
════════════	..............Minor Road - unsealed
────────────	...................................City Road
────────────	...................................City Street
────────────	.... City Lane
▭▭▭▭▭▭▭▭▭	.... Steps on Street
▨▨▨▨▨▨▨▨	.........................Path thru a park
··················	.............................Walking Tour
────────────	...............................Ferry Route
────────────	.... Walking Track

AREA FEATURES

▬▬▬▬	.....................................Building
✝✝✝✝✝	..................................Cemetery
░░░░░	....Beach
▦▦▦▦	.... Market
✿	.........................Park, Gardens
～～～	.... Reef
▬▬▬▬	.... Urban Area

HYDROGRAPHIC FEATURES

～～～	...................................Coastline
～～～	.... Creek, River
⬮ ⬮	..............Lake, Intermittent Lake
≫──≫≫──	.... Rapids, Waterfalls
⬮	....Salt Lake
⚘ ⚘ ⚘ ⚘ ⚘	.... Swamp

SYMBOLS

❂	**CAPITAL**	.........National Capital	✈	......................Airport	▲	..........Mountain or Hill
◉	**CAPITAL**	......Provincial Capital	⸪	....Archaeological Site	⌒⌒	.... Mountain Range
●	**CITY**	...................................City	❺	.........................Bank	🏛	..................Museum
●	**Town**	...................................Town	🏖	......................Beach	←	.........One Way Street
●	Village	...................................Village	ᴔ	...............Bicycle Track	🅿	....................Parking
			⌒	.........................Cave	)(	.... Pass
■		............Place to Stay	🏛	......................Church	⛽	............Petrol Station
🏕		.... Camping Ground	⌒⌒⌒	.... Cliff or Escarpment	★	.... Police Station
🚐		...........Caravan Park	◓	................Embassy	✉	.... Post Office
🏠		............Hut or Chalet	⚑	..........................Golf	❖	.... Shopping Centre
			⊕	....................Hospital	☎	.................Telephone
▼		..............Place to Eat	✳	....................Lookout	▣	.......................Tomb
🍺		.... Pub or Bar	🗼	.... Lighthouse	❶	....Tourist Information
			◪	.... Marae	⬭	.... Transport
			⚱	.................Monument	☤	.... Shipwreck

Note: not all symbols displayed above appear in this book

Introduction

The tiny and remote Cook Islands are Polynesia in a conveniently handy, though widely scattered, package. They offer something for nearly everyone. Rarotonga, the main island, is a spectacularly beautiful island – mountainous like Tahiti and cloaked in dense jungle. Surrounded by a protective coral reef, it has idyllic soft white-sand beaches fringed by rustling coconut palms and clear turquoise waters full of colourful tropical fish. It also has everything from modern resort facilities to backpackers' hostels, excellent restaurants and great entertainment, all on an island just 32km around. 'Raro' is the entry point for 99% of visitors to the Cooks as it is the location for the international airport.

Rarotonga is only the starting point for exploring the Cook Islands. From Raro you can fly or, if you're feeling hardy and adventurous, ship by passenger freighter to the other islands of the southern group. Aitutaki is by far the best known with its huge turquoise lagoon fringed but, picture-postcard islets. Aitutaki is a combination of high island and atoll and is a frequent nominee for any 'most beautiful island in the Pacific' award. If Raro is the Tahiti of the Cooks then Aitutaki is the Bora Bora.

Few visitors go farther than these two principal islands but that's a great shame because some of the others are equally interesting. Atiu, Mitiaro, Mauke and Mangaia are geological curiosities with fringing, raised-fossil reefs known as *makatea*, weird and beautiful areas of razor-sharp coral formations riddled with limestone caves. Stalactites and stalagmites may seem a

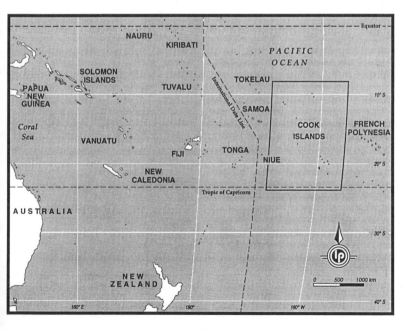

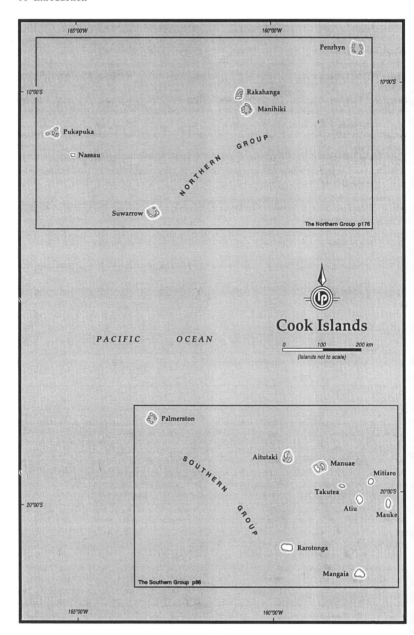

strange thing to find on a tropical island but the caves are full of them. There's also a cave on Atiu inhabited by a tiny, unique swallow known as the *kopeka* and the island has countless burial caves.

Finally, there are the remote islands of the northern group. These are the classic low atolls of the Pacific and you need persistence to explore them. Though airstrips were built on a couple of them during WWII, they subsequently went without air connections for many decades due to their isolation and it's only within the past few years that three of them – Manihiki, Penrhyn and Pukapuka – have been reached by regular air services. It takes quite a while and costs quite a bit to get there, so most of the travel to the northern group is still done by sea; these remote coral atolls are still seldom visited.

Of course islands aren't all there is to the

Cooks – there are also the Cook Islanders themselves. Some say these handsome, easy-going people are the friendliest folk in the Pacific. They certainly have some of the most spectacular dancers and an evening at an 'island night' is an experience you will long remember.

There are plenty of activities to keep you busy if you're so inclined – swimming, snorkelling, diving, deep-sea fishing, canoeing, sailing, windsurfing, cycling, motorcycling, walking, hiking and climbing are all possibilities. Somehow though, time seems to go slower in the Cooks than in other places and you may soon find that the most enjoyable thing to do is to slow down, take it easy and relax into the peaceful way of life and the voluptuous beauty all around you. 'The Cooks are like Tahiti as it was 20 years ago,' say the promoters. It's a great place.

Facts about the Country

HISTORY

Although the Cook Islands only have a written history from the time of the arrival of Europeans, they have a rich oral history that has been passed on for many generations. Archaeologists have discovered many early religious ceremonial grounds, or *marae*, and traces of early settlements many centuries old on several of the islands.

Polynesian Settlement

The Cook Islanders are Polynesians, people of the 'many' (*poly*) islands of the South Pacific. They are Maori people, distantly related to the New Zealand Maori, and their language is Cook Islands Maori, closely related to New Zealand Maori and also to the Polynesian languages of Tahiti and Hawaii.

It is thought that 40,000 years ago the Pacific region was totally uninhabited. Around that time people started to move down from Asia and settled Australia and Melanesia – the 'black islands' which include modern Papua New Guinea. The Australian Aboriginals and the tribes of Papua New Guinea are the descendants of this first wave of Pacific settlers. The islands of Micronesia ('tiny islands') and Polynesia ('many islands') remained uninhabited until around 5000 to 6000 years ago. At this time the Austronesian people of South-East Asia started to move beyond Papua New Guinea to the islands which now comprise the Solomons, Vanuatu and Fiji.

The Austronesian language group includes the languages of South-East Asia (from Indonesian to Vietnamese) and the languages of the Pacific which developed as a sub-group as people moved into the Pacific. Around 1500 BC people moved on from Fiji to Tonga and this group is assumed to have included the ancestors of all the Polynesian people. Their language gradually diverged to become Polynesian as settlers moved to Samoa around 300 BC and to the Society Islands and Marquesas (now both part of French Polynesia) in the early years AD. The final great waves of Polynesian migration are thought to have taken place around 400 AD to Easter Island and between 500 and 800 AD to the other islands of modern French Polynesia, the Cook Islands and to New Zealand. Pukapuka in the Cooks, however, is thought to have been settled directly from Samoa or even earlier from Tonga.

It's uncertain exactly when the first settlers did reach the Cook Islands, but modern historians believe that the Polynesian migrations through the Cook Islands began around the 5th century AD. Oral history traces Rarotongan ancestry back about 1400 years.

The 'Great Migration'

One of Rarotonga's most notable historical moments occurred around 1350 AD, when Avana Harbour in Ngatangiia was the starting point for the fleet of canoes now often referred to in New Zealand as the 'Great Migration'. It was in this year that the Maori canoes voyaged to Aotearoa ('the land of the long white cloud'), bringing the settlers that became the great ancestors of the present-day New Zealand Maori tribes.

These New Zealand Maori tribes, named after the canoes on which their ancestors came, all trace their genealogies to an ancestor that arrived on one of the 'Great Canoes'. You can go to Avana Harbour and see the spot from where the canoes departed. Opposite the big white Ngatangiia CICC church at Avana Harbour is a circle of seven stones, commemorating seven canoes that completed the voyage: *Takitumu, Tokomaru, Kurahaupo, Aotea, Tainui, Te Arawa* and *Mataatua*. Some of these canoes came from Rarotonga, some from other islands, but they all gathered here to receive a blessing before setting out for Aotearoa. ■

In 1997 a team of Japanese archaeologists came upon a marae estimated to be about 1500 years old on Motutapu (one of the small islands off the coast of Rarotonga). On Rarotonga the ancient road, known as Ara Metua, still encircling most of Rarotonga, is about 1000 years old.

The oldest archaeologically dated item in the Cook Islands is a dog skull dated at 2300 years old, found on the island of Pukapuka. Dogs are not native to the Cook Islands. How did that dog skull show up here?

In common with other Polynesian peoples, Cook Islanders' legends say that the ancestors of ancient times originated from the legendary homeland of Avaiki (spelt Hawai'i, Hawai'iki etc in other parts of Polynesia). The exact location of Avaiki has been lost in history; it isn't modern-day Hawaii, but the similarity of names suggests that modern Hawaii was probably named after the ancestral homeland.

Early Cook Islands Society

Rarotonga has always been the most important island of the Cooks and it's assumed the culture of its early inhabitants was largely duplicated on the other islands.

Pre-European Rarotonga was divided into three districts (Te Au O Tonga, Puaikura and Takitumu), each of which was governed by a hierarchy of chiefs, the most important of whom was the *ariki*, or paramount high chief. The districts were subdivided into *tapere* populated by a related group known as *ngati* and headed by a chief ranking directly below the ariki, known as a *mataiapo*. Next in rank, just below and answerable to the ariki or mataiapo, were the *rangatira*.

Tapere were typically around 150 hectares in area and had a population of around 100 to 200. Each tapere had its own marae, an open-air religious meeting ground marked by stones. The *koutu* was a similar centre, used for secular meetings and political functions. Larger marae and koutu served entire districts.

Although in some respects this pattern of relationship and land ownership was firmly

entrenched, in other ways it was quite flexible. The line of chieftainship, for example, was not totally based on the male line and early European visitors gravely misunderstood the Rarotongan system by trying to translate what they observed into purely European terms. Hereditary titles could also be created and an ariki who became particularly powerful might could create rangatira titles as a reward for his faithful supporters.

A chief's control over his people was related to his *mana*, a sort of supernatural power which he was believed to possess. A person's mana came not only from his birth but also from his achievements and status. Mana could not only be gained; it could also be lost. An ariki who became unpopular (eg by interfering excessively in the distribution of crops) might suddenly find that his followers perceived a dramatic decline in his mana, which could even lead to his losing control.

Control of *tapu* was a powerful weapon for an ariki. For supernatural reasons, certain activities were tapu, or forbidden, and since a chief could often decide what was or was not tapu this gave him considerable power. It was the people's strong belief in an ariki's combination of inherent mana and control of tapu which made the ariki so powerful and allowed them to exert control over their people without necessarily having the physical means to enforce their will. The early missionaries failed to fully understand the structure of the Rarotongan society and virtually ignored the operations of the pre-European religion.

Within the ariki system was another class of people with tremendous power – the *taunga*. Taunga were experts, and there were taunga in many fields; there could be a taunga for woodcarving, another for agriculture, another for navigation etc. Most powerful of all, even more powerful than the ariki in certain ways, was the taunga in charge of spiritual matters. The principal connection between the people and the powerful spirits of gods and ancestors, these taunga could have even more mana than the ariki they served under – for while an ariki could gain or lose mana through his actions in relation to the people, a powerful taunga had the much greater powers of the spirit world on his side and only a more powerful taunga would dare to challenge him. Another very important taunga was the one charged with memorising the tribal history and genealogy. These taunga were like living libraries in a society where there was no written word. Taunga were trained rigorously from childhood in their particular skills.

The islands were not as extensively cultivated as the first missionaries' reports may

---

Cannibalism

At one time the Cook Islanders certainly practised cannibalism. Although the early islanders rarely ate meat (their pigs were poor specimens and difficult to breed) there were plenty of fish and cannibalism was not, as it has been in some areas of the world, a protein supplement. It appears that in the Cooks it was an activity more closely associated with the supernatural acquisition of the *mana*, or power, of one's adversaries. It was also a way of exacting revenge: to eat your defeated opponent was probably the most telling indignity you could subject him to. The pioneering missionary William Wyatt Gill reported the following cannibal recipe:

The long spear, inserted at the fundament, ran through the body, appearing again with the neck. As on a spit, the body was slowly singed over a fire, in order that the entire cuticle and all the hair might be removed. The intestines were next taken out, washed in sea-water, wrapped up in singed banana leaves (a singed banana-leaf, like oil-silk, retains liquid), cooked and eaten, this being the invariable perquisite of those who prepared the feast. The body was cooked, as pigs now are, in an oven specially set apart, red-hot basaltic stones, wrapped in leaves, being placed inside to insure its being equally done. The best joint was the thigh.

If you really want to learn something about the practice of cannibalism in the Cooks, read *Cannibals & Converts* by Maretu (see the Books section of the Facts for the Visitor Chapter), who is the only author who has written not only as a historian but also as a participant. ■

---

have indicated and many crops were disastrously susceptible to the occasional severe hurricanes. A bad storm could completely destroy an island's crops and lead to terrible famines until replanting could be completed.

European Explorers

The Spanish explorers Alvaro de Mendana and Pedro Fernandez de Quiros were the first Europeans to sight islands in the group. Pukapuka in the north was the first, sighted by Alvaro de Mendana on 20 August 1595. Eleven years later, on 2 March 1606, Pedro Fernandez de Quiros stopped at Rakahanga, also in the northern group, to take on provisions.

There is no record of further European contact for over 150 years, until in his expeditions of 1773 and 1777 Captain James Cook explored much of the group, although the only island that he personally set foot on was the tiny atoll of Palmerston, which was uninhabited at the time.

Remarkably, Captain Cook never sighted the largest island, Rarotonga. That honour was left to the mutineers on HMS *Bounty* who touched upon Rarotonga in 1789. The mutiny actually took place after the *Bounty* sailed from Aitutaki. From Rarotonga the mutineers sailed on to Pitcairn Island in their search for a refuge far from the reach of the long arm of the British navy.

Cook, following what was virtually an English tradition of attaching truly terrible names to truly exotic places, dubbed the southern group islands the Hervey Islands in honour of a British Lord of the Admiralty. Half a century later a Russian cartographer, Admiral John von Krusenstern, published an atlas, the *Atlas de l'Océan Pacifique*, in which he renamed the islands to honour Captain Cook, who had been killed in Hawaii in 1779, a couple of years after his final visit to the Herveys. The northern group islands were called variously the Penrhyn Islands, the Manihiki Islands and a few other names. It was not until the turn of the century when the islands were annexed by New Zealand that the whole southern and northern group became known by one name.

Captain James Cook

Missionaries

Missionaries followed the explorers. Reverend John Williams of the London Missionary Society (LMS) made his first appearance in the Cooks at the island of Aitutaki in 1821, after sailing from French Polynesia. He left two Polynesian 'teachers' behind and when he returned two years later they had made remarkable progress. Indeed, the conversion of the Cook Islanders, generally accomplished in its initial stages by Polynesian converts, went far faster and more easily than it had done in the Society Islands, from where these missionaries generally came.

Papeiha, the most successful of these original missionaries, was moved to Rarotonga in 1823 and he laboured there for the rest of his life. In that period the missionaries totally swept across the islands and established religious control which has held strong to this day. They did their best to completely wipe out the original island religion, establishing what was virtually a religious police state. The height of their power was from 1835 to

1880 when their rigid and fiercely enforced laws were backed up by a system in which money from fines imposed on wrongdoers was split between the police and judges. Naturally this turned police work into an extremely lucrative profession and in parts of Rarotonga one person in every six was in the police force, ready and willing to turn in their neighbours for a cut in the proceeds. The missionary 'Blue Laws' included strict limitations on what you could do and where you could go on a Sunday. There was even a law requiring any man who walked with an arm around a woman after dark to carry a light in his other hand!

Although their influence was huge, the missionaries left the actual government of the islands to the tribal chiefs, or ariki. Therefore while Rarotonga, established as the Cook Islands' headquarters for the LMS, became an important administrative and religious centre for the islands, it was not a government centre. The individual Cook Islands remained as separate and independent political entities. Due to their relative isolation, small populations, lack of economic importance and their generally poor harbour facilities the islands were largely neglected and ignored by traders, whalers and the European powers. The missionaries also worked hard at keeping other Europeans at arm's length.

The fact that the ariki system, the traditional system of land inheritance, the indigenous language and many other cultural attributes have remained intact shows that the missionaries did not completely obliterate the original island culture, despite the drastic changes they brought. Even the traditional religion, which had been abandoned by the entire population as far as the missionaries knew, continued to survive among a select few.

Disease, Population Decline & Slavers

The missionaries intended to bring far more than just Christianity to the islands of Polynesia: they planned to bring peace, an end to cannibalism and infanticide, and a general improvement in living standards. They also brought previously unknown diseases and did many things to destroy the islanders' traditional culture. The consequences were a drastic and long-lasting population decline. The Cook Islanders took the onslaught of deadly new diseases as a message from above to abandon their old religion and fall in with the new.

Undoubtedly the diseases would have soon arrived – courtesy of traders and whalers – whether or not the missionaries had brought them, but the statistics are nevertheless horrifying. When the missionaries first arrived on Rarotonga in 1823 the population was probably around 6000 to 7000 (it's around 11,000 today). The first major assault on the population was the arrival of dysentery from Tahiti in 1830, which killed nearly 1000 people in a single year. Common European diseases, from whooping cough to measles, smallpox and influenza, followed. Each was previously unknown in the Cooks and each took a terrible toll.

Throughout the 19th century deaths exceeded births and by 1854, when an accurate census was finally taken, the population of Rarotonga was less than 2500 – about two-thirds of the population had died in just 31 years. By 1867 the population had dropped to just 1856, and although migration from other islands began to create an artificial increase in the population of Rarotonga the decline in the group's total population did not start to level out until the late 19th century. It was not until early in the 20th century that a real increase in population began.

The trend of migrating from the outer islands to Rarotonga which commenced in the 19th century continued, so that although the population decline on Rarotonga slowed, it was only due to a greater decline on other islands. Many islanders left for work on other Pacific islands, particularly Tahiti, but also on various plantation islands established by European traders. This migration continues to the present day as islanders move first to Rarotonga and then on to New Zealand or Australia.

The new housing designs introduced by the missionaries were damp and poorly ventilated and probably contributed to the death rate. However, disease was not the only cause of the drop in population. A brutal Peruvian slave trade took a terrible toll on the islands of the northern group, despite only lasting a mere seven months from late 1862. At first the traders may have genuinely operated as labour recruiters but they quickly turned to subterfuge and outright kidnapping to round up their human cargoes. The Cook Islands were not the only ones visited by the traders but Tongareva (Penrhyn) was their first port of call and it has been estimated that three-quarters of the population was taken. Rakahanga and Pukapuka also suffered tremendous losses.

Few of the recruits, whether they went freely, as many did in the beginning, or through baser methods, ever returned to the islands. Over 90% died in transit to Peru, died in Peru, or died while being repatriated. At the time of repatriation efforts Peru was suffering from a terrible smallpox epidemic and many Polynesians died from this while travelling back or, far worse, introduced the disease to their islands.

The islanders' limited contact with westerners, and the fact that what little contact they had experienced had been relatively benign, were major factors in why they were easy prey for the South Americans. As the missionary William Wyatt Gill commented:

Their simplicity of character, their kindness to visitors, their utter ignorance of the depths of depravity and deceit in the hearts of wicked white men, render them the easy dupes of designing characters.

Protectorate & Annexation

Despite their considerable influence through the missionaries, the British did not formally take control of the Cook Islands until 1888. In that year the islands were declared a British protectorate by a Captain Bourke who arrived off Rarotonga in the warship HMS *Hyacinth*. To some extent this inevitable, although reluctant, extension of British control was due to fears that the French might extend their power from neighbouring Tahiti in the Society Islands.

It is indicative of the hasty manner in which the British finally took over the islands that they failed to make a firm decision on just which islands would be included in the protectorate. The unfortunate Captain Bourke also got the ceremony wrong and *annexed* the islands rather than simply bringing them under British protection! This caused some embarrassment and later the process had to be reversed in the southern islands where he had hoisted the flag, although for some reason Aitutaki remained annexed. One by one the islands in the southern and northern groups were brought under British control.

The first British Resident (the representative of the British government in a British protectorate), FJ Moss, arrived in 1891 but his period in the islands was not a great success. In part this was due to his basic failure to understand the complexities of the ariki system, and the inappropriate application of European economic assumptions. FJ Moss was given the shove with some lack of ceremony in 1898 and the new Resident, WE Gudgeon, adopted a totally different method of running the islands. He ruled with an iron hand but his methods were also far from universally successful.

In the late 1890s the question of whether the islands should be associated with Britain or New Zealand was batted back and forth. Finally, in 1900 Rarotonga and the other main southern islands were annexed to New Zealand, and in 1901 the net was widened to encompass all the southern and northern islands.

Population & Economics

A major problem facing the islands during the early years of British power was the steadily declining population. The combination of disease, slavery and migration meant that the islands' population had fallen to less than half the precontact level. Gudgeon, whose opinion of the islanders under his charge was far from complimentary, was convinced they were a dying race. In the early part of the 20th century the population started to slowly increase, although there were continuing migration losses, first to Tahiti and later to New Zealand.

Economics was another major problem and an answer to the islands' economic difficulties is still far away. Prior to their takeover, the New Zealand Government was convinced that the Cooks could easily be made self-sufficient but this turned out to be a frequently repeated fallacy. The easy-going Polynesian nature, combined with shipping difficulties which continue to this day, defeated all attempts to tap the obvious agricultural richness of the islands, particularly the volcanic islands of the south.

Improvement of the islands' economic situation was felt by some officials to be hampered by the ariki system and land-ownership patterns. Since land was traditionally controlled by the ariki, commoners did not have land to grow produce and the ariki often preferred to leave land unused rather than set a precedent for use by outsiders. The power of the ariki has gradually been weakened but they wield a lot of influence even today and the land-ownership system is still a major disincentive to improving the use of agricultural land.

Independence

During WWII the USA built airstrips on Penrhyn and Aitutaki, but essentially the Cooks remained a quiet and forgotten New Zealand dependency. In the 1960s it was belatedly realised that colonies were becoming an aberration and the path to independence was plotted with considerable haste. In 1965 the Cook Islands became internally self-governing but foreign policy and defence were left to New Zealand. The continuing problem of the population drain accelerated after independence.

The close links with New Zealand have precluded the Cook Islands from taking a seat in the United Nations, although the islanders derive a number of benefits from their relation to New Zealand, including New Zealand citizenship and the right to come and go at will from both New Zealand

and Australia. Not only is the population of Cook Islanders in New Zealand actually greater than in the Cook Islands themselves but it is also a very important source of income for the nation.

Modern Politics

Elections in 1968 installed Albert Henry, leader of the Cook Islands Party and a prime mover in the push for independence, as the Cooks Islands' first prime minister. In 1972 he was once again elected prime minister and in January 1974 he was knighted by Queen Elizabeth II. Sir Albert was an Aitutakian and it's said that the people of this island are such keen arguers and debaters that they'll get themselves into trouble simply for the joy of talking their way out of it. In the 1978 elections Sir Albert got himself into deep trouble.

The problem revolved around the great number of Cook Islanders living overseas, principally in New Zealand. Sir Albert feared that the forthcoming election was going to be a close one and dreamt up the ingenious plan of organising a series of charter flights from Auckland, New Zealand, to Rarotonga, bringing back hordes of Cook Islanders for a short vacation and a quick visit to the polling booths – where they would gratefully vote for the provider of their free tickets. It worked wonderfully: 445 Cook Islanders were flown back by the Australian airline Ansett at a cost of A$290,000 and Sir Albert was duly re-elected.

Then came the protests of electoral fraud. A High Court case followed and eventually Sir Albert was kicked out of office by the Chief Justice for misappropriation of public funds. In 1980 he was stripped of his knighthood and in early 1981 he died, some say broken-hearted. (You can see his unusual grave in the Avarua CICC church graveyard, complete with a bronze bust peering down at you wearing Sir Albert's own black spectacles.)

A truly multidimensional man, Dr Tom Davis, leader of the Democratic Party, became the new prime minister. Before returning to the Cook Islands to enter politics he'd qualified as a doctor in New Zealand,

become Chief Medical Officer to the islands, written a book titled *Doctor to the Islands*, studied in Australia, sailed a yacht to the USA, studied at Harvard and become an expert on space medicine with NASA.

In the next election in 1983, however, the Democratic Party was bundled out and another Henry took over as prime minister. Dr Davis had become Sir Thomas Davis during his period in power but in the 1983 election he even lost his seat in parliament. Unfortunately for the new leader, Geoffrey Henry, a cousin of Albert Henry, politics in the Cook Islands is a family affair and his family quickly turned against him. When another important Henry withdrew his support Geoffrey Henry soon found he'd lost his parliamentary majority. Parliament was dissolved, a new election was called and this time around the Democratic Party squeezed back in with Sir Thomas Davis once more prime minister. In his own electorate Sir Thomas' majority was just five votes in this second 1983 election.

In 1984, a split occurred in the governing Democratic Party. As a result, they lost their majority, and the loyal Democrats started lobbying with the opposing Cook Islands Party (CIP). This led to the first coalition, with the Democrat and CIP members aligning against the rebel Democrats. Also in 1984, Geoffrey Henry came in again, this time as deputy prime minister under Sir Thomas.

It was not to last for long. In 1985, just a couple of days before the South Pacific Forum convened on Rarotonga, Sir Thomas sacked Geoffrey Henry, and Terepai Maoate, the former deputy leader of the opposition under Geoffrey, took over as the deputy prime minister. This caused another split, resulting in another coalition, this time with loyalist Democrat and CIP members in alliance against a mixture of rebels from both parties.

In 1987, yet another split occurred. The entire cabinet was sacked by parliament and Sir Thomas was booted out as prime minister. Then the Democrat/CIP coalition elected all the same cabinet ministers back in again, with Dr Pupuke Robati, the former minister from the northern group island of Rakahanga, as prime minister. The deputy prime minister, Terepai Maoate, retained his seat.

In 1989 Geoffrey Henry was again returned to power as prime minister after five years in opposition. However, the CIP only managed to secure 12 out of the 24 contested seats.

Geoffrey, who became Sir Geoffrey during his five-year term of office, presided over the construction of the Sir Geoffrey Henry National Cultural Centre in Avarua and the 6th international Festival of Pacific Arts, known as the Maire Nui, in October 1992. Though his administration enjoyed many successes, as the 1994 election approached there was widespread public discontent with his government for various reasons.

Nevertheless, Sir Geoffrey's party, the CIP, won a landslide victory in the March 1994 election, winning 20 of the 25 parliamentary seats. The Democratic Party secured three seats and the Alliance – the new coalition party formed by a mixture of former Democrats and CIPs – won two. Norman George, leader of the Democratic Party, kept his seat as MP from Atiu, but former prime minister Sir Thomas Davis, who had returned from the USA to lead the Alliance Party, did not win even the seat he sought. Now in his mid-80s, author of several books and with a long and varied career behind him, Papa Tom said he thought he'd give the political fray a rest for a while.

Since 1994

Problems continued and escalated following the 1994 elections. A controversy concerning the Cook Islands' offshore banking industry and alleged international tax evasion, which had begun before the election, ripened into an international scandal known as the 'winebox affair', with New Zealand the principal complainant. Although wrongdoing was never proved in court, it made the Cook Islands look bad.

The biggest problem the Cook Islands faced during this period, though, was economic. When New Zealand decided it could no longer afford to go on supporting the Cook Islands' negative-cashflow economy with massive amounts of aid, a radical economic adjustment had to be made. In April 1996 Sir Geoffrey announced a severe economic stabilisation program which included a 50% reduction in government departments and ministries, a 50% reduction in pay for all remaining public sector workers, the privatisation of several government-owned enterprises and the closure of several overseas diplomatic missions.

Altogether Sir Geoffrey sacked about 2000 public servants, which in a country of around 20,000 inhabitants is a great proportion of the working population. A 'transition' project was set up to assist the newly unemployed workers, but with nowhere near enough work available in the private sector to accommodate all of these people, masses of them had no alternative but to leave the country in search of jobs elsewhere. Families throughout the Cook Islands were broken up as wage earners were forced to leave the country; in many cases, entire families were forced to emigrate. Most went to New Zealand and Australia, where they have working rights. Whether these people will ever be able to return to live in their homeland remains to be seen.

There was divided opinion about Sir Geoffrey's action. Many people said the government had become swollen with excess workers, and that the 'downsizing' of government was actually a 'rightsizing', for the benefit of the country. Many other people, quite understandably, were extremely dissatisfied with the state of affairs as the country was hit with massive unemployment and privation, an exodus of much of its population and a sharp decline in public services.

The bad news about the state of affairs in the Cooks went abroad to New Zealand and Australia, and resulted in yet further economic hardship as tourism, the Cook Islands' biggest money earner, suffered a sharp decline. Tourism figures did eventually recover, but only gradually.

In order to have a leader of the opposition a party must have a minimum of five members in parliament, so the Democratic and Alliance parties, with their two and three parliamentary seats respectively, merged during this term to form the Democratic Alliance Party. The leader of the opposition, Norman George, acted as a gadfly to the government in general and to the prime minister in particular. By late 1997, still with over a year to go before the 1999 elections, George was continually hounding Sir Geoffrey, using the press and every other means at his disposal to try to make Henry look bad. 'I want your job!' he continually exclaimed.

George was a blustery leader who did a number of things that embarrassed or aggravated his party. In November 1997 he received a severe shock when the members of the DAP caucus voted four to two to oust him from leadership, replacing him with Dr Terepai Maoate as the leader of the opposition in parliament and Dr Robert Woonton as the deputy opposition leader.

Norman George claimed his ousting was illegal and that since he was still officially the leader of the DAP party as a whole, he should still be the opposition leader in parliament as well. Nevertheless, his office in parliament, and his salary, had already been transferred to Dr Maoate. The annual DAP convention, which had long been scheduled for December 1997, continued despite the Maoate faction suddenly saying it was postponed until sometime in 1998. Amidst raging accusations by each side claiming the other had broken the rules of the party constitution, Norman George continued with the scheduled convention, which reconfirmed him as party leader and elected a new national council. Dr Maoate's faction, however, did not recognise either the convention or its outcome, and Maoate continued as the opposition leader in the parliament.

Many further dramas can be expected leading up to the 1999 election.

Politics may be colourful but the Cook Islands are generally quite stable, despite all the ins and outs of the various characters.

The government's biggest problem is managing the economy and trying to keep some sort of balance between the meagre exports and the avalanche of imports.

GEOGRAPHY

The Cook Islands have a total land area of just 241 sq km – that's about a quarter of the area of the Australian Capital Territory or of Rhode Island (the smallest US state). This inconspicuous land mass is scattered over about two million sq km of sea, an area as large as Western Europe. The islands are south of the equator, slightly east of the International Date Line and about midway between American Samoa and Tahiti. Rarotonga, directly south of Hawaii and about the same distance south of the equator as Hawaii is north, is 1260km from Tahiti and 3447km from Auckland, New Zealand.

The 15 islands are conveniently divided into northern and southern groups, separated by as much as 1000km of empty sea. The islands are:

Island	Land Area (in sq km)	Type
Southern Group		
Rarotonga	67.2	high volcanic
Mangaia	51.8	raised island
Atiu	26.9	raised island
Mitiaro	22.3	raised island
Mauke	18.4	raised island
Aitutaki	18.1	almost atoll
Manuae*	6.2	coral atoll
Palmerston	2.0	coral atoll
Takutea*	1.2	coral cay
Northern Group		
Penrhyn	9.8	coral atoll
Manihiki	9.8	coral atoll
Pukapuka	5.1	coral atoll
Rakahanga	4.1	coral atoll
Nassau	1.2	coral cay
Suwarrow	0.4	coral atoll

* unpopulated

There are some clear differences between the two groups quite apart from their geographical separation. The southern islands are younger volcanic islands, while the northern group islands are older coral atolls. The southern islands, constituting about 90% of the total land area of the Cook Islands, are generally larger, more heavily populated, economically better off and more closely connected with the outside world.

GEOLOGY

The Cook Islands lie on the Pacific Plate, a huge tectonic plate at the bottom of the Pacific Ocean. This plate is moving north-westwards at a rate of around 10cm a year. The creation of all the volcanic islands of the South Pacific is related to this geological movement in one way or another.

The southern group islands are actually a continuation of the Austral Islands in the south of French Polynesia, lying along the same north-west to south-east fracture in the earth's crust. Only Rarotonga, which is the youngest island in the Cooks group, is a straightforward volcanic, mountainous island like Tahiti in French Polynesia. Aitutaki has one small mountain, actually more of a large hill, but also a surrounding atoll reef like Bora Bora in French Polynesia. Technically, Aitutaki is properly called an 'almost atoll'.

Four of the southern group islands – Atiu, Mauke, Mitiaro and Mangaia – are raised islands. They were formed as volcanic islands in the distant past, and like other volcanic islands gradually became encircled by coral reefs. Over time the volcanic cones in their centres were eroded and slowly sank. About two million years ago, Rarotonga was formed in volcanic paroxysms which caused a buckling of the sea floor in the region nearby, causing these islands to be raised above sea level. This exposed the fringing reefs, which became rocky coastal areas known as *makatea*, surrounding central regions of volcanic soil. In Atiu and Mangaia the makatea surround hilly central plateaus while Mauke and Mitiaro are virtually flat with swampy central regions. Two of the southern group islands, Manuae and Takutea, are uninhabited and very small, and Palmerston is a coral atoll like the northern

group, and indeed is often included with those islands.

All the northern group islands are coral atolls and most take the classic Pacific form with an outer reef. encircling a lagoon and small islands dotting this reef. An atoll of this type is basically an old volcano that has come up from the sea floor and broken the surface as an island, with coral growing around the shallow edge. Over time, with a combination of erosion, gradual sinking and other factors, the volcanic cone becomes flattened to near sea level or even below it, while the large coral rim continues to grow.

All the northern islands except Penrhyn rise from the Manihiki Plateau, an area of the ocean bottom 3000m deep. Penrhyn rises from east of this platform where the ocean is 5000m deep. The Penrhyn volcano is thus much taller than those of the other northern group islands. Nassau is unique in the northern group because it is simply a single island with an encircling reef, not a group of islands around a lagoon. All the northern group atolls are very low – waves can wash right over them in hurricanes and you have to be very close to see them from a ship.

CLIMATE

The climate of the Cook Islands is very similar to that of Hawaii, although the seasons are reversed: January is the middle of summer, and August the middle of winter.

The Cooks have a pleasantly even climate year-round with no excesses of temperature, humidity or rainfall, although it can rain quite often. Rarotonga, with its high mountains, is very likely to be wet. Although you'd have to be unlucky to suffer one of the rare week-long rainy periods, be sure to bring rain gear with you at any time of year. The wettest months are usually December to March when around 25cm of rain can fall each month. These are also the hottest months, although the seasonal variation is slight, ranging from high/low temperatures of 29/23°C in February, the hottest month, down to 25/18°C in the coldest months of June, July, August and September. The summer months can feel quite warm and humid,

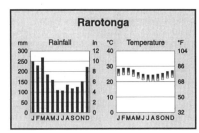

and the winter nights can sometimes be quite cool, even chilly.

Hurricane season is from November to March. On average a mild hurricane will pass by two or three times a decade but extremely severe hurricanes are a much rarer occurrence, averaging once every 20 years.

ECOLOGY & ENVIRONMENT

Waste management is a big issue in the Cook Islands, especially on Rarotonga which receives a high volume of packaged imported goods. Glass, plastic and aluminium are collected in special bins for recycling, but there's still a lot of rubbish and it must go somewhere.

Septic tanks are used for sewage waste, but when the septic tank is pumped out, where is the waste to go? So far, it has been used as fertiliser on agricultural plantations.

Water supplies and management are another big concern, both for agriculture and domestic use, and droughts have occurred in recent years.

Air pollution is unknown here; nevertheless, unleaded fuel has been introduced in order to reduce emissions into the atmosphere.

Government departments are assigned to handle issues such as erosion and deforestation. Following devastating fires on Mangaia in the early 1990s which left much of the island's hilly interior barren, much of the area was replanted with Caribbean pine trees, a species found to thrive here. Planted and cared for by the forestry service, the trees have prevented erosion and they are also expected to become a valuable timber crop.

Native flora and fauna are under siege on many fronts in the Cook Islands, as in many parts of the world. Clearing of land for agriculture and building, use and overuse of chemicals (eg herbicides, pesticides and fertilisers), introduced species that harm or compete with native species (eg mynah birds, cats and rats) are all factors that native species must contend with. Even the fish in the sea and lagoons are threatened by overfishing, destructive fishing methods and the leaching of chemicals and waste into the water.

The Cook Islands is trying to do something about all of this, but education and changes are needed, and they are needed fast.

Conservation programs have been established to protect some of the Cook Islands' rare native species of flora and fauna. For example, the Rarotonga flycatcher, or *kakerori*, until recently on the verge of extinction, is now making a comeback due to the efforts of a kakerori recovery program. It was discovered that rats were the primary threat to the kakerori's survival, so the program has focused on the elimination of rats from the kakerori's breeding area. The kakerori's population has grown from 29 birds in 1989 to over 140 in 1997, and is still increasing.

The Cook Islands Natural Heritage Project has been working for several years to identify and catalogue all the hundreds of species of flora and fauna in the Cook Islands, collecting traditional names and

Kakerori (Rarotonga flycatcher)

Traditional Conservation Methods

The Cook Islands had a system of conservation in place long before most of the rest of the world was familiar with the concept, and *ra'ui*, this traditional method of conservation, is once again coming into use.

A ra'ui is called by the traditional leaders (the ariki, mataiapo and rangatira) for the purpose of conservation of a particular area or resource. It is designated for a particular place, purpose, and period of time.

During a period of ra'ui, nothing can be taken from the designated ra'ui area. It gives a chance for nature to replenish itself without human interference, and it can apply to many situations. Examples of ra'ui might include establishing a time for ground to lie fallow, a ra'ui in the lagoon to allow fish and shellfish to breed, or even on coconut trees, to allow more coconuts to grow.

On Rarotonga, a ra'ui for certain sections of the lagoon was called by the Koutu Nui (Rarotonga's assembly of mataiapo and rangatira) in 1997, and is expected to be implemented, area by area, during 1998.

The first area of implementation will be at Tikioki, a section of Titikaveka on the south-east side of the island, in the lagoon behind the Beach Cargo packing shed. The ra'ui is scheduled to begin early in 1998 and to last for two years, and it's highly likely to be renewed once the two years are up. During the period of ra'ui, the designated area of the lagoon will be signposted on land and marked by buoys in the water. Swimming and snorkelling will be allowed, but nothing can be taken – fishing and gathering of shellfish from the reef will be prohibited. The purpose is to allow the fish and other species a protected breeding area.

Subsequent areas of ra'ui are expected to be established in the lagoon at Muri, at the Rarotongan Beach Resort, at the Social Centre on the west end of the airport, and at Panama on the east end of the airport.

Dorice Reid (Te Tika Mataiapo), president of the Koutu Nui, can answer questions about ra'ui or any other aspects of traditional leadership in the Cook Islands. Contact her at the Little Polynesian on Rarotonga (☎ 24-280, fax 21-585, PO Box 366, Rarotonga). ■

knowledge associated with them, and promoting their conservation and protection.

Organisations working on conservation in the Cook Islands include:

Cook Islands Environment Services (Tuanga Taporoporo; ☎ 21-256, fax 21-134), PO Box 371, Rarotonga – the arm of government that administers the Rarotonga Environment Act, passed in 1995, monitoring development and waste management, and conducting environmental impact assessments

Cook Islands Natural Heritage Project (☎ 20-959, fax 24-894, gerald@nature.gov.ck), PO Box 781, Rarotonga – does research, is compiling a database of species, and produces pamphlets, booklets, posters and other informative materials

Ministry of Marine Resources (☎ 28-722, 28-730, fax 29-721, rar@mmr.gov.ck), PO Box 85, Rarotonga – a government ministry that handles marine resources and marine reserves

Takitumu Conservation Area (☎/fax 29-906, kakerori@tca.co.ck), PO Box 817, Rarotonga – involved in eco-tourism, awareness education, the kakerori recovery program and the preservation of native species

Taporoporoanga Ipukarea Society Inc (☎ 26-189, fax 22-189, passfiel@gatepoly.co.ck), PO Box 649, Rarotonga – promotes environmental education and awareness, and other projects

FLORA & FAUNA

Flora

Although the flora varies widely from island to island, the two most noticeable features are probably the coconut palm and the great variety of flowers, and they seem to grow with wild abandon almost everywhere.

Rarotonga has a wide variety of vegetation in a number of distinct vegetation zones. Gerald McCormack of the Cook Islands Natural Heritage Project has identified several types of 'plant communities', varying according to elevation and the types of terrain where they live. Communities include valley forest, native fernland, native slope forest, native ridge forest, native rockface and highest of all, a native cloud-forest community; the damp, mountainous central part of the island is densely covered in a luxuriant jungle of ferns, creepers and towering trees. Look for the book *Rarotonga's Mountain Tracks and Plants* by Gerald McCormack & Judith Künzle for more about Rarotonga's plant life and a number of interesting walks on the island.

The raised islands of the southern group, such as Mangaia or Atiu, are particularly interesting for the sharp dividing line between the fertile central area with volcanic soil, the swampy transition zone between the fossil coral makatea and the central region, and the wild vegetation on the makatea itself. Although the makatea is rocky, it's covered with lush growth and a considerable variety of plants that are supported by pockets of volcanic soil. Pandanus trees, whose leaves are so important in traditional handicrafts of the islands (mats, baskets etc) grow on the makatea; they used to grow on all the southern group islands but are now rare on Rarotonga and Atiu. On the atolls of the northern group the soil is usually limited and infertile and there is little vegetation apart from the coconut palms.

Fauna

In common with most other Pacific islands the fauna is limited.

Mammals The only mammals considered native are Pacific fruit bats (formerly known as flying foxes), which are found only on Mangaia and Rarotonga. The bats were introduced from Mangaia onto Rarotonga in the 1870s; recent archaeological evidence indicates that these mammals were already present on Mangaia when the Polynesians arrived.

Rats and pigs were also introduced to the islands. Today there are many domestic pigs which are usually kept by the simple method of tying one leg to a coconut tree. Rarotonga also has many dogs, some cats and goats, and a few horses and cattle. The island of Aitutaki has the distinction of having no dogs at all.

Birds The number of native land birds is limited, and on Rarotonga you have to get up

into the hills to see them. They have been driven up there by a number of human-related factors, including changes in the natural vegetation, cats, guns and the ubiquitous mynah bird.

A native of India, the mynah was introduced to Rarotonga from Tahiti in 1906 to control coconut stick insects. These green insects, about 10 to 15cm long, were once a great destroyer of the coconut trees on the island. The mynah bird was so successful in reducing the number of coconut stick insects that you rarely see one of these insects today, and they never reach plague proportions. Other islands also wanted the mynah to control their coconut stick insect problems, and today the mynah is found in great numbers on all the inhabited southern group islands except Mitiaro. Although the coconut stick insect is no longer a problem, the sometimes obnoxious mynah birds have proliferated, becoming quite a nuisance and have contributed to the lack of native birds in the lowlands.

Despite the limited number of birds there are some of great interest to birdwatchers including a surprising number of endemic birds – species found only in the one localised area. Of particular interest are the cave-dwelling Atiu swiftlet (*kopeka*) on the island of Atiu, the chattering kingfisher of Atiu and Mauke and the Mangaia kingfisher. The most colourful endemic bird is the Cook Islands fruit dove, found in the inland areas of Rarotonga and on Atiu. The Rarotonga flycatcher, or kakerori, which is found only on a limited area of Rarotonga and is on the endangered species list, is slowly making a comeback.

The *Guide to Cook Islands Birds* by DT Holyoak is an illustrated field guide to the birds of the islands. The Cook Islands Natural Heritage Project has published a photographic poster of all the significant birds of the Cook Islands.

Fish & Marine Dwellers Of course there are many fish in the waters around the islands. Snorkellers in the lagoons inside the reefs and divers outside the reefs will find plenty

Unga Putua (Chocolate Hermit) (JK)

by the Cook Islands Natural Heritage Project, is helpful for identifying species.

Around Rarotonga, on the sandy lagoon bottom of Aitutaki and on other islands there are great numbers of sea cucumbers, also known as bêches-de-mer or, in Maori, as *rori*. There are about 15 species of rori in the Cooks, about six of which are common; certain varieties of these strange slug-like creatures are a noted delicacy. Large, bright-blue starfish are also a common sight. On land as well as in the water the Cooks have a great number of crabs – over 200 species at last count – ranging from tiny, amusing hermit crabs to large coconut crabs.

Humpback whales visit Rarotonga and other Cook Islands every year in August and September. Humpbacks, which can reach up to 11m in length, are the 'singing whales' – various recordings have been made of the males singing to attract the females during the mating season. Only around 12 to 20 humpbacks come up from Antarctica each year to mate and calf. With an 11-month gestation period, the whales mate one year, bear young the next, rear their young in Antarctica during that year and mate again the following year. Oddly enough the whales don't eat much while they're here; during most of the year, they live in Antarctica

of colourful tropical fish to keep them enthralled. Fortunately for swimmers, sharks are not a problem – the islands of the southern group generally have such shallow lagoons that sharks and other large fish are usually found only outside the reef. Sharks are present outside the reef, mainly nonaggressive white-tipped reef sharks (and they are rare), but there are none which pose a danger to humans. The coral structures support a variety of fish and other reef life, and the high visibility makes wonderful opportunities for scuba divers. *Cook Islands Reef Life*, a colourful poster printed in 1992

U'u (Parrotfish) *Scarus spp* (JK)

where their food is plentiful, they build up a lot of blubber, and mostly survive off their blubber during their time in the Cooks.

GOVERNMENT & POLITICS

The Cook Islands is a semi-independent nation, in free association with New Zealand. It has its own government responsible for all internal affairs, while its international relations and defence matters are handled by New Zealand.

The Cook Islands has a Westminster parliamentary system of government like that of England, Australia and New Zealand. Of course with a population of 20,000 it's on a small scale. The Cook Islands Parliament inhabits an inconspicuous building beside the Rarotonga airport; it was originally built as a hostel for airport workers during the airport's construction in 1974. The prime minister has an office here and another one in Avarua.

The parliament has two houses. The lower house or Legislative Assembly has 25 elected members, with 24 from the various districts of the Cook Islands and one 'overseas constituency' seat representing the thousands of Cook Islanders living in New Zealand. The upper house, or House of Ariki, represents the island chiefs but they have only advisory powers. Her Majesty the Queen of England is represented by a Queen's Representative (QR), whose residence on the south side of Rarotonga is a stately affair overlooking the lagoon.

Away from Rarotonga each island has at least one elected member of parliament (MP), plus a resident appointed chief administrative officer (CAO). This is a direct carryover from the position of Resident (the representative of the British government in a British protectorate) of colonial times, and the CAO's house on each island is still known as The Residency. The CAO generally has more power than the elected Island Council.

ECONOMY

The Cook Islands' economy is far from balanced – exports are far lower than imports.

The biggest factor in making up the shortfall is good old foreign aid, particularly from 'big brother' New Zealand but also from Australia and other countries. Considerable amounts of money are also sent back by Cook Islanders living abroad – remember there are more Cook Islanders living overseas than there are in the Cooks.

Pearls are the Cook Islands' most lucrative export. Pearl farming is a relatively new industry in the Cooks, only appearing on the economic charts since 1989, but the black pearls of Manihiki have become internationally famous and are a highly prized product. Pearl shell is another significant export. Pearls are cultivated in the lagoons of Manihiki and Pehrhyn, and there's talk of expanding the industry into the lagoons of other northern group islands as well.

Second in importance for export are fruits and vegetables. Citrus fruits are the major agricultural export, although tropical fruits such as papaya (pawpaw) and bananas, and vegetables such as beans, tomatoes, capsicums (peppers) and zucchini (courgettes) are also exported. Much of this produce is airfreighted out; an important plus for tourism is that agriculture creates an additional demand for aircraft. Copra (dried coconut), produced throughout the Pacific, is another important export.

Clothing and footwear, the islands' principal export in the early 1980s, has declined in recent years. However, in addition to pearls a couple of other new industries have arisen to become significant exports. Live fish and fresh or chilled fish are growing export items, as are aromatic *maire eis* (necklaces) made on the island of Mauke and flown each week to Hawaii.

Exports have been almost totally dependent on New Zealand so if the Kiwis sneeze the Cook Islanders catch a cold. New Zealand is a small market and for the Cooks it has sometimes been a fickle one. Although New Zealand is still by far the Cooks' most important trading partner, there's been a little more diversification in recent years, with Australia, Fiji, Hong Kong and the USA becoming significant trading partners.

The most important money earner for the Cooks, however, is tourism. Tourism expanded rapidly in the late 1980s and early 1990s, and despite a dropoff in the number of visitors in 1995, it's estimated that over 46,000 tourists visited Rarotonga in 1996, with a 2% increase expected for 1997. Though this figure is slightly less than in the boom years of 1993 and 1994, it's still a significant number for a small island with a population of only around 11,000. Other important money earners include offshore banking and the status of the islands as a tax haven, revenue from taxes on imports, and the Cook Islands' beautiful and cleverly marketed postage stamps.

For the casual visitor it's very hard to get any sort of handle on the economy of the Cooks, or more particularly of Rarotonga. On one hand the balance of trade is undoubtedly pretty horrific and the Cook Islanders live far beyond their means. On the other hand everybody is undeniably well fed. There's definitely a lot of food around, even a surplus, with exotic fruits growing in profusion all around the island. Avocados, pawpaws and coconuts grow in such abundance that they're often used as pig food. It's a popular joke that when *Merry Christmas Mr Lawrence* (a WWII prison camp drama starring David Bowie) was filmed on Rarotonga it proved impossible to find 500 people who looked thin enough to appear as prison camp extras. Extras had to be flown in from New Zealand.

POPULATION & PEOPLE

In a provisional estimate the population of the Cook Islands was 18,904 in 1996, up from 18,617 in the 1991 census. The figure for Cook Islanders living outside the Cook Islands is even greater; most of the expatriate Cook Islanders live in New Zealand and Australia, where Cook Islanders have residence and working rights. The story of the Cook Islands' population is a story of continuing movement from the outer islands to Rarotonga and from there to New Zealand, and to a lesser extent to Australia.

Over 90% of the population lives on the southern group islands, with over 50% of the country's population on Rarotonga alone. Population estimates are:

Island	Population in 1991	Population in 1996
Southern Group		
Rarotonga	10,886	11,100
Aitutaki	2357	2332
Mangaia	1214	1104
Atiu	1006	960
Mauke	639	646
Mitiaro	247	319
Northern Group		
Pukapuka	670	780
Manihiki	663	662
Penrhyn	503	600
Rakahanga	262	249
Nassau	102	99
Palmerston	49	49
Suwarrow	6	4

There are a number of unpopulated islands in both the northern and southern groups. These islands are not normally visited by anyone – locals or tourists – and the only way to access them is by private yacht.

Over 90% of the population is Polynesian. There's also a small minority of people of European descent, principally New Zealanders, and some Fijian, Indian and Chinese families.

Strange Names

To most people's ears the Cook Islanders have some pretty strange given names. There's no differentiation between male or female names and they're often given to commemorate some event that happened around the time the name's recipient was born. Big brother just left your island to go off to school on another island? Well you might end up as 'Schooltrip'. The school was far away in Whangarei, New Zealand? You could be named 'Whangarei'. Big brother won a medal in the Commonwealth Games? You're 'Silver Medal'! But why would somebody be named 'Tipunu' or 'Teaspoon'? And why 'Sore Leg', or 'Bad Man'? ∎

There are often subtle differences between the islands, in some cases due to their isolation. The people of Pukapuka in the north, for example, are in some ways more closely related to Samoa than to the other islands of the Cooks group; geographically the northern Cook Islands are closer to Samoa than they are to the southern Cook Islands.

EDUCATION

Education is free and compulsory for children from ages five to 15. There are 28 primary schools throughout the islands and seven secondary schools, with secondary school education available on all the inhabited islands of the southern group providing education up to the level of the New Zealand School Certificate. Tertiary education is available in the Cooks at a nursing school, a teacher-training college and through an apprenticeship program, and the Cook Islands Christian Church has a theological college. The New Zealand government offers Cook Islanders scholarships for secondary and tertiary education and career training programs in New Zealand, Australia, Fiji, Papua New Guinea and Samoa. The University of the South Pacific (USP), based in Suva, Fiji, has a small extension centre in Avarua.

ARTS
Dance

Dancing in the Cook Islands is colourful, spectacular and popular. The Cook Islanders are reputed to be the best dancers in Polynesia, even better than the Tahitians, say the connoisseurs. You'll get plenty of opportunity to see dancing as there are dance performances all the time, particularly at the ubiquitous 'island nights'. If you arrive at an 'island night' around 9 pm, after the buffet the entry charges to see the performances are usually only about NZ$5 or NZ$10.

The dancing is often wonderfully suggestive and, not surprisingly, this upset the Victorian European visitors. You can almost sense William Wyatt Gill, the observant early missionary, raising his eyebrows as he reported that:

Respecting the *morality* of their dances, the less said the better; but the 'upaupa' dance, introduced from Tahiti, is obscene indeed.

Things haven't changed much!

The sensual nature of Cook Islands dance is rooted in its history when dances were performed in honour of Tangaroa, god of fertility and of the sea. This also explains the similarity in the dances of the Cook Islanders, Tahitians and Hawaiians, all of whom shared the same religion, taking their god Tangaroa with them as they migrated from one island group to another.

If you go to the annual dance championships on Rarotonga the things which judges watch for will probably be outlined. They include the difficulty of the dance, the movements of the hands which must express the music, the facial expressions and the grace with which the dance is done. Male dances tend to be aggressive and energetic, female dances are often all languid suggestiveness and gyrating hips.

'Island nights' performances are a lot of fun. Don't concentrate solely on the dancers – the musicians are wonderful to watch and the audience often gets involved in a big way. Some of the fat mamas are simply superb and, despite their weight, can shake a hip as well as any young *vaine* (woman). Take note of how it's done though; a feature of almost every 'island night' is dragging some unsuspecting *papa'a*, or foreigners, up on stage to perform!

As western ideals of beauty have gained considerable ascendancy these days, it's only as they get older that some Polynesian women start to widen so dramatically. In the missionary period William Wyatt Gill wrote:

The greatest requisite of a Polynesian beauty is to be fat and as fair as their dusky skin will permit. To insure this, favourite children in good families, whether boys or girls, were regularly fattened and imprisoned till nightfall, when a little gentle exercise was permitted. If refractory, the guardian would even whip the culprit for not eating more, calling out 'Shall I not be put to shame to see you so slim in the dance?'

Another interesting thing to see is how much the traditional dance movements permeate even the modern 'western-style' dancing. Go to any nightclub and you'll see disco, pop, rock-n-roll and even sometimes ballroom dancing spiced with hip-swaying, knee-knocking and other classic island movements. Don't be afraid to join in and try it yourself – the locals will love it and you'll have a great time too!

Traditional Arts & Crafts

Although the arts and crafts of the Cook Islands today are only a shadow of their former importance, they were once widespread and of high quality. The early missionaries, in their passion to obliterate all traces of heathenism, did a comprehensive job of destroying much of the old art forms. Fortunately, however, they also saved some of the best pieces, many of which can now be found in European museums.

There was no real connection between the southern volcanic islands and the northern atolls in the pre-European period and the art of the small islands to the north was much more limited. Domestic equipment and tools, matting, and inlaid pearl shell on canoes and canoe paddles were about the extent of their work. In the south, however, a variety of crafts developed, with strong variations between the individual islands.

A number of fine books have been published about the arts and crafts of the Cook Islands; see the Books section in the Facts for the Visitor chapter.

Many arts and crafts are still practised in the islands today. See the Things to Buy section in the Facts for the Visitor chapter, and in each individual island chapter, for an idea of the types of arts and crafts that are found in the islands today.

Woodcarving Figures of gods carved from wood were amongst the most widespread art forms and were particularly common on Rarotonga. These squat figures, variously

described as fisherman's gods or as images of specifically named gods such as Tangaroa, were similar to the Tangaroa image which has become symbolic of the Cook Islands today. Staff gods with repetitive figures carved down a pole, war clubs and spears were other typical Rarotongan artefacts. The incredibly intricately carved mace gods, often from Mangaia, and the slab gods from Aitutaki, were other examples of woodcarving which are no longer found today.

Ceremonial Adzes Making Mangaian ceremonial adzes was an important craft. At first, these axe-like hand tools probably had an everyday use but with time they became purely ceremonial objects and more and more stylised in their design. Each element of these adzes was beautifully made – from the stone blade to the carefully carved wooden handle and the intricate sennit binding that lashed the blade to the handle. Some of the best examples of Mangaian ceremonial adzes are on exhibit in some of the world's great museums. Some people believe that the art of ceremonial adze making has died out. Not so – on Mangaia there are woodcarvers who still make the ceremonial adzes in the traditional way.

Canoes Canoes, or *vaka*, were carved with great seriousness and ceremony in pre-European times. Not only did the canoes have to be large and strong enough for long-distance ocean voyages, they also had to be made in accordance with strict rules of tapu. Taunga, or experts, not only in the matter of canoes and woodcarving but also in spiritual matters, had to guide every step of the process. A suitable tree had to be found, chosen and cut, with proper supplication to the god of the forest. Once cut, the carving had to proceed in a certain way, all the way to the launching of the canoe, which once again had to be done in accordance with all the proper spiritual as well as physical laws and requisites. None of the huge, pre-European canoes survive in the Cook Islands today.

Buildings Houses and other buildings were made of natural materials which decayed rapidly, so no ancient buildings survive to the present day and very few buildings of traditional construction remain on any of the southern islands. Woodcarving was only rarely used in houses, although some important buildings, including some of the first locally built mission churches, had carved and decorated wooden posts. Artistically impressive sennit lashing was, however, found on many buildings – since nails were not available the wooden framework of a building was tied together with carefully bound sennit rope. Each island or area had its own distinctive style of sennit binding and this is still followed today. If you are on the island of Mangaia you can see fine sennit lashing on the roof beams of the CICC church in Tamarua village.

Other Crafts Woven fans, feathered headdresses bound with sennit, woven belts and baskets, and wooden seats from Atiu were other common artefacts of the pre-European period. Some of these crafts have survived but others are found only in museums.

SOCIETY & CONDUCT
Traditional Culture
Visitors to the Cooks often get a superficial impression of the place and are disappointed upon seeing close-cut lawns, western-style clothing and New Zealand-type houses that there is so little sign of Polynesian culture. Yet right underneath this thin western veneer, layer upon layer of the old Cook Islands culture survives. It's in the land system – how it's inherited, how it's managed, how it's leased but never sold. It's in the way people transact business. It's in the concept of time. Tradition survives intact in hospitality, in how to dance and make music and celebrate, in the preparation of food, the wearing of flowers, the language and in many other day-to-day ways of doing things.

Every native Cook Islander is part of some family clan, and each family clan is connected in some distinct way to the ancient system of chiefs (ariki, mataiapo and rangatira) which has survived for centuries in an unbroken line. Rarotonga's six ariki clans are still based on the original land divisions from when the Maori first arrived on the island many centuries ago.

Even today, when an ariki is installed, the ceremony takes place on an ancient family marae. The new ariki and all the attendants are dressed in the traditional ceremonial leaves, and the ancient symbols of office – a spear, woven shoes, a feather-shell-tapa cloth headdress, a woven fan, a huge mother-of-pearl shell necklace and other emblems – are presented. You'll see these things in museums, but for Cook Islanders, they are not just museum pieces.

You'll see many graves of the ancestors beside modern houses. For many Cook Islanders, the spirits of the ancestors are an ever-present reality. The spirits are not feared as ghosts are in some other cultures. It is simply a fact of life that they live here along with everyone else.

Dos & Don'ts

Friendliness and respect for others are highly valued in Cook Islands culture; a soft, friendly demeanour will smooth your way here in every interaction with others. Always be politely respectful of everyone, including old people and children. Don't be rude to people; such behaviour will definitely get you nowhere here. When you interact with others, offer a greeting and a smile before anything else.

Be modest and respectful in dress. Women should see the Women Travellers section, in the Facts for the Visitor chapter, for tips on dress; also see the following Religion section for tips on how to dress when you visit a CICC church.

RELIGION

Only a few people today know much about the pre-European religion of the Cook Islands, with its sophisticated system of 71 gods, each ruling a particular facet of reality, and its 12 heavens – seven below the sun, five above it, plus another dominion below the earth – each the dwelling place of particular gods and spirits.

The early missionaries held 'pagan beliefs' in such utter contempt that they made virtually no effort to study, record or understand the traditional religion. They did, however, make great efforts to wipe it out and destroy any heathen images they came across. Fortunately some fine pieces of religious art were whisked away from the islands and are now prized pieces in European museums.

The Cook Islands today are overwhelmingly Christian – in fact people from Christian cultures who haven't been to church for years (weddings and funerals apart) suddenly find themselves going back to church for fun! The major local denomination is the Cook Islands Christian Church or CICC. Founded by those first LMS missionaries who came to the islands in the early 1820s, it's a blend of Church of England, Baptist, Methodist and whatever else was going on at the time – Roman Catholicism definitely excepted. Today the CICC still attracts about 70% of the faithful, on Rarotonga at least, and probably a higher percentage on the outer islands. The remaining 30% is squabbled over by the Roman Catholics, the Seventh-Day Adventists, the Church of the Latter-Day Saints (Mormons, looking as out of place in their white shirts and ties as ever), Jehovah's Witnesses, Assembly of God, Apostolic Revival Fellowship and various other groups, plus a small but avid following of Baha'is.

The CICC still has an overwhelming influence on local living habits and in many cases the pattern is exactly that established by those original British missionaries in the 19th century. Rarotongan villages are still divided into four sections which take turns in looking after the village church and its minister. Each family in the congregation contributes a monthly sum into the church fund which goes towards church costs. The church minister is appointed for a five-year period after which he moves to another church. He gets a small weekly stipend but in addition the village group responsible for that week also collects to provide him with a more reasonable weekly salary.

This village responsibility has two sides for the church minister. He is responsible for far more than just his church: if the village teenagers are playing up or hanging around the local bars the blame is likely to be laid at the CICC minister's door! And if he doesn't do something about it then a pitifully low weekly contribution can be interpreted as a strong hint to get on with the job. In fact islanders say that they prefer to have a minister with no local connections – someone from an outer island, say. That way if they decide to keep him in line by cutting the money supply he's not going to find it so easy to fall back on the food from his local gardens!

Visitors are more than welcome to attend a Sunday church service and it's a delightful event. You're looked upon as a useful way of augmenting the collection and anyway, there's nothing much else happening on a Sunday morning. The service is held mostly in Maori, although there will be a token welcome in English and parts of the service may be translated into English as well. The islanders all dress in their Sunday best and the women all wear strikingly similar wide-brimmed hats. When you go, show respect by observing a few simple rules of dress: no shorts for men or women and no bare shoulders. CICC services throughout the islands are held at 10 am on Sunday, with other services held on Sunday evening and early on several mornings throughout the week.

The major attraction of a CICC service is the inspired hymn singing – the harmonies are superb and the volume lifts the roof! This wonderful singing has a pre-European origin. When the missionaries arrived they found the people were already singing praise to their gods, so they simply put Christian words to the existing songs. Thus the harmony, rhythm and basic structure of the music you hear has its roots in a time long before the arrival of Christianity. Of course you will also hear a familiar tune or two, but sung in a distinctively Cook Islands style.

Early Missionaries

Important figures in the early spread of Christianity through the islands included:

Aaron Buzacott Following in John Williams' footsteps, Buzacott not only did most of the work in translating the Bible into Maori, he also composed most of the hymns in the CICC Maori hymn book. Buzacott also supervised the construction of the church in Avarua, Rarotonga, and died in 1864 after 30 years' work in the Cook Islands. The story of his life and labours is told in *Mission Life in the Islands of the Pacific*.

William Gill Author of *Gems from the Coral Island*, William Gill built the present CICC church at Arorangi, Rarotonga, and also its predecessor, destroyed by a hurricane in 1846. He worked at Arorangi from 1839 to 1852 when he returned to England. His brother George was the first resident missionary on Mangaia.

William Wyatt Gill Author of *From Darkness to Light in Polynesia*, William Wyatt Gill was no relation to William Gill. He spent 20 years on Mangaia – see the Books section of the Facts for the Visitor chapter for more details.

Maretu Maretu's accounts of the spread of Christianity are particularly interesting because they are by a Cook Islander rather than a European (see the Books section of the Facts for the Visitor chapter). A native of Rarotonga, Maretu later worked as a missionary on the islands of Mangaia, Manihiki and Rakahanga.

Papeiha Probably the most successful of the local mission workers, Papeiha was brought to the Cook Islands from Raiatea in the Society Islands, now part of French Polynesia, in 1821 by John Williams. Papeiha introduced Christianity to the Cook Islands – to Aitutaki in 1821 and to Rarotonga in 1823. He died on Rarotonga in 1867, having spent 46 years in the Cook Islands.

John Williams A pioneer mission worker in the Pacific, he was instrumental in the spread of Christianity to the Cook Islands. He was killed (and eaten) on the Vanuatu island of Erromanga in 1839.

LANGUAGE

The language of the Cook Islands is Cook Islands Maori, but English is spoken as a second language by virtually everyone and you'll have no trouble at all getting by with English.

Among themselves, however, the people speak their own language. If you'd like to learn some yourself, pick up a copy of *Kai*

TONY WHEELER

TONY WHEELER

TONY WHEELER

NANCY KELLER

NANCY KELLER

A: Heliconia
B, C, D: Varieties of Hibiscus
E: Pink Frangipani

Tivaevae
All photographs by Nancy Keller

Korero: A Cook Islands Maori Language Coursebook by Tai Tepuaotera Turepu Carpentier & Clive Beaumont, which is available in Rarotonga with an accompanying audio tape. It's a good way to start. If you'll be here for some time and are serious about learning the language, the Cook Islands Library & Museum Society in Avarua has a number of books for learning the language, and the University of the South Pacific (USP) centre in Avarua offers classes.

English can present its own special difficulties for Cook Islanders. In their language there is no differentiation between male and female; 'he', 'she', 'him' and 'her' are all expressed by the one word *aia*. You'll frequently hear Cook Islanders mix up all the different English words to express what they have only one word for, calling men 'she' and women 'he'!

Although each island has its own distinctive speech, people from all the Cook Islands can understand one another. Cook Islands Maori is also closely related to the Maori language of New Zealand and to the other eastern Polynesian languages including Hawaiian, Marquesan and Tahitian. A Cook Islander would have little trouble understanding someone speaking those languages.

Cook Islands Maori was traditionally a spoken language, not a written one. The language, in its Rarotongan form, was first written down by the missionaries in the 1830s. Later they produced a Rarotongan version of the Bible, which is still used today.

Pronunciation

The Cook Islands alphabet has only 13 letters: *a, e, i, k, m, n, ng, o, p, r, t, u, v*. The *ng* sound is pronounced the same as in English (eg running, singing) but in Cook Islands Maori it's often at the beginning of a word (eg Nga, Ngatangiia). Practise by pronouncing the sound in an English word and see how it feels in the throat, then try saying it alone. Aim at making the sound at the beginning of a word, and you'll have it. All the other consonants are pronounced as they are in English.

Vowels The pronunciation of vowels is very important. Each vowel has both a long and a short sound. Using the wrong one results in a completely different word and meaning (eg *pupu* means 'class', 'group' or 'team'; *pūpū* means 'a type of small shell'). Sometimes the long vowels carry a macron over them when written (ā, ē, ī, ō, ū), but not always; the language can correctly be written either with or without the macrons. The long and short pronunciation of the vowels is like this:

Short

a	as the 'a' in 'about'
e	as in 'pet'
i	as in 'sit'
o	as in 'cot'
u	as in 'put'

Long

ā	as in 'all'
ē	as in 'play'
ī	as in 'bee'
ō	as in 'worn'
ū	as in 'tune'

Another symbol used in the written language is a glottal stop, represented by an apostrophe before or between vowels (eg *ta'i*). It indicates a stop in the enunciation – a similar sound in English is heard in the expression 'oh-oh', where the throat closes momentarily. Consider the words *tai* (pronounced with one syllable, as the English 'tie') and *ta'i*, (pronounced with two syllables – 'ta' plus 'ee').

The classic joke about the confusion that mispronunciation of Cook Islands Maori vowels can create, is that if you pronounce the word *ika* with a longish 'i' it means 'fish', while pronounced with a clipped 'i' (*'ika*) it means 'the female genitalia'! If you want to say 'fish', pronounce it as if it had an 'e' sound in front of it – *e ika*.

Greetings & Civilities

Hello. (all purpose greeting, lit: 'may you live!')	*Kia orana!*

How are you? (to one person)	*Pe'ea koe?*	mother	*mama*
		brother	*tungane*
How are you? (to two people)	*Pe'ea korua?*	sister	*tua'ine*
		friend	*oa, taeake*
How are you? (to three or more people)	*Pe'ea kotou?*		
		me/I	*au*
		you (one person)	*koe*
Good. (also 'Thank you.')	*Meitaki.*	you (two people)	*korua*
		you (three or more)	*koutou*
Very good. (also 'Thank you very much.')	*Meitaki ma'ata.*	him/her/he/she	*aia*
		we (two)	*taua, maua*
		we (three or more)	*tatou, matou*
Goodbye. (to person leaving, lit: 'Go along.')	*Aere ra.*	they (two)	*raua*
		they (three or more)	*ratou*
Goodbye. (to person staying, lit: 'Remain.')	*E no'o ra.*	beautiful	*manea*
		ugly	*vi'ivi'i*
Welcome!	*Turou!*	The mountain is beautiful.	*Manea te maunga.*
Good luck! (a toast)	*Kia manuia!*		

Around Town

Please. (used at the end of a statement)	*Ine.*	beach	*tapa ta'atai*
		church	*ekalesia; are pure*
Thank you.	*Meitaki.*	house	*are*
Thank you very much.	*Meitaki ma'ata.*	island; lagoon islet	*motu*
		lagoon	*roto*
		land	*enua*

Small Talk

		mountain	*maunga*
Yes.	*Ae.*	ocean	*moana*
No.	*Kare.*	reef	*akau*
Maybe.	*Penei ake.*	sky	*rangi*
		store; shop	*toa*
What's your name?	*Ko'ai to'ou ingoa?*	town	*taoni*
My name is …	*Ko … toku ingoa.*	village	*tapere*
Where are you from?	*No'ea mai koe?*		
I'm from …	*No … mai au.*		
Where are you going?	*Ka aere koe ki'ea?*	**Time**	
		day	*ra*
I'm going to (Aitutaki).	*Te aere nei au ki (Aitutaki).*	night	*po*
		hour	*ora*
		one o'clock	*ora ta'i*
		two o'clock	*ora rua*
person; people	*tangata*		
man, husband	*tane*		
woman, wife	*vaine*	**Numbers**	
children	*tamariki*	1	*ta'i*
boy	*tamaiti, tamaroa*	2	*rua*
girl	*tama'ine*	3	*toru*
baby	*pepe*	4	*a*
father	*papa*	5	*rima*

6	*ono*
7	*itu*
8	*varu*
9	*iva*
10	*ta'i-nga'uru*
11	*ta'i-nga'uru-ma-ta'*
	(one ten plus one)
12	*ta'i-nga'uru-ma-rua*
	(one ten plus two) etc, to
20	*rua-nga'uru* (two tens)
21	*rua-nga'uru-ma-ta'*
	(two tens plus one) etc, to
99	*iva-nga'uru-ma-iva*
100	*ta'i-anere*
101	*ta'i-anere-ma-ta'i*
	(one hundred plus one) etc, to
110	*ta'i-anere e ta'i-nga'uru*
	(one hundred plus one ten) etc, to
999	*iva-anere e iva-nga'uru-ma-iva*
1000	*ta'i-tauatini*
1001	*ta'i-tauatini-ma-ta'i*
	(one thousand plus one) etc

Days of the Week

Monday	*Monite*
Tuesday	*Ru'irua*
Wednesday	*Ru'itoru*
Thursday	*Paraparau*
Friday	*Varaire*
Saturday	*Ma'anakai*
Sunday	*Tapati*

Months of the Year

January	*Tianuare*
February	*Peperuare*
March	*Mati*
April	*Aperira*
May	*Me*
June	*Tiunu*
July	*Tiurai*
August	*'Aukute*
September	*Tepetema*
October	*'Okotopa*
November	*Noema*
December	*Titema*

Facts for the Visitor

PLANNING
When to Go

Anytime is a good time to visit the Cook Islands. Seasonal variations are slight (see the Climate section in the Facts about the Country chapter).

What Kind of Trip?

The Cook Islands can be visited as a destination on its own, as a stopover when crossing the Pacific, or as part of a Circle Pacific or round-the-world trip (see the Getting There & Away chapter). From some places, the Cooks are a pleasant and affordable spot for a package tour lasting a week or two.

Some people travel to the Cooks to pursue special interests such as diving, snorkelling, hiking, caving, dancing and handicrafts. Others come on a variety of research or aid projects.

You can have a fine trip to the Cooks if you visit Rarotonga alone, or a combination of Rarotonga and Aitutaki, the two islands most visited by tourists. Or you can get right off the tourist highway and visit the other islands of the southern group, or even, if you're hardy, the northern group islands, which most tourists never see.

Maps

New Zealand's Department of Lands & Survey produces excellent 1:25,000 topographical maps of each of the Cook Islands, showing physical features, roads, villages, walking tracks, lagoons, reefs, etc. These maps are available at many places on Rarotonga, and from the Department of Lands & Survey in New Zealand. The Tourist Authority office in Avarua hands out a couple of free publications containing good tourist maps. See the Rarotonga chapter for details on where to find maps.

What to Bring

The Cook Islands' even and moderate climate makes clothing choice a breeze. You rarely need anything warmer than a short-sleeve shirt or T-shirt, but bring along a jumper (sweater) or jacket just to be on the safe side, especially during the cooler months of June to September. Bring rain gear at any time of year.

You'll need an old pair of running shoes or sneakers for walking on the reefs – there are some things you'd rather not step on, and coral cuts take a long time to heal. You'll also need those runners, or a pair of sturdy shoes or hiking boots, if you intend to go walking or climbing on Rarotonga, or across the razor-sharp *makatea* (raised coral reefs) of Atiu, Mauke, Mitiaro or Mangaia.

A torch (flashlight) will come in handy, especially if you visit the outer islands, where the power goes off at midnight. There are also caves to explore, for which a torch is essential.

The Cook Islands are, of course, wonderful for snorkelling and diving. You can bring your own equipment with you or rent or buy it on Rarotonga.

The Cook Islands are a major supplier of clothes to New Zealand so there's a pretty good choice of clothes locally, although prices tend to be high.

Most western consumable commodities are readily available but, again, somewhat expensive. It may be more economical to bring a spare tube of toothpaste or another spool of film rather than buy it locally.

Don't forget sunscreen or suntan lotion, although these are readily available. You may find you prefer the age-old local favourite, pure coconut oil. It does wonders for both skin and hair and smells good too, whether it's the plain variety or scented with local flowers. Mauke Miracle Oil, a little more expensive, contains herbs which act as a natural sunscreen.

SUGGESTED ITINERARIES

If you only have a week to spend in the Cooks, you'll probably get no farther than the two principal islands: Rarotonga and Aitutaki. It's worth visiting both, as they are both wonderful islands and they are quite different from one another.

You can easily visit both Rarotonga and Aitutaki in a one or two-week holiday. From Rarotonga there are three flights a day to Aitutaki, plus a one-day tour, every day except Sunday, when there are no flights at all. When you visit Aitutaki, be sure to go on a lagoon cruise – Aitutaki's lagoon is one of the wonders of the Cook Islands.

If you have a little more time, it's worth making a visit to other islands of the southern group: Atiu, Mauke, Mitiaro and/or Mangaia. These islands are quite different from both Rarotonga and Aitutaki, and all have plenty of interesting features and activities.

Visiting the northern group islands requires more time. The northern islands are right off the beaten track and while few visitors ever go there, those that do usually come back enchanted.

HIGHLIGHTS

Some of your most enjoyable times will probably be when you're just relaxing and enjoying the simple pleasures of life, like watching the sunset, lazing on the beach, lolling in the lagoon, bicycling along the back roads or talking with someone you've met. For some reason it seems easier to relax in the Cooks than in many other places.

Many of the highlights of the Cook Islands are listed in the Activities section. Everything mentioned here is covered in more detail in the individual island chapters.

Physical Beauty

The top highlight of the Cook Islands would have to be the physical beauty of the islands. With their soft white-sand beaches, swaying coconut palms, turquoise lagoons replete with colourful tropical fish, their lush vegetation and flowers and the velvety-warm air – what more could anyone ask for?

The lush, craggy mountains of Rarotonga and the large turquoise lagoon of Aitutaki are unforgettable beauties and definite high-

lights of the Cooks. But every other island also has its own characteristics and beauty: the weird makatea and caves of several southern group islands, the red earth and grey cliffs of Mangaia, the rich agriculture practised on all the islands and the coral reefs.

Music & Dance

The Cook Islands is famous for its dancing. Be sure to attend at least one dance performance; they're held several nights a week at 'island nights' on Rarotonga and Aitutaki, accompanied by lavish buffets of traditional Cook Islands foods.

Cook Islands music is magnificent, too, with a variety of styles including string-band music, drumming on wooden slit drums, rousing church singing, action songs and other styles.

Cultural Events

Many kinds of cultural events are held on the islands. There are public events, like Gospel Day, the 10-day Constitution Day celebrations, the Island Dance Festival week, Tiare Festival week and many sporting competitions, which everyone is welcome to attend – don't miss them if they happen while you're here. Then there are also a number of more family-based traditions, like hair cutting ceremonies, investiture ceremonies, weddings, funerals and so on. It's a privilege to be invited to these kinds of events so if you do get invited, take the chance to attend.

Cook Islands Cultural Village

You can probably learn more about Cook Islands culture in one day at the Cook Islands Cultural Village on Rarotonga, especially if you also take the Circle Island Tour, than you will on any other day of your stay.

Food

Be sure to try some traditional Cook Islands food while you're here – preferably prepared in a traditional Maori underground oven (*umu*). Sample some fresh tropical fruits and tasty seafood, try the raw fish in coconut sauce (*ika mata*), taro, taro leaves (*rukau*) and breadfruit (*kuru*), drink coconut water fresh from the coconut, or a tropical fruit juice like passionfruit or mango.

'Island nights' on Rarotonga and Aitutaki feature lavish buffets of traditional island foods. Or you can participate in an *umukai* – a traditional Cook Islands Maori underground oven feast – assisting in the preparation and learning how it's done. Piri Puruto on Rarotonga and Tauono's on Aitutaki both offer this, and there may be others. It's a memorable experience.

TOURIST OFFICES
Local Tourist Offices
The Cook Islands Tourist Authority is in the centre of Avarua; see the Rarotonga chapter for details. You can contact them for printed information and free maps before you arrive and stop in when you're here.

Tourist Offices Abroad
Overseas offices or representatives of the Cook Islands Tourist Authority include:

Australia
    Tourism Cook Islands (☎ (02) 9955-0446, fax 9955-0447), 56 Dustaffenge St, PO Box H95, Hurlstone Park, NSW 2193
Benelux
    (☎ (32) 2-538-2930, fax 2-538-2885) Rue Americaine 27, 1050 Brussels, Belgium
France
    (☎ (35) 76-700617, fax 76-700918) 13 Rue d'Alembert, 3800 Grenoble
Germany
    (☎ (49) 30-238-17628, fax 30-238-17641) Dirkenstrasse 40, 1020 Berlin
Hong Kong
    Pacific Leisure (☎ (852) 524-7065), Tung Ming Building, 40 Des Voeux Rd, Central, PO Box 2382
New Zealand
    Tourism Cook Islands (☎ (09) 366-1100, fax 309-1876), 1/127 Symonds St, PO Box 37391, Parnell, Auckland
United Kingdom
    (☎ (44) 81-392-1838, fax 81-392-1318), 375 Upper Richmond Rd West, London SW14 7NX

In places where the Cook Islands has no tourist office, tourist information is available from Cook Islands consulates (see the Embassies & Consulates section later in this chapter).

VISAS & DOCUMENTS
Passport
Every international visitor to the Cook Islands must be in possession of a valid passport.

Visas & Visitor's Permits
No visa is required to visit the Cooks. A visitor's permit, good for 31 days, is granted on arrival for all nationalities. The only things you need do are present a valid passport, an onward or return airline ticket, and honour the loosely policed 'prior booking' arrangement (see the Accommodation section later in this chapter).

Extensions If you want to stay longer than the initial 31 days you should have no problems so long as you can show you've got adequate finances and still have your vital onward or return air ticket. Extensions cost NZ$70 for up to three months, or NZ$120 for up to six months. If you want to stay more than six months, you must apply in advance from outside the country to the Principal Immigration Officer, Ministry of Foreign Affairs & Immigration, PO Box 105, Avarua, Rarotonga (☎ 29-347, fax 21-247).

Visitor's permits can be extended on Rarotonga at the Ministry of Foreign Affairs & Immigration office on the top floor of the government building, the big three-storey white building behind the Banana Court in Avarua. Come in a week before your current visitor's permit expires.

If you are intending to visit the outer islands you'd be wise to extend your permit beforehand as there are often delays. One long-stay visitor wrote that extending his family's visas in Aitutaki took forever:

The immigration officer was always waiting for information from Rarotonga and we finally got our visas in order three days before we left the Cooks and three months after they had officially expired!

Photocopies

Whenever you travel, make photocopies of all your vital documents, ie passport data pages, airline tickets and other travel documents, travel insurance policy, credit cards and travellers cheque serial numbers. Keep at least one copy in a separate place in your luggage, and leave a copy with someone back home for safekeeping.

Travel Insurance

However you're travelling, it's worth taking out travel insurance. Work out what you need. You may not want to insure that grotty old army-surplus backpack – but everyone should be covered for the worst possible case: an accident, for example, that will require hospital treatment and a flight home. It's a good idea to make a copy of your policy, in case the original gets lost. If you are planning to travel for a long time, the insurance may seem very expensive – but if you can't afford it, you certainly won't be able to afford to deal with a medical emergency overseas.

Medical care is very basic in the Cooks. Even the locals don't depend solely on the medical care available here; their national health system provides for them to fly to New Zealand for medical treatment when necessary. As a foreigner, though, you're not covered by this same protection unless you have personal insurance. See the Health section for more on this.

Driving Licence

The only document you'll need in the Cook Islands, aside from your valid passport and visitor's permit, is a Cook Islands driving licence if you want to drive. See Rental Cars in the Getting Around section of the Rarotonga chapter for details on getting a Cook Islands driving licence.

EMBASSIES & CONSULATES
Cook Islands Consulates Abroad

The Cook Islands has consulates, but not embassies, in various countries. Consulates deal with relations between governments and individuals, whereas embassies deal with relations between governments and governments. Since the Cook Islands' international relations fall under the umbrella of New Zealand, the Cook Islands has only consul representatives in foreign countries. They include:

Australia
> Sir Ian Graham Turbott, Honorary Consul (☎ (02) 9907-6567, fax (02) 9949-6664), 8/8 Lauderdale Avenue, Fairlight, NSW 2094

New Zealand
> HE Mr Iaveta Short, High Commissioner (☎ (4) 472-5126, 472-5127, fax 472-5121), Cook Islands High Commission, 56 Mulgrave St, PO Box 12-242, Thorndon, Wellington
> Mr William Teariki, Consul General (☎ (9) 366-1100, fax (9) 309-1876), 1st Floor, 127 Symonds St, PO Box 37-391, Auckland

Norway
> Mr Hallbjorn Hareide, Honorary Consul General (☎ (2) 430-910, 446-721, fax (22) 444-611), Bydgoy Alle 64, 0265 Oslo 2

USA
> Mr Robert Worthington, Honorary Consul (☎ (808) 842-8999, fax 842-3520), Cook Islands Consulate, Kamehameha Schools, c/o 144 Ke Ala Ola Rd, Honolulu, Hawaii 96817
> Ms Karla Eggleton, North America Representative (☎ (310) 641-5621, toll-free (888) 994-COOKS, fax (310) 338-0708, cooks@itn-aps.iom), Integrated Travel Resources Inc, 5757 West Century Blvd, Suite 660, Los Angeles, CA 90045-6407

Foreign Consulates in the Cook Islands

Foreign consulates in the Cook Islands are all in Avarua. They include:

France
> Mrs Marie Melvin, Honorary French Consul (☎ 20-919, fax 22-031), c/o Island Craft Ltd, PO Box 28, Avarua, Rarotonga

Germany
> Dr Wolfgang Losacker, Honorary German Consul (☎ 23-206, fax 23-305), beside the Banana Court, PO Box 125, Avarua, Rarotonga

New Zealand
> New Zealand High Commission, (☎ 22-201, fax 21-241) upstairs over the Philatelic Bureau, beside the post office, Avarua; PO Box 21, Avarua, Rarotonga

CUSTOMS

The usual customs restrictions of 2L of spirits or 2L of wine or 4.5L of beer, plus 200 cigarettes or 50 cigars or 250g of tobacco apply. The usual agricultural quarantines also apply: bringing in plants or plant products, and animals or animal products is restricted or prohibited, and used camping or sporting equipment may have to be fumigated. Firearms, weapons and drugs are prohibited.

MONEY

All prices in this book are quoted in New Zealand dollars (NZ$) since the Cook Islands dollar is tied to and valued the same as the New Zealand dollar.

Costs

Thumbing through the pages of this book will show you the costs for everything from accommodation and dining out to hiring a motorcycle, riding the bus or going diving.

The Cook Islands are more expensive than Fiji, but they're nowhere near the horrendous levels of Tahiti and French Polynesia.

The New Zealand connection is both a factor for and against the steep costs. The Cook Islands are heavily dependent upon New Zealand for their imports so there's a healthy slug on top of New Zealand prices to cover the shipping costs. Shipping is a major element in the high prices of most Pacific islands. Additionally, and again like many other Pacific islands, there's a sad lack of self-sufficiency. It's something of a shock to see the tins of mackerel and tuna in every trade store when the reef abounds with fish. The plus point about the Cook Islands' strong links to New Zealand is that for a number of years the New Zealand dollar has not been the world's strongest currency. So if the New Zealand dollar sinks, relative to your home market currency, then prices in the Cook Islands also translate into that much less.

Camping out is not allowed, but cheaper accommodation can also help to cut costs.

Most importantly, nearly all accommodation offers opportunities for preparing your own food which is substantially cheaper than eating out. See the Accommodation and Food sections later in this chapter for details.

Many visitors to the Cooks come on all-inclusive package holidays. Check out the package holidays available from travel agents; sometimes you can get accommodation-and-airfare packages for about the same price as airfare only, or even less.

Credit Cards

Visa, MasterCard and Bankcard are readily accepted at most places in Rarotonga. The Westpac bank in Avarua gives cash advances on all three cards; ANZ bank in Avarua gives cash advances on Visa and MasterCard. American Express and Diners Club are accepted at the better hotels and restaurants.

Currency

New Zealand and Cook Islands coins and paper money are used interchangeably in the Cooks. The only Cook Islands note is the $3 note – a rarity, only one other country has such a note. There is also a complete set of Cook Islands coins – 5c, 10c, 20c, 50c, $1, $2 and $5. Most of the coins are the same size and shape as the New Zealand coins (and Australian ones for that matter) so you can use New Zealand coins for pay phones or other such uses quite easily. The old huge $1 Tangaroa coin is now a collectors' item – they're available at the Philatelic Bureau on Rarotonga – having been replaced by a smaller, wavy-edged $1 coin, still bearing Tangaroa's image. The $2 coin is also an oddity, it's triangular! The $5 coin is larger than the rest and made of brass.

Cook Islands money, whether coins or paper bills, cannot be changed anywhere else in the world, so be sure to either spend it or change it back into New Zealand or other currency before you leave the country. It will only be good for a souvenir when you arrive somewhere else.

Currency Exchange

The Cook Islands use both Cook Islands and New Zealand currency, which are equal in value. The exchange rates are:

Australia	A$1	=	NZ$1.14
Canada	C$1	=	NZ$1.89
Fiji	Fiji$1	=	NZ$1.11
France	FF1	=	NZ$0.27
Germany	DM1	=	NZ$0.94
Japan	¥100	=	NZ$1.34
French Polynesia	CFP100	=	NZ$1.57
UK	UK£1	=	NZ$2.79
USA	US$1	=	NZ$1.71

You get about 4% more for travellers cheques than for cash. There are not many places you can change money – the Westpac and ANZ Banks in Avarua, the Administration Centre in Aitutaki and at some hotels. You're better off changing all your money on Rarotonga rather than hoping to be able to change money on the outer islands. Westpac has a branch at the Rarotonga international airport, open for all arriving and departing international flights.

Tipping & Bargaining

Tipping and bargaining are not customs in the Cook Islands. The price marked on items for sale, or on the bill in restaurants, is the price the merchant expects to receive. Haggling over prices is considered very rude.

Consumer Taxes

A 12.5% VAT (value added tax) is figured into the quoted price of just about everything. If a price is quoted to you 'plus tax' or 'plus VAT', you must add 12.5% to see what you'll actually pay.

POST & COMMUNICATIONS

Post

Postage stamps are a major source of revenue for the government. Some beautiful stamps are produced and, by limiting the supply and availability, they've managed to make many of them valuable collectors' items. The Philatelic Bureau office, next to the post office in Avarua, offers a wide selection of stamps, coins and bills.

As an ideal souvenir, you can send some attractively stamped postcards home from the Cooks. Postage rates include:

To	Postcards	Letters	Time
New Zealand, Australia & the South Pacific	NZ$0.80	NZ$0.85	7 days
USA, Canada, Latin America & Asia	NZ$0.85	NZ$1.05	10 days
Europe & Africa	NZ$0.90	NZ$1.15	10 days

You can receive mail care of poste restante at the post office, where it is held for 30 days. To collect mail at the post office in Avarua it should be addressed to you, c/o Poste Restante, Avarua, Rarotonga, Cook Islands. Poste restante services are available on the other islands.

Telephone

All the southern group islands, including Rarotonga, have modern telephone systems. The front pages of the telephone directory contain a section with details on international telephone calls. International collect calls can be made free from any telephone. Other international calls can be made from private phones, pay phones or from Telecom offices. Each island has a Telecom office. On Rarotonga, the Telecom office in Avarua is open 24 hours, seven days a week; hours are more limited on other islands. In addition to international and interisland telephone services, Telecom also offers fax, telegram and telex services.

The cost per minute for telephone calls is:

Destination	Operator-Assisted	Direct-Dial
all Cook Islands	NZ$1.20	NZ$1.00
New Zealand	NZ$2.53	NZ$2.30
Australia & the Pacific Islands	NZ$3.63	NZ$3.30
USA & Hong Kong	NZ$6.16	NZ$4.99
Other Countries	NZ$6.16	NZ$5.83

International and interisland calls are always charged at the same rate – there is no cheaper time to call, with the exception of direct-dial calls to New Zealand, which are reduced to NZ$1.85 per minute every night between midnight and 7 am.

The country code for the Cook Islands is 682. There are no local area codes.

Country codes for other countries are listed in the telephone directory. To direct dial from the Cook Islands to another country, dial '00', then the country code, city code and number.

No code is required for interisland calls. Dial the international operator '015' for international and interisland operator-assisted calls. International information is '017'; the local information operator is '010'.

Collect calls may be made only to the following countries: Australia, Canada, Fiji, French Polynesia, Hong Kong, India, Niue, Netherlands, New Zealand, Sweden, Tonga, UK, USA and Vanuatu.

BOOKS

There have been a surprising number of books written about the Cooks or in which the Cooks make an appearance. Unfortunately some of the most interesting are out of print and you will have to search libraries or second-hand bookshops if you want to find them. There's also an increasing number of interesting books about the Cook Islands being written today.

Some books are published in different editions by different publishers in different countries. As a result, a book might be a hardcover rarity, or even completely unheard of, in one place, while it's readily available in paperback in bookstores somewhere else. Many of the books mentioned below are readily available in the Cook Islands, but they may be difficult to find in other countries.

All the bookshops in the Cook Islands are in Avarua; see the Rarotonga chapter. The University of the South Pacific (USP) centre has the largest selection of books about the Cook Islands.

You can borrow books from the Cook Islands Library & Museum Society – including their extensive Pacific Collection – and from the National Library, both in Avarua, by signing up for a Temporary Borrower's Card. See the Rarotonga chapter for more information.

Lonely Planet

If you're travelling farther afield in the Pacific, check out the many other Lonely Planet books on Pacific nations.

Guidebooks

If you can read German, *Die Südsee: Inselwelten im Südpazifik* by Sabine Ehrhart (Du Mont Buchverlag, Köln, Germany) is an excellent overall guide to the South Pacific, with well-written history, natural history and culture sections and superb illustrations.

Cook Islands Companion by Elliot Smith (Pacific Publishing, Albany, California) is a guide to the Cook Islands.

Travel

Across the South Pacific by Iain Finlay & Trish Shepherd (Angus & Robertson, Sydney, 1981) is an account of a trans-Pacific jaunt by a family of four. The section on the Cook Islands is particularly interesting.

How to Get Lost & Found in the Cook Islands by John & Bobbye McDermott (Orafa, Honolulu, 2nd edition 1986) is another in the Air New Zealand funded series by a Hawaiian ex-adman, with a concentration on the Cooks' many colourful characters.

Exploring Tropical Isles & Seas by Frederic Martini (Prentice-Hall, Englewood Cliffs, New Jersey, 1984) makes interesting reading if you want to know more about what types of islands there are, how they are formed and what lives in the sea around them.

Best-selling travel writer Paul Theroux has a chapter on his trip to Aitutaki in *The Happy Isles of Oceania: Paddling the Pacific* (Penguin, 1992).

History

Alphons MJ Kloosterman's *Discoverers of the Cook Islands & the Names they Gave* (Cook Islands Library & Museum Society, Rarotonga, 1976) gives a brief history of each island, the early legends relating to that island and a record of its European contact. It makes interesting reading and there's an exhaustive listing of the early descriptions of the islands by European visitors.

History of Rarotonga, up to 1853 by Taira Rere (Rangitai Taira, Rarotonga, 1981, reprinted 1991) is a short, locally written history of Rarotonga. *The Gospel Comes to Rarotonga* by the same author (Rarotonga, 1980) is a concise account of the arrival of Christianity in the Cook Islands, particularly in Rarotonga, with interesting thumbnail sketches of the various important participants in this chapter of the islands' history.

The Cook Islands, 1820-1950 by Richard Gilson (Victoria University Press, Wellington, 1980) is a rather starchy and dry history of the Cooks, focusing almost exclusively on Rarotongan history, especially economics and politics after annexation by New Zealand up to 1950; little mention is made of the other islands in the group.

Years of the Pooh-Bah: A Cook Islands History by Dick Scott (Cook Islands Trading Corporation, Rarotonga, and Hodder & Stoughton, Auckland, 1991) is a newer and more readable book. Illustrated with plenty of historical photos, it tells the history of the Cooks with an emphasis on how they have been administered by Britain and New Zealand.

HE Maude's *Slavers in Paradise* (Australian National University Press, Canberra, and Stanford University Press, Stanford, 1981) provides a readable yet detailed analysis of the Peruvian slave trade which wreaked havoc in Polynesia from 1862. Some of the atolls in the northern group were particularly badly hit by this cruel and inhumane trade.

They Came for Sandalwood by Marjorie Crocombe (Wellington, 1964) is the story of Philip Goodenough and the *Cumberland* on Rarotonga, written for children.

Missionaries' Accounts

The Reverend William Gill turned up on Rarotonga in 1839 and lived in the Cooks for the next 30 years. His book *Gems of the Coral Islands* (1858) is perceptive but heavily slanted towards the missionary view of life.

The Cooks had a second William Gill: William *Wyatt* Gill was no relation at all to the other William Gill (he was only 11 years old when the older Gill started his missionary career) but he lived on the island of Mangaia for 20 years from 1852 and wrote several important studies. His book *From Darkness to Light in Polynesia* was originally published in 1894 but has been reissued (University of the South Pacific, Suva, 1984). *Cook Islands Custom* by William Wyatt Gill (University of the South Pacific, Suva, 1979) is a direct reprint of a fascinating illustrated manuscript originally published in 1892, telling of the customs of the Cook Islanders as the missionaries found them when they arrived.

Mission Life in the Islands of the Pacific by Aaron Buzacott (University of the South Pacific, Suva, 1985) is another recently reissued missionary account. It traces the life and work of Buzacott, who arrived on Rarotonga in 1828 and laboured as one of Rarotonga's foremost missionaries until his death in 1864. On Rarotonga his name is remembered in the Avarua CICC church which he constructed, the Maori Bible which he helped to translate and in the many hymns which bear his name in the CICC hymn book.

Amongst these reports on the Cook Islands by foreign-born missionaries there are also a couple of interesting books telling the story from an islander's point of view. One author, Maretu, was born in the Ngatangiia area of Rarotonga sometime around 1802. He was an older child when Europeans first visited Rarotonga in 1814 and a young man when the missionaries first arrived in 1823. Maretu later became a missionary himself and worked on several other islands in the Cooks. In 1871 he sat down to write, in Rarotongan Maori, an account of the extraordinary events he had witnessed during his lifetime. Translated into English and extensively annotated, his illuminating work has been published as *Cannibals & Converts* (University of the South Pacific, Suva, 1983).

Another Ngatangiia-born native son, Taunga, was about five years old when the missionaries arrived. He attended the mission school and became one of its star pupils, subsequently spending most of his long life as a missionary in the Pacific. *The Works of Taunga: Records of a Polynesian Traveller in the South Seas 1833-1896* by Ron & Marjorie Crocombe (Australian National University Press, Canberra, 1968; reprinted by University of the South Pacific, Suva, 1984) presents Taunga's accounts of his adventures, with notes putting his writings into historical perspective. *If I Live: The Life of Taunga* by Marjorie Tuainekore Crocombe (Lotu Pasifika Productions, Suva) is a short, simple story of Taunga's life, based on the larger book.

Impressions of Tongareva (Penrhyn Island), 1816-1901, edited by Andrew Teariki Campbell (University of the South Pacific, Suva, 1984) is an interesting book reproducing 48 historical references and accounts of visits to Penrhyn by missionaries, seafarers and others.

Residents' Accounts

A number of Cook Islands residents have gone into print with their tales of life in the South Pacific.

Wild Life Among the Pacific Islanders by EH Lamont, Esq, is a lively tale of the author's travels in the Pacific. He was shipwrecked and stranded on a remote island while on a ship heading for California and subsequently married three Polynesian women. The book was originally published in London in 1867 and has recently been re-published (University of the South Pacific, Suva, 1994).

Mangaia and the Mission by Sir Peter H Buck, originally published in 1934 as *Mangaian Society*, is an interesting ethnological study which Buck wrote about his time as the Resident Agent of Mangaia from 1929 to 1930 (University of the South Pacific, Suva, 1993).

Robert Dean Frisbie's books *The Book of Puka-Puka* (1928) and *The Island of Desire* (1944) are classics of South Pacific life. Frisbie was born in the USA and ran a store on Pukapuka. His first book, subtitled 'A Lone Trader on a South Sea Atoll', is a collection of articles he wrote for *Atlantic Monthly* and is now available in paperback. Frisbie's eldest daughter Johnny also wrote of the Cook Islands in *Miss Ulysses from Puka-Puka* (1948) and *The Frisbies of the South Seas* (1959).

One of the best known residents would have to be Tom Neale, who wrote of his life as the hermit of Suwarrow in *An Island to Oneself* (Holt, Rinehart & Winston, New York, 1966; Fontana Silver Fern, Auckland, 1975; Avon paperback). Tom Neale lived by himself on the beautiful but totally isolated northern atoll of Suwarrow for a total of six years in two three-year spells, in the late 1950s and early 1960s; his book recounts these periods. He then returned to Suwarrow and lived there for most of the 1970s until he was brought back to Rarotonga, shortly before his death in 1977. Many Rarotongan residents have anecdotes or opinions of him and it seems that his book, which was actually ghost written, makes him out to be a much more reasonable fellow than he actually was. One person's opinion was that he was so cantankerous that an uninhabited island was the only place for him! See the Suwarrow section of the Northern Islands chapter for more details.

Isles of the Frigate Bird (Michael Joseph, London, 1975) and *The Lagoon is Lonely Now* (Millwood Press, Wellington, 1978) were both written by the late Rarotongan resident Ronald Syme. The first book is mainly autobiographical and relates how the author came to the Cook Islands in the early 1950s and eventually settled down. The second book is more anecdotal, relating legends, customs and incidents of island life. Both books make interesting reading.

There are countless other early accounts of life in the Cooks, few of them currently available. FJ Moss, for example, wrote of the islands in 1888 in his book *Through Atolls & Islands*. Julian Dashwood (Rakau, or 'wood' in Maori) was a long time islands character who wrote two books about the Cooks. *I Know an Island* was published in the 1930s and he followed that with a second book in the 1960s published as *Today is Forever* in the USA and as *Island Paradise* in England. *Sisters in the Sun* by AS Helm & WH Percival (Robert Hale, London, 1973) tells of Suwarrow and Palmerston.

A more recent book, *From Kauri Trees to Sunlit Seas: Shoestring Shipping in the South Pacific* by Don Silk (Godwit Publishing, Auckland, 1994), co-owner (with Bob Boyd) of the Silk & Boyd interisland shipping based in the Cook Islands for many years, tells of the author's life and adventures in the Pacific over nearly four decades.

Politics & Politicians

Cook Islands Politics: the Inside Story (Polynesian Press, Auckland, 1979) is an anthology of articles by 22 writers. Representing many points of view, it tells the story of the toppling of Prime Minister Sir Albert Henry from power: the historical background, the intrigues, the corruption and the bribery.

Sir Thomas Davis, KBE (known as 'Sir Tom' or 'Papa Tom' in the Cooks), prime minister of the Cook Islands from 1978 to 1987, has written a number of books. *Island Boy – An Autobiography* (University of the South Pacific, Suva, 1992) tells the story of his life up to 1992. Another autobiographical book, *Doctor to the Islands* by Tom & Lydia Davis (Michael Joseph, London, 1955) is an earlier autobiographical work by Sir Tom and his wife, about his years as an island doctor. Sir Tom has also written another book, *Vaka* (see Legends, Literature, Poetry & Song later in this section).

Legends, Literature, Poetry & Song

Once you're in the Cooks you'll see numerous paperback books about the traditional legends of the various islands. Many of these have been published by the University of the South Pacific's Institute of Pacific Studies. *Cook Islands Legends* (University of the South Pacific, Suva, 1981) and *The Ghost at Tokatarava and Other Stories from the Cook Islands* (Ministry of Cultural Development, Rarotonga, 1992) are both written by notable Cook Islands author Jon Jonassen. *Te Ata O Ikurangi – The Shadow of Ikurangi* by JJ MacCauley (Cook Islands Library & Museum Society, Rarotonga) is another collection of legends. *Atiu Nui Maruarua* (University of the South Pacific, Suva, 1984) presents legends and stories from the island of Atiu in two languages, Atiuan Maori and English.

Vaka: Saga of a Polynesian Canoe by Tom Davis, KBE (University of the South Pacific, Suva, 1992) is a historical novel based on the story of the *Takitumu* canoe, one of the canoes of the 'great migration' to New Zealand around 1350 AD, over a span of 12 generations. It's a novel, not a history book, so it doesn't stand as solid history, but it makes fascinating reading.

The late Manihikian author and poet Kauraka Kauraka published a number of books of legends, stories and poetry. *Oral Tradition in Manihiki* (1989) is a fascinating scholarly analysis of the Maui myth (Maui being an important figure in the legends of many parts of the Pacific), Manihiki culture and the relation between the two. Kauraka's books of Cook Islands legends, principally from his home island of Manihiki, include *Legends from the Atolls* (1983) and *Tales of Manihiki* (1991). His poetry books include *Return to Havaiki/Fokihanga ki Havaiki* (1985), *Dreams of a Rainbow* (South Pacific Creative Arts Society, Rarotonga, 1987) and *Manakonako/Reflections* (1991). All of these books are bilingual, with the text published side by side in English and Manihikian Maori; all are published by the University of the South Pacific, Suva, except as noted.

Korero by Makiuti Tongia (Mana Publications, Suva, 1977, reprinted 1991) is another book of poetry, all in English this time.

Te Rau Maire: Poems and Stories of the Pacific, edited by prominent Cook Islands authors Marjorie Tuainekore Crocombe, Ron Crocombe, Kauraka Kauraka and Makiuti Tongia (Cook Islands Ministry of Cultural Development, Rarotonga, University of the South Pacific, Suva et al, 1992) is a sampling of stories and poetry from many Pacific nations, with several poems and one story from the Cook Islands.

E Au Imene Tamataora: Songs and Song-writers of the Cook Islands by John J Herrmann (University of the South Pacific, Suva, 1988) presents the lyrics (in Cook Islands Maori) to six songs by each of seven Cook Islands composers, with a brief story (in English) about each song, its composition and composer.

Arts & Crafts

Cook Islands Art by Dale Idiens (Shire Publications, Buckinghamshire, 1990) is illustrated with black and white photos of all kinds of arts and crafts from around the Cook Islands, explaining how they are or were used and their cultural significance. *The Art of Tahiti* by Terence Barrow (Thames & Hudson, London, 1979) is more accurately a guide to the art of Polynesia and includes an interesting chapter on the Cook Islands.

Tivaevae: Portraits of Cook Islands Quilting by Lynnsay Rongokea (Daphne Brasell Associates Press, Wellington, 1992) introduces 18 Cook Islands women from five islands, with colour photos of the women, their environment and the colourful *tivaevae* (appliqué works) they sew.

Patterns of Polynesia: The Cook Islands by Ailsa Robertson (Heinemann Education, Auckland, 1989) is a collection of patterns for things you can make yourself, including tivaevae and Mangaian masks.

Cook Islands Drums by Jon Jonassen (Cook Islands Ministry of Cultural Development, Rarotonga, 1991) gives information about Cook Islands drums and drumming, including rhythms, cultural significance and diagrams of how to make the various kinds of drums.

Pareu and Its Many Ties (Te Pua Inano, Rarotonga, 1992) gives colour photos and instructions on how to tie *pareu* (sarongs) in a variety of ways for both men and women.

The culinary art of the Cook Islands is celebrated in the *Cook Islands Cook Book* by Taiora Matenga-Smith (University of the South Pacific, Suva, 1990), a collection of Cook Islands recipes side by side in English and Maori. If you ever wanted to learn how to make raw fish in coconut sauce (*ika mata*), curried octopus in coconut sauce (*eke takare i roto ite akari*), stuffed breadfruit (*anga kuru akaki ia*) or Cook Islands fruit pudding (*poke*), here's your chance.

Cook Islands Photographs

Visions of the Pacific by David Arnell & Lisette Wolk (Ministry of Cultural Development, Rarotonga, 1993) is a coffee table-style book of truly exceptional colour photographs showing all the different Pacific island peoples who gathered in Rarotonga for the 6th Festival of Pacific Arts (Maire Nui festival) in October 1992.

South Seas Cook Islands by Dr Wolfgang Losacker, physician and honorary German consul on Rarotonga, is another coffee table-style book of colour photos of all the Cook Islands and their peoples, including the northern group islands. The book is available at Dr Wolfgang's office beside the Banana Court in Avarua and at Bounty Bookshop.

Nature, Plants & Birds

Rarotonga's Mountain Tracks and Plants by Gerald McCormack & Judith Künzle (Cook Islands Natural Heritage Project, Rarotonga, 1994) is a guide to the mountain tracks of Rarotonga and the plants you'll see when you walk them, as well as a general guide to the island's flora. Also look for *Rarotonga's Cross-Island Walk* by the same authors (Cook Islands Natural Heritage Project, 1991).

Guide to Cook Islands Birds by DT Holyoak (1980) has colour photos and text for identification of a number of local birds. *Kakerori: Rarotonga's Endangered Flycatcher* by Gerald McCormack & Judith Künzle (Cook Islands Conservation Service, Rarotonga, 1990) is a small illustrated book on the efforts to save one of Rarotonga's rare birds.

Academic Reports

Akatokamanava: Myth, History and Society in the Southern Cook Islands by Jukka Siikala (University of Auckland, Auckland, 1991) is an anthropological study of the cosmology of the southern Cook Islands, with analyses of their myths and history, written by a Finnish anthropologist.

People of the Cook Islands: Past and Present (Cook Islands Library & Museum Society, Rarotonga, 1988) is a report of the physical anthropological and linguistic research conducted in the Cook Islands from 1985 to 1987 by a group of Japanese scholars.

Richard Walter's *Prehistory of Mauke: An Ethnoarchaeological Report* (Cook Islands Library & Museum Society, Rarotonga, 1989) gives archaeological reports on 39 sites on Mauke, together with traditional stories connected with each site and other archaeological observations about the island. There's also *An Archaeological Survey of Pukapuka Atoll, 1985 (Preliminary Report)* by Masashi Chikamori & Shunji Yoshida (Keio University, Tokyo, 1988). All of these publications are on sale at the Cook Islands Library & Museum Society in Avarua.

Agriculture in the Cook Islands: New Directions by Saifullah Syed & Ngatokorua Mataio (University of the South Pacific, Suva, 1993) is a specialists' report on the topic.

Language & Dictionaries

Kai Korero: A Cook Islands Maori Language Coursebook by Tai Tepuaotera Turepu Carpentier & Clive Beaumont (Pasifika Press, Auckland, 1995) gives a good general introduction to the language of Rarotonga. A cassette audio tape accompanies the text. *Say it in Rarotongan* by Mana Strickland (Pacific Publications, Sydney, 1979) and *Conversational Maori* by Taira Rere (Rarotonga, 1980) are similar but older books. A visit to the Cook Islands Library & Museum Society in Avarua will turn up a number of other resources for tackling the language.

The *Cook Islands Maori Dictionary* by Jasper Buse with Raututi Taringa (Ministry of Education, Rarotonga, 1995), a Maori-English dictionary, is available in paperback on Rarotonga and is extremely helpful. *A Dictionary of the Maori Language of Rarotonga* by Stephen Savage (University of the South Pacific, Suva, 1980) is an older, more dated tome published many years after its author's death in 1941.

General

Television and Video in the Pacific Islands edited by Michael R Ogden & Linda S Crowl (University of the South Pacific, Suva, 1993) features one chapter about the Cook Islands ('Introducing Television: Seven Lessons from the Cook Islands' by Duane Varan) and other references to the Cooks throughout the book, with other chapters about the new experience of TV and video in a number of other Pacific countries.

The island of Suwarrow gets a chapter in *Ships, Sharks & Pirate Gold* by Graeme Wise (Random House, Auckland, 1997), a collection of true stories about the Pacific.

INTERNET RESOURCES

Email and Internet connections are available in the Cooks. Polyaccess in Avarua offers a walk-in service where you can connect; see the Rarotonga chapter for details. If you'll be staying longer in the Cooks and have your own computer, ask Telecom how you can get hooked up.

NEWSPAPERS & MAGAZINES

Rarotonga's daily newspaper, the *Cook Islands News*, is published every day except Sunday and provides coverage of local events and a brief summary of international events. The Saturday edition has a pull-out entertainment section with dining and nightlife guides, plus feature articles and the upcoming week's cinema and TV programming. There's another newspaper called the

Cook Islands Press that is published on Sunday only.

International subscriptions are available to both papers, and are a good way to keep up on local news when you're abroad. Contact:

Cook Islands News (☎ (682) 22-999, fax 25-303, editor@cinews.co.ck), PO Box 15, Avarua, Rarotonga, Cook Islands

Cook Islands Press (☎ (682) 24-865, fax 24-866, cipress@gatepoly.co.ck), PO Box 741, Avarua, Rarotonga, Cook Islands

The daily *New Zealand Herald* is sold on Rarotonga the day after it's published. A small selection of foreign magazines is also available, principally at the Bounty Bookshop in Avarua.

RADIO & TV

The Cooks have two local radio stations, one AM frequency and the other FM frequency, the first FM station in the South Pacific. The AM station reaches all the Cook Islands. Apart from local programs it also broadcasts Radio New Zealand news and Radio Australia's overseas world news service. The less powerful FM station can be received on most (but not all) of Rarotonga.

TV arrived on Rarotonga on Christmas Day, 1989. On Rarotonga there are broadcasts weekdays from 2.30 pm until around 11 pm, starting earlier on Sunday (12.30 pm) and later on Saturday (5.30 pm), with a couple of hours of CNN news early in the morning each day. On weekdays, the *Te Rongo Veka* local news program (half in Maori, half in English) provides local coverage. Later in the evening there's a half-hour news program from New Zealand's Channel One.

Each evening, the TV broadcast is taped and sent by airplane to Aitutaki, where it is shown the following evening. TV has reached other outer islands in recent years; most of the southern group islands now get TV, and sometimes the northern group gets it too – whenever a tape gets sent over from Raro.

Check the *Cook Islands News* for TV and radio schedules, which are published every day. A weekly schedule is published in the Saturday newspaper.

Shooting Video

Properly used, a video camera can give a fascinating record of your holiday. As well as videoing the obvious things – sunsets, spectacular views – remember to record some of the ordinary everyday details of life in the country. Often the most interesting things occur when you're actually intent on filming something else. Remember too that, unlike still photography, video 'flows' – so, for example, you can shoot scenes of countryside rolling past the bus window, to give an overall impression that isn't possible with ordinary photos.

Video cameras these days have amazingly sensitive microphones, and you might be surprised how much sound will be picked up. This can also be a problem if there is a lot of ambient noise – filming by the side of a busy road might seem OK when you do it, but viewing it back home might simply give you a deafening cacophony of traffic noise. One good rule to follow for beginners is to try to film in long takes, and don't move the camera around too much. Otherwise, your video could well make your viewers seasick! If your camera has a stabiliser, you can use it to obtain good footage while travelling on various means of transport, even on bumpy roads. And remember, you're on holiday – don't let the video take over your life, and turn your trip into a Cecil B de Mille production.

Make sure you keep the batteries charged, and have the necessary charger, plugs and transformer for the country you are visiting. In most countries, it is possible to obtain video cartridges easily in large towns and cities, but make sure you buy the correct format. It is usually worth buying at least a few cartridges duty free to start off your trip.

Finally, remember to follow the same rules regarding people's sensitivities as for still photography – having a video camera shoved in their face is probably even more annoying and offensive for locals than a still camera. Always ask permission first. ■

Video was present on Rarotonga several years before TV. Perhaps this explains the large number of video shops around – TV sets were on the island years before there was any broadcast TV, so videos became enormously popular. On Rarotonga you can rent video tapes, a video machine and even the colour TV to go with it.

PHOTOGRAPHY & VIDEO

You can buy colour print, colour slide (transparency) film and videos at Cocophoto, in the CITC Pharmacy in Avarua. Prices are considerably higher than what you'd pay back home, so it's a good idea to bring your film with you. You'll also need to bring film with you if visit the other islands, because film is only available on Rarotonga.

Cocophoto has a good selection of Kodak, Fuji and Agfa films and it also sells cameras and does photo processing. Film costs around NZ$16/24 for a roll of 24/36 colour prints and NZ$15/17 for a roll of 24/36 colour slides. Same-day colour print processing costs NZ$14/19 per roll of 24/36 colour prints. They don't do slide processing, or black and white; if you need these services, you'll have to send your film out of the country to get it done. Videos costs around NZ$10 per 180-minute cassette.

There is no film or film processing available on the outer islands – they have to send their film to Rarotonga to be done.

The Cook Islanders are generally quite happy to be photographed but the usual rule applies – it's polite to ask first. It's also worth bringing some high speed film with you. If you're taking photos in the densely forested mountain country of Rarotonga, or in the makatea of Atiu or Mauke, it can be surprisingly dark. Bring a flash if you plan to take photos in the caves on any of the outer islands.

TIME

The Cook Islands are east of the International Date Line. This is effectively one of the last places in the world; tomorrow starts later here than almost anywhere else. More precisely, when it's noon in the Cooks the time in other places (making no allowances for daylight saving and other seasonal variations) is:

London, England	9 pm same day
New York & Toronto	5 pm same day
San Francisco &	
Los Angeles, USA	2 pm same day
Tahiti & Hawaii	noon (same time)
Samoa	11 am same day
Tonga	11 am next day
Auckland, New Zealand	10 am next day
Sydney &	
Melbourne, Australia	9 am next day

Remember, however, that in common with many other places in the Pacific the Cook Islands also have Cook Islands Time, which means 'sometime, never, no hurry, no worries'.

The International Date Line
The early LMS missionaries generally came to the Cook Islands from Sydney, Australia, and were unaware that they had crossed the International Date Line and should have turned the calendar back a day. This anomaly continued for 78 years until 1899 when Christmas was celebrated two days in a row and the Cooks came into line with the rest of the world. Or at least some of the Cooks came into line; it took a bit longer for the message to get to all the other islands and for it to be accepted. Accounts of visiting ships at that time indicate that considerable confusion existed for a while. ∎

ELECTRICITY

Electricity is 240V, 50Hz AC just like in Australia and New Zealand, and the same three-pin plugs are used.

On Rarotonga and Aitutaki the power supply operates 24 hours a day; it's usually regular and quite dependable.

On other islands the availability of power may be more limited. The other southern group islands have power only from 5 am to midnight. The outer islands also have great fluctuations of current, so unless you have a voltage regulator, don't plug in a sensitive appliance like a computer. Even a surge protector may not help, as the spikes in the current can be very extreme, and a surge protector cannot protect the appliance against fluctuating low voltage.

WEIGHTS & MEASURES
The Cook Islands uses the metric system. See the conversion table at the back of this book.

LAUNDRY
Most accommodation places make some provision for their guests' laundry needs. On Rarotonga there's a laundry in Avarua with another branch in Arorangi.

TOILETS
Toilets in the Cooks are the same as in most western countries. You won't see public toilets on the streets but if you're out in public and nature calls, you can easily duck into any restaurant and ask permission to use the facilities.

HEALTH
The Cook Islands is generally a healthy place for locals and visitors alike. Food and water are generally good, fresh, clean and readily available, there are few endemic diseases, and the most serious health problem visitors may experience is sunburn from overdoing it at the beach. Nevertheless, it never hurts to know some basic travel health rules, anytime you travel.

Travel health depends on your predeparture preparations, your daily health care while travelling and how you handle any medical problem that does develop. While the potential dangers can seem quite frightening, in reality few travellers experience anything more than upset stomachs.

Predeparture Planning
Immunisations Plan ahead for getting your vaccinations: some of them require more than one injection, and some vaccinations should not be given together. It is recommended you seek medical advice at least six weeks before travel.

Record all vaccinations on an International Health Certificate, available from your doctor or government health department.

No vaccinations are required for travel in the Cook Islands, but discuss your requirements with your doctor. Vaccinations you should consider for this trip include:

- **Hepatitis A** The most common travel-acquired illness, after diarrhoea, which can put you out of action for weeks. Havrix 1440 is a vaccination which provides long term immunity (possibly more than 10 years) after an initial injection and a booster at six to 12 months.
  Gamma globulin is not a vaccination but is ready-made antibody collected from blood donations. It should be given close to departure because, depending on the dose, it only protects for two to six months.
- **Diphtheria & Tetanus** Diphtheria can be a fatal throat infection and tetanus can be a fatal wound infection. Everyone should have these vaccinations. After an initial course of three injections, boosters are necessary every 10 years.
- **Hepatitis B** This disease is spread by blood or by sexual activity. Travellers who should consider a hepatitis B vaccination include those visiting countries where there are known to be many carriers, where blood transfusions may not be adequately screened or where sexual contact is a possibility. It involves three injections, the quickest course being over three weeks with a booster at 12 months.
- **Polio** Polio is a serious, easily transmitted disease, still prevalent in many developing countries. Everyone should keep up to date with this vaccination. A booster every 10 years maintains immunity.

Health Insurance Make sure that you have adequate health insurance. See Travel Insurance under documents in the Facts for the Visitor chapter for details.

Travel Health Guides If you are planning to be away or travelling in remote areas for a long period of time, you may like to consider taking a more detailed health guide.

Staying Healthy in Asia, Africa & Latin America, Dirk Schroeder (Moon Publications, 1994) – probably the best all-round guide to carry; it's compact, detailed and well organised

Travellers' Health, Dr Richard Dawood (Oxford University Press, 1995) – comprehensive, easy to read, authoritative and highly recommended, although it's rather large to lug around

Travel with Children, Maureen Wheeler (Lonely Planet Publications, 1995) – includes advice on travel health for younger children

There are also a number of excellent travel health sites on the Internet. From the Lonely Planet home page (www.lonelyplanet.com /health/health.htm) there are links to the World Health Organisation, the US Center for Diseases Control & Prevention and Stanford University Travel Medicine Service.

Other Preparations Make sure you're healthy before you start travelling. If you are going on a long trip make sure your teeth are OK. If you wear glasses take a spare pair and your prescription.

If you require a particular medication take an adequate supply, as it may not be available locally. Take part of the packaging showing the generic name, rather than the brand, which will make getting replacements easier. It's a good idea to have a legible prescription or letter from your doctor to show that you legally use the medication.

Basic Rules

Food Good food is readily available in the Cook Islands so getting proper nutrition presents no special problems.

Whenever you travel, make sure your diet is well balanced. Fish, eggs and dairy products, pork, chicken, beef and mutton chops, as well as nonanimal products including tofu, beans, lentils and nuts, are all available in the Cook Islands and all are good ways to get protein. Fresh fruits and vegetables are a good source of vitamins. Try to eat plenty of grains and bread, preferably wholemeal bread. Remember that overcooked food loses much of its nutritional value. If your diet isn't well balanced or if your food intake is insufficient, it's a good idea to take vitamin and mineral supplements.

Water Tap water is usually safe to drink on Rarotonga and on most of the outer islands.

Do ask about it, though. In Aitutaki, for example, there are some places where you should take your drinking water from a rainwater tank beside the house or hotel, rather than from the tap. Even on Rarotonga, the tap water is not chlorinated and while most visitors like the water and have no complaints, some seem to be sensitive to it. If you suffer any upsets (diarrhoea, for example) you might try boiling your water before drinking it. Remember that if you are sensitive to the water, ice is just as suspect.

On rare occasions when rainfall has been either unusually heavy or unusually light, tap water can become cloudy. Very hard rain can cause mud and silt to enter the water supply, and drought can cause stored water to be dirty from the silt at the bottom of the tank. If you are suspicious of water for any reason, boil it for about five minutes before drinking. In heavy rain, remember you can always collect rainwater.

In hot climates always make sure you drink enough – don't rely on feeling thirsty to indicate when you should drink. Not needing to urinate or very dark yellow urine is a danger sign. Excessive sweating can lead to loss of salt and therefore muscle cramping. Salt tablets are not a good idea as a preventative, but in places where salt is not used much, adding salt to food can help.

Water Purification The simplest way of purifying water is to boil it thoroughly. Vigorously boiling for about five minutes should be satisfactory.

Consider purchasing a water filter for a long trip. There are two main kinds of filter. Total filters take out all parasites, bacteria and viruses, and make water safe to drink. They are often expensive, but they can be more cost effective than buying bottled water. Simple filters (which can be just a nylon mesh bag) take out dirt and larger foreign bodies from the water so that chemical solutions work much more effectively; if water is dirty, chemical solutions may not work at all. It's very important when buying a filter to read the specifications, so that you know exactly what it removes from the water and what it doesn't. Simple filtering will not remove all dangerous organisms, so if you cannot boil water it should be treated chemically. Chlorine tablets (Puritabs, Steritabs or other brand names) will kill many pathogens, but not some parasites like giardia and amoebic cysts. Iodine is more effective in purifying water and is available in drops or tablet form (such as Potable Aqua). Follow the directions carefully and remember that too much iodine can be harmful.

Medical Problems & Treatment

Self-diagnosis and treatment can be risky, so you should always seek medical help. Although we do give drug dosages in this section, they are for emergency use only. Correct diagnosis is vital.

Antibiotics should ideally be administered only under medical supervision. Take only the recommended dose at the prescribed intervals and use the whole course, even if the illness seems to be have been cured. Stop immediately if there are any serious reactions and don't use the antibiotic at all if you are unsure that you have the correct one. Some people are allergic to commonly prescribed antibiotics such as penicillin or sulpha drugs; carry this information when travelling, eg engraved on a bracelet.

In some places standards of medical attention are so low that for some ailments the best advice is to get on a plane and go somewhere else. Basic medical care is available in the Cook Islands – every island has a hospital, though on the outer islands the hospitals are quite primitive. Patients on the outer islands are often sent to the hospital on Rarotonga for care. Rarotonga has a hospital, an outpatient clinic and several private doctors. For serious conditions, however, Cook Islanders go to New Zealand for treatment. See the Health Insurance section earlier in this chapter.

Environmental Hazards

Fungal Infections Fungal infections occur more commonly in hot weather and are usually found on the scalp, between the toes or fingers, in the groin and on the body (ringworm). You get ringworm (which is a fungal infection, not a worm) from infected animals or other people. Moisture encourages these infections.

To prevent fungal infections wear loose, comfortable clothes, avoid artificial fibres, wash frequently and dry carefully. If you do get an infection, wash the infected area at least daily with a disinfectant or medicated soap and water, and rinse and dry well. Apply an antifungal cream or powder like tolnifate (Tinaderm). Try to expose the infected area to air or sunlight as much as possible and wash all towels and underwear in hot water, change them often and let them dry in the sun.

Heat Exhaustion Dehydration and salt deficiency can cause heat exhaustion. Take time to acclimatise to high temperatures, drink sufficient liquids and do not do anything too physically demanding.

Salt deficiency is characterised by fatigue, lethargy, headaches, giddiness and muscle cramps; salt tablets may help, but adding extra salt to your food is better.

Heat Stroke This serious, occasionally fatal, condition can occur if the body's heat-regulating mechanism breaks down and the body temperature rises to dangerous levels. Long, continuous periods of exposure to high temperatures and insufficient fluids can leave you vulnerable to heat stroke.

The symptoms are feeling unwell, not sweating very much (or at all) and a high body temperature (39°C to 41°C, or 102°F to 106°F). Where sweating has ceased the skin becomes flushed and red. Severe, throbbing headaches and lack of coordination will also occur, and the sufferer may be confused or aggressive. Eventually the victim will become delirious or convulse. Hospitalisation is essential, but in the interim get victims out of the sun, remove their clothing, cover them with a wet sheet or towel and then fan continually. Give fluids if they are conscious.

Prickly Heat Prickly heat is an itchy rash caused by excessive perspiration trapped under the skin. It usually strikes people who have just arrived in a hot climate. Keeping cool, bathing often, drying the skin and using a mild talcum or prickly heat powder or resorting to air-conditioning may help.

Sunburn In the tropics you can get sunburnt surprisingly quickly, even through cloud. Use a sunscreen, hat, and barrier cream for your nose and lips. Calamine lotion, Stingose and aloe vera are good for mild sunburn. Protect your eyes with good quality sunglasses, particularly if you will be near water or sand.

Jet Lag Jet lag is experienced when a person travels by air across more than three time zones (each time zone usually represents a one-hour time difference). It occurs because many of the functions of the human body (such as temperature, pulse rate and empty-ing of the bladder and bowels) are regulated by internal 24-hour cycles. When we travel long distances rapidly, our bodies take time to adjust to the 'new time' of our destination, and we may experience fatigue, disorienta-tion, insomnia, anxiety, impaired concentration and loss of appetite. These effects will usually be gone within three days of arrival, but to minimise the impact of jet lag:

- Rest for a couple of days prior to departure.
- Try to select flight schedules that minimise sleep deprivation; arriving late in the day means you can go to sleep soon after you arrive. For very long flights, try to organise a stopover.
- Avoid excessive eating (which bloats the stomach) and alcohol (which causes dehydration) during the flight. Instead, drink plenty of noncarbonated, nonalcoholic drinks such as fruit juice or water.
- Avoid smoking.
- Make yourself comfortable by wearing loose-fitting clothes and perhaps bringing an eye mask and ear plugs to help you sleep.
- Try to sleep at the appropriate time for the time zone you are travelling to.

Motion Sickness Eating lightly before and during a trip will reduce the chances of motion sickness. If you are prone to motion sickness try to find a place that minimises movement – near the wing on aircraft, close to midships on boats, near the centre on buses. Fresh air and looking off into the distance or at the horizon usually help; reading, stale air and cigarette smoke make it worse. Commercial motion-sickness prep-arations, which can cause drowsiness, have to be taken before the trip commences – once you're feeling sick, it's too late. Ginger (available in capsule form) and peppermint (including mint-flavoured sweets) are natural preventatives.

Infectious Diseases
Diarrhoea Simple things like a change of water, food or climate can all cause a mild bout of diarrhoea, but a few rushed toilet trips with no other symptoms is not indica-tive of a major problem.

Dehydration is the main danger with any diarrhoea, particularly in children or the elderly as dehydration can occur quite quickly. Under all circumstances fluid replacement (at least equal to the volume being lost) is the most important thing to remember. Weak black tea with a little sugar, soda water, or soft drinks allowed to go flat and diluted 50% with clean water are all good. With severe diarrhoea a rehydrating solution is preferable to replace lost minerals and salts. Commercially available oral rehy-dration salts (ORS) are very useful; add them to boiled or bottled water. In an emergency you can make up a solution of six teaspoons of sugar and a half teaspoon of salt to a litre of boiled or bottled water. You need to drink at least the same volume of fluid that you are losing in bowel movements and vomiting. Urine is the best guide to the adequacy of replacement – if you have small amounts of concentrated urine, you need to drink more. Keep drinking small amounts often. Stick to a bland diet as you recover.

Lomotil or Imodium can be used to bring relief from the symptoms, although they do not actually cure the problem. Only use these drugs if you do not have access to toilets, eg if you *must* travel. For children under 12 years Lomotil and Imodium are not recommended. Do not use these drugs if the person has a high fever or is severely dehydrated.

In certain situations antibiotics may be required: diarrhoea with blood or mucous (dysentery), any fever, watery diarrhoea with fever and lethargy, persistent diarrhoea not improving after 48 hours and severe diarrhoea. In these situations gut-paralysing drugs like Imodium or Lomotil should be avoided.

A stool test is necessary to diagnose which kind of dysentery you have, so you should seek medical help urgently. Where this is not possible the recommended drugs for dysentery are norfloxacin 400mg twice daily for three days or ciprofloxacin 500mg twice daily for five days. These are not recommended for children or pregnant women. The drug of choice for children would be co-trimoxazole (Bactrim, Septrin, Resprim) with dosage dependent on weight. A five-day course is given. Ampicillin or amoxycillin may be given in pregnancy, but medical care is necessary.

Amoebic Dysentery This is more gradual in the onset of symptoms, with cramping abdominal pain and vomiting less likely; fever may not be present. It will persist until treated and can recur and cause other health problems.

Giardiasis This is another type of diarrhoea. The parasite causing this intestinal disorder is present in contaminated water. The symptoms are stomach cramps, nausea, a bloated stomach, watery, foul-smelling diarrhoea and frequent gas. Giardiasis can appear several weeks after you have been exposed to the parasite. The symptoms may disappear for a few days and then return; this can go on for several weeks. Tinidazole, known as Fasigyn, or metronidazole (Flagyl) are the recommended drugs. Treatment is a 2g single dose of Fasigyn or 250mg of Flagyl three times daily for five to 10 days.

Hepatitis Hepatitis is a general term for inflammation of the liver. It is a common disease worldwide. The symptoms are fever, chills, headache, fatigue, feelings of weakness and aches and pains, followed by loss of appetite, nausea, vomiting, abdominal pain, dark urine, light-coloured faeces, jaundiced (yellow) skin and the whites of the eyes may turn yellow. **Hepatitis A** is transmitted by contaminated food and drinking water. The disease poses a real threat to the western traveller. You should seek medical advice, but there is not much you can do apart from resting, drinking lots of fluids, eating lightly and avoiding fatty foods. People who have had hepatitis should avoid alcohol for some time after the illness, as the liver needs time to recover.

Hepatitis E is transmitted in the same way, and it can be very serious in pregnant women.

There are almost 300 million chronic carriers of **Hepatitis B** in the world. It is spread through contact with infected blood, blood products or body fluids, for example through sexual contact, unsterilised needles and blood transfusions, or contact with blood via small breaks in the skin. Other risk situations include having a shave, tattoo, or having your body pierced with contaminated equipment. The symptoms of type B may be more severe and may lead to long term problems. **Hepatitis D** is spread in the same way, but the risk is mainly in shared needles.

Hepatitis C can lead to chronic liver disease. The virus is spread by contact with blood usually via contaminated transfusions or shared needles. Avoiding these is the only means of prevention.

HIV & AIDS HIV (Human Immunodeficiency Virus) develops into AIDS (Acquired Immune Deficiency Syndrome) which is a fatal disease. HIV is a major problem in many countries. Any exposure to blood, blood products or body fluids may put the individual at risk. The disease is often transmitted through sexual contact or dirty needles – vaccinations, acupuncture, tattooing and body piercing can be potentially as dangerous as intravenous drug use. HIV/AIDS can also be spread through infected blood transfusions; some developing countries cannot afford to screen blood used for transfusions.

If you do need an injection, ask to see the syringe unwrapped in front of you, or take a needle and syringe pack with you.

Fear of HIV infection should never preclude treatment for serious medical conditions.

Intestinal Worms These parasites are most common in rural, tropical areas. The different worms have different ways of infecting people. Some may be ingested in food including undercooked meat and some enter through your skin. Infestations may not show up for some time, and although they are generally not serious, if left untreated some can cause severe health problems later. Consider having a stool test when you return home to check for these and determine the appropriate treatment.

Sexually Transmitted Diseases Gonorrhoea, herpes and syphilis are among these diseases; sores, blisters or rashes around the genitals, discharges or pain when urinating are common symptoms. In some STDs, such as wart virus or chlamydia, symptoms may be less marked or not observed at all, especially in women. Syphilis symptoms eventually disappear completely but the disease continues and can cause severe problems in later years. While abstinence from sexual contact is the only 100% effective prevention, using condoms is also effective. Gonorrhoea and syphilis can be treated with antibiotics; the different sexually transmitted diseases require specific antibiotics. There is no cure for herpes or AIDS.

Insect-Borne diseases
Dengue Fever There is no preventative drug available for this mosquito-spread disease which can be fatal in children. A sudden onset of fever, headaches and severe joint and muscle pains are the first signs before a rash develops. Recovery may be prolonged. Travellers are advised to prevent mosquito bites at all times by using mosquito repel-

lents containing the compound DEET on exposed areas, wearing long pants and long sleeved shirts and using a mosquito net at night. With any type of dengue, aspirin-based drugs should be avoided.

Filariasis This is a mosquito-transmitted parasitic infection found in many parts of Africa, Asia, Central and South America and the Pacific. Possible symptoms include fever, pain and swelling of the lymph glands; inflammation of lymph drainage areas; swelling of a limb or the scrotum; skin rashes and blindness. Treatment is available to eliminate the parasites from the body, but some of the damage already caused may not be reversible. Medical advice should be obtained promptly if the infection is suspected.

Malaria Malaria is not present in the Cook Islands.

Cuts, Bites & Stings
Bedbugs & Lice Bedbugs live in various places, but particularly in dirty mattresses and bedding, evidenced by spots of blood on bedclothes or on the wall. Bedbugs leave itchy bites in neat rows. Calamine lotion or Stingose spray may help.

All lice cause itching and discomfort. They make themselves at home in your hair (head lice), your clothing (body lice) or in your pubic hair (crabs). You catch lice through direct contact with infected people or by sharing combs, clothing and the like. Powder or shampoo treatment will kill the lice and infected clothing should then be washed in very hot, soapy water and left in the sun to dry.

Insect Bites & Stings Mosquitoes can be a real nuisance in the Cooks at certain times of year, particularly during the rainy season from around mid-December to mid-April. Use repellent, and carry some with you if you'll be tramping through the bush or in caves. Mosquito coils are available everywhere in the Cook Islands and lighting one will make your room free of mosquitoes for several hours, or you can use insect spray. Screens on windows or mosquito nets over beds are also helpful.

The most effective insect repellent is called DEET; it is an ingredient in many commercially available insect repellents. Look for a repellent with at least a 28% concentration of DEET. Be warned that DEET breaks down plastic, rubber, contact lenses and synthetic fabrics, so be careful what you touch after using it. It poses no danger to natural fibre fabrics. Other good repellents include Off! and Repel, which come in a stick or a spray and will not eat through plastic the way repellents containing DEET do. Or you can mix up a half-and-half combination of Dettol (the bathroom cleaner) and baby oil, mineral oil or coconut oil. Kerosene is another effective repellent; mix kerosene with baby oil, mineral oil or coconut oil and rub it all over you. You'll certainly stink to high heaven but at least you won't have to worry about being bitten by insects.

Bee, wasp, centipede and other insect stings are usually painful rather than dangerous. However in people who are allergic to them severe breathing difficulties may occur and require urgent medical care. Large centipedes can give a painful or irritating bite but it's no more dangerous to your health than a bee or wasp sting. Large red-and-yellow wasps are easily spotted and easy to avoid. Tiny red ants have an annoying but not dangerous sting.

Calamine lotion or Stingose spray will relieve insect bites and stings; ammonia is also effective. Ice packs or antihistamine cream will reduce the pain and swelling. Or you can reduce the itch by using a local remedy: pick a frangipani leaf and rub the white liquid oozing from the stem onto the bite. Aloe vera may also help. If you are allergic to bee or wasp stings, be sure to carry your medication with you.

Snakes There are no land or shallow-water snakes in the Cook Islands. The one snake species lives in the open sea.

Jellyfish & Other Sea Creatures Jellyfish are not a big problem in the Cook Islands because most swimming is done in protected lagoons, inside the coral reefs. However, on rare occasions when there have been particularly high or rough seas, jellyfish have been washed into the lagoons.

Local advice is the best way of avoiding contact with these sea creatures with their stinging tentacles. Stings from most jellyfish are simply rather painful. Dousing in vinegar will neutralise the venom, relieve the pain and de-activate any stingers which have not 'fired'. Calamine lotion, antihistamines and analgesics may also reduce the reaction and relieve the pain. The most effective folk remedy for jellyfish stings, used all over the world, is to apply fresh urine to the stings as soon as possible – something in the urine neutralises the jellyfish venom. Methylated spirits or alcohol increases firing of stinging cells and increases the pain. Avoid benzocaine, which can sensitise the skin.

On very rare occasions someone will see a poisonous stonefish or stingray in a lagoon. Stonefish look exactly like stones, hence their name; when they are hanging around coral or stony areas, as they usually do, their natural camouflage makes it practically impossible to see them. If you do get stung by a stonefish, go to the hospital, where they will give you an injection.

More commonly encountered inside the lagoon is stinging coral – it's the bright, sulphur yellow-coloured coral with a smooth surface. Don't touch this coral. If you do, however, the sting is only bothersome, not dangerous. Applying vinegar or fresh urine will neutralise the sting.

If you're out reef walking don't thrust your arm into deep tidepools, as eels sometimes lurk there. Certain cone shells found in the Pacific can sting dangerously or even fatally. Again, local advice is the best suggestion.

There are no sharks in the lagoons but they do live in the open sea beyond the reefs. The sharks that live around here are not the human-eating variety so they pose no danger to divers.

Cuts & Scratches Wash well and treat any cut with an antiseptic such as povidone-iodine. Where possible avoid bandages and Band-aids, which can keep wounds wet. Coral cuts are notoriously slow to heal and if they are not adequately cleaned small pieces of coral can become embedded in the wound. Avoid coral cuts by wearing shoes when walking on reefs, and clean any cut thoroughly with an antiseptic. Severe pain, throbbing, redness, fever or generally feeling unwell suggest infection and the need for antibiotics promptly as coral cuts may result in serious infections.

Women's Health

Gynaecological Problems Sexually transmitted diseases are a major cause of vaginal problems. Symptoms include a smelly discharge, painful intercourse and sometimes a burning sensation when urinating, but with some STDs women may observe no symptoms at all. Male sexual partners must also be treated. Medical attention should be sought and remember in addition to these diseases HIV or hepatitis B may also be acquired during exposure. Besides abstinence, the best thing is to practise safe sex using condoms.

The use of antibiotics, synthetic underwear, sweating and contraceptive pills can lead to fungal vaginal infections when travelling in hot climates. Maintaining good personal hygiene, and wearing loose-fitting clothes and cotton underwear will help prevent these infections.

Fungal and yeast infections, characterised by a rash, itch and discharge, can be treated with a vinegar or lemon-juice douche, or with yoghurt. Nystatin, miconazole or clotrimazole pessaries or vaginal cream are the usual treatment.

Pregnancy It is not advisable to travel to some places while pregnant as some vaccinations normally used to prevent serious diseases are not advisable in pregnancy, eg yellow fever. In addition, some diseases are much more serious for the mother (and may increase the risk of a stillborn child) in pregnancy, eg malaria. Neither of these are present in the Cook Islands, but keep it in mind if you will be travelling further afield.

Most miscarriages occur during the first three months of pregnancy. Miscarriage is not uncommon, and can occasionally lead to severe bleeding. The last three months should also be spent within reasonable distance of good medical care. A baby born as early as 24 weeks stands a chance of survival, but only in a well-equipped, modern hospital. Pregnant women should avoid all unnecessary medication, vaccinations and malarial prophylactics should still be taken where needed. Additional care should be taken to prevent illness and particular attention should be paid to diet and nutrition. Alcohol and nicotine should be avoided.

Less Common Diseases

The following pose a small risk to travellers, and so are only mentioned in passing. Seek medical advice if you think you may have these diseases.

Tetanus Tetanus occurs when a wound becomes infected by a germ which lives in soil and in the faeces of horses and other animals. It enters the body via breaks in the skin. All wounds should be cleaned promptly and adequately and an antiseptic cream or solution applied. Use antibiotics if the wound becomes hot, throbs or pus is seen. The first symptom may be discomfort in swallowing, or stiffening of the jaw and neck; this is followed by painful convulsions of the jaw and whole body. The disease can be fatal.

Typhus Typhus is spread by ticks, mites and lice. It begins with fever, chills, headache and muscle pains followed a few days later by a body rash. There is often a large painful sore at the site of the bite and nearby lymph nodes are swollen and painful. Typhus can be treated under medical supervision.

WOMEN TRAVELLERS

It's tempting to say that the Cooks present no special problems for women travellers, and leave it at that. Most of the time and in most situations women travellers will never have a problem in the Cooks. As a visitor to the islands, you will usually be treated with courtesy and kindness.

Nevertheless, you should be aware that the threat of rape does exist. Be cautious about going alone to deserted places, such as tramping in the mountains; be cautious about swimming alone in the lagoon late at night, or even walking down some deserted stretch of beach late at night. As in other parts of the world, your best protection is to be accompanied – go with a friend, or get a group of travellers together at the place you're staying.

On Rarotonga there's a 24-hour women's counselling centre, Punanga Tauturu (☎ 21-133).

What to Wear
Like everywhere, as a woman your travelling experiences will go a lot smoother if you observe the local customs of dress and don't offend people by your appearance. This is easy to do in the Cooks by observing a few basic courtesies.

Swimming wear is for swimming; it's fine at the beach or by the pool but elsewhere you should cover up. Don't swim or sunbathe topless or in the nude, as you will cause grave offence to locals if you do. Sleeveless blouses and shorts are fine to wear anywhere, but 'short shorts' up to your bum will cause many raised eyebrows in disapproval. Wearing a pareu is fine.

If you visit the outer islands, remember that their standards of dress are more conservative than on Rarotonga and Aitutaki, which have been visited by plenty of foreign tourists.

If you go to church, be sure to wear sleeves, so your shoulders and upper arms are covered. Don't wear a pareu or shorts to church; a skirt or dress is best, preferably with the hemline at or below the knee. It's customary for women to wear hats in the Cook Islands Christian Church (CICC), so wear one if you can, but don't worry about it if you don't have one – everyone under-

stands that visitors to the islands are not usually travelling with hats! Flowers can be worn any other time, but not to church.

GAY & LESBIAN TRAVELLERS
Homosexuality is an accepted fact of life in the Cook Islands, as in most of Polynesia. There's no need for gays or lesbians to hide their sexuality. Public displays of sexual affection are frowned upon, though, whether gay or straight, so don't put on a demonstration with your lover in public.

There are no particular 'gay bars' or places for gay people to gather; you can meet gay people everywhere.

DISABLED TRAVELLERS
Special facilities for the disabled are few and far between in the Cook Islands, however the newly renovated Rarotongan Beach Resort on Rarotonga is fully accessible. All of its rooms and public areas are wheelchair accessible, and a couple of rooms are specially equipped with facilities for the disabled.

SENIOR TRAVELLERS
Many senior travellers visit the Cooks – the warm climate, the relaxed pace of life and the easy-going friendliness of the Cook Islanders are all ideal for seniors. Older people are respected and venerated in the Cooks, and seniors are treated well here.

Many local seniors are very spry – it's not unusual for people in their 70s and 80s to have lifestyles just as active as their children and grandchildren. The 'Golden Oldies' have rugby and cricket tournaments every year, and also the occasional event such as song and dance competitions. If you stop by to watch a Golden Oldies cricket game you'll probably be invited to join in!

TRAVEL WITH CHILDREN
Children are loved in the Cook Islands and travelling with them presents no special problems. Some hotels allow children to stay free of charge, others have a reduced children's rate, and a few do not accept children at all. Be sure to ask the policy when you make your bookings.

There are plenty of things to do that will keep children happy in the Cooks. Soft, sandy beaches on calm lagoons couldn't be safer for children to swim in, though of course they must still be supervised; if they like snorkelling they'll be enthralled. Be sure they understand not to touch the coral. There are plenty of other activities such as walking, cycling, horse riding and canoeing that children will like. An 'island night' performance would be fun for the kids, as would a visit to the Cook Islands Cultural Village, and there's plenty more. Children dance in some of the 'island night' dance troupes, and they do very well!

Bring along a baby carrier if you'll need one. Nappies (diapers) are expensive, so you might want to bring some of these along too. For protection from sun, bring sunscreen and light clothes which cover the whole body. If your child is sensitive to local water, you can boil the drinking water, or buy bottled water. Make sure your health and travel insurance also covers your child.

Travel With Children by Maureen Wheeler, co-founder of Lonely Planet, is a helpful book for travel with children anywhere in the world.

DANGERS & ANNOYANCES

The Cook Islands are safer than most places in the world, but a certain amount of common sense is still called for. In general, you will find the Cooks to be just as idyllic as the tourist brochures lead you to expect and the people to be some of the friendliest you will ever meet. As anywhere, crime does exist but with normal, minimal caution you should have no problems.

Theft

Theft has unfortunately become quite a problem on Rarotonga, though it's nothing like the levels of many other parts of the world. It's practically unheard of for anyone to be attacked or robbed, or even to be robbed sneakily from their person; it is more likely to happen if you leave things laying around. Don't leave all your money in your wallet on the beach and then go off swimming. Even theft of clothes from clotheslines at night is a problem; it's best to bring your clothes in at night. It's not a bad idea to check your valuables with your hotel management, just as you would when travelling in other places, to prevent theft from your room when you're not there.

Swimming

In the sheltered lagoons swimming could hardly be safer but be very wary of the passages and breaks in the surrounding reef. Currents are especially strong here; the lagoon waters sweep swiftly out to the open sea and often straight downwards due to the very steep drop-offs just off the reef. Rarotonga has several such passages, notably at Avana Harbour, Avaavaroa, Papua and Rutaki, and they exist on other islands as well. Check the Rarotonga map for the position of reef passages before you go swimming. Several unnecessary deaths have occurred when people have been swept away in these passages. Venturing outside the reef should only be done if you are fully aware of the tidal flow and currents, and then only with great care.

Check the Health section earlier in this chapter for advice on other things you should watch out for when swimming.

Insects & Other Creatures

At certain times of year mosquitoes can be a real nuisance. They are not malarial, but they can carry dengue fever, so it's important to avoid being bitten. Bring repellent.

Other insects that bite or sting include bees, wasps and small red ants. The insect most people fear the most is the large centipede. Though it looks very frightening – they can reach about 15cm (six inches) long – their sting is no more dangerous than a bee or wasp sting. Jellyfish are not pleasant, either, but they are not usually found inside the lagoons where most people swim. Stonefish are poisonous but they are rarely encountered. See the Health section earlier in this chapter for more on insects and other creatures found in the Cook Islands, their stings and what to do if you do get stung.

Not really a danger, but definitely an annoyance if there are many around, are the large cockroaches that live in the Cooks, as in the tropics all over the world. They won't hurt you, but do make sure they don't crawl over your food at night as they can spread germs. Insect spray is sold at every grocery shop. It's said that if the cockroaches are flying, it means it will rain the next day.

BUSINESS HOURS

Monday to Friday, 8 am to 4 pm is the usual business week, and shops are also open on Saturday morning until noon. Small local grocery stores keep longer hours, often from around 6 or 7 am until around 8 or 9 pm. The Westpac and ANZ banks in Avarua are open Monday to Friday from 9 am to 3 pm; Westpac also opens from 9 to 11 am on Saturday.

Nearly everything is closed on Sunday – bars close at midnight on Saturday and even the local airline doesn't fly on Sunday. The only exceptions, again, are the small local grocery stores, some of which open for a couple of hours very early Sunday morning and for a few hours again in the evening. A couple of shops are operated by Seventh-Day Adventists, who celebrate the Sabbath on Saturday rather than Sunday, so they're closed on Saturday and open on Sunday. Even many restaurants are closed on Sunday, except for hotel restaurants, which are open seven days a week. Several of the larger hotels serve up special Sunday meals – brunches in late morning, barbecues in late afternoon.

PUBLIC HOLIDAYS & SPECIAL EVENTS

The Cook Islands have many public holidays, and they're good opportunities to see dancing and other activities.

New Year's Day
　1 January
Good Friday & Easter Monday
　March/April – the two principal Easter days
Anzac Day
　25 April – as in New Zealand and Australia, this is an annual memorial day for the soldiers of the two world wars, with a parade and services

Queen's Birthday
　First Monday in June – as in New Zealand and Australia, the Queen's 'official' birthday is celebrated as a public holiday
Gospel Day (Rarotonga only)
　26 July – Rarotonga celebrates the arrival of the gospel to its shores
Constitution Day
　4 August – Cook Islands' independence is celebrated by 10 days of festivities (see Cultural Events, below); Constitution Day is a national holiday
Gospel Day (Cook Islands)
　26 October – Nuku religious plays are performed to commemorate the arrival of Christianity to the Cook Islands, when British missionary John Williams and Raiatean missionary Papeiha arrived on 26 October 1823; every major church participates with Biblical dramatisations involving music, processions and colourful costumes
Flag Raising Day
　27 October – the raising of the British flag over Rarotonga on 27 October 1888 by Captain Bourke of the HMS *Hyacinth* is celebrated with traditional drumming and string-band competitions
Christmas Day
　25 December
Boxing Day
　26 December

Special Events

In addition to the annual holidays, many other island-wide events occur. 'Any excuse for a good time' seems to be the motto, and the locals exuberantly turn out to support all manner of marches, runs, walks, sports competitions, music/dance/art/cultural events, youth rallies, religious revivals, raffle drawings, international mobilisations for one cause or another – you name it! Don't be shy about attending any function – visitors are always welcome.

The following are some of the more interesting and important festivals and events.

Australia Day Golf Tournament
　26 January – a golf tournament with Australia-oriented prizes held at the Rarotonga Golf Club on Australia Day
Waitangi Day Golf Tournament
　6 February – a golf tournament with New Zealand-oriented prizes held at the Rarotonga Golf Club; New Zealand's Waitangi Day commemorates the signing of the Treaty of Waitangi on 6 February 1840

Cultural Festival Week
    Second week of February – a week of festivities featuring *tivaevae* quilt competitions, and arts and crafts displays

Cook Islands Sevens Rugby Tournament
    Mid-February – international and local teams compete in this tournament

Island Dance Festival Week
    Third week of April – dance displays and competitions including the important individual male and female Dancer of the Year competition

Song Quest
    Held over five weeks beginning in July – this event culminates in a big finale during the final two weeks where singers, musicians and performers from all the Cook Islands come to Rarotonga to compete for stardom

Masters' Golf Tournament
    Mid-July – this golf tournament is for those aged 40 years and over, and visitors are welcome to enter

Lawn Bowling Tournament
    Mid-July to the first week in August – this tournament has both local and overseas participants

Constitution Celebration
    Beginning on the Friday before 4 August – this 10-day festival celebrates the 1965 declaration of independence with sporting activities, dances, musical performances, historical and cultural displays, and many other events; this is the country's major festival of the year

Aitutaki Open Golf Tournament
    Mid-September – this open golf tournament is held on Aitutaki

Rarotonga Open Golf Tournament
    Late September – another open golf tournament held just after the Aitutaki tournament

Linmar's 15km Road Race
    Late September – a 15km foot race sponsored by Linmar's shop

Round Rarotonga Road Race & Round the Rock Relay
    Early October – these popular fun runs, one for individual runners and a few days later for teams, circle the island on the coast road; the record for the 32km distance is just over 98 minutes, and visitors are welcome to run with the locals

All Souls Day (Turama)
    1 November – the Catholic community decorates graves with flowers and candles

Tiare (Floral) Festival Week
    Final week of November – Tiare Festival Week is celebrated with floral float parades, a Miss Tiare pageant, a Mama Muumuu pageant, flower display and arrangement competitions, and all the public businesses on Rarotonga decorate their premises with flowers; the week starts off with an official opening and an international food festival

New Year's Eve
    31 December – the new year is welcomed with dancing and other entertainment

ACTIVITIES

The Cook Islands are relaxed, slow and easy-going. But there are plenty of activities to keep you busy if you're so inclined. All the activities mentioned here are covered in more detail in the individual island chapters.

Swimming

Of course with all the water around, water sports are the most obvious activity in the islands, and swimming is the first water sport on most people's minds. All the islands have at least some sort of sheltered lagoon where you can swim, and some sandy beaches.

The two most visited islands, Rarotonga and Aitutaki, are great for swimming. Most other islands of the southern group are surrounded by reefs that are very close to the land, so the swimming possibilities are fewer, but even these islands have somewhere or other to swim – sometimes in caves! The various island chapters point out the best places to swim on each island.

Snorkelling & Diving

Rarotonga and Aitutaki both have excellent possibilities for snorkelling in the lagoons inside the reef, and for diving outside the reef.

There are many features that make diving on Rarotonga and Aitutaki particularly attractive, especially the high 30m to 60m (100 to 200-foot) visibility and the variety of things to be seen down below. Diving and instruction prices in the Cooks are quite reasonable.

Diving operators on both islands offer daily diving trips, and if you aren't already a certified diver you can take a four-day course and receive NAUI or PADI certification that will permit you to dive anywhere in the world.

Snorkelling is enjoyable on both islands. Snorkelling gear is sold on Rarotonga and is available for hire on Rarotonga and Aitutaki. Both islands have lagoon cruise operators to take you to some of the best snorkelling spots. See the Rarotonga and Aitutaki chapters for more information.

There aren't as many possibilities for snorkelling on the other islands of the southern group; their reefs are so close to shore that the lagoons are narrow and shallow. If you venture to the islands of the northern group, be sure to bring your snorkelling gear because most of the islands have large lagoons with clear water, abundant fish and exotic shells.

Other Water Sports

The sheltered lagoons of Rarotonga and Aitutaki are also great for other water sports. On Rarotonga, head to Muri Beach where sailing boats, windsurfers, outrigger canoes, kayaks, surfboards and other equipment are available for hire. Sailing races are held at Muri beach on Rarotonga every Saturday, starting at 1 pm. Aitutaki has less paraphernalia but an even bigger lagoon.

Lagoon Cruises

Aitutaki must be one of the best places in the world for lagoon cruises. The lagoon is large, warm, brilliantly turquoise, and full of brightly coloured tropical fish and a variety of living corals. The main island is surrounded by a number of *motu* (smaller islands) and cruises to these islands, with swimming, snorkelling and a barbecue fish lunch, stopping at some of the lagoon's best snorkelling spots on the way, operate every day except Sunday. Don't miss taking a lagoon cruise if you go to Aitutaki.

Rarotonga's lagoon is smaller, so you don't really need a boat to get around on the lagoon. Glass-bottom boats operate from Muri Beach and cruise to some of the best places to see coral and tropical fish. The cruises provide snorkelling gear, and conclude with barbecue lunches. Also on Rarotonga, Reef Runner individual craft and the Reef Sub both enable you to see the coral from outside the reef, without going diving.

Deep-Sea Fishing

Boats for deep-sea fishing, equipped with everything you need, are available for charter on Rarotonga and Aitutaki. If you visit some of the other outer islands, where tourism is not as organised, you might get some of the locals to take you fishing the way they do it, in outrigger canoes!

Hiking & Walking

All the islands have innumerable possibilities for walking, tramping and exploring. Rarotonga, with its craggy interior mountains, lush valleys and beautiful white-sand beaches, has something for everyone, from challenging mountain treks to easy strolls through valleys and along beaches and streams. Even expert rock climbers can find plenty to challenge them on Rarotonga. See the Walking & Climbing section in the Rarotonga chapter.

Rarotonga is the only mountainous island in the Cooks; the other islands offer less strenuous walking possibilities. Atiu, Mauke, Mitiaro and Mangaia all have caves to visit, a good reason to take off tramping through the makatea to reach them. Aitutaki, with its single small mountain Maungapu and limitless beaches and trails, is also great for walking and exploring.

Cycling

Cycling is a popular activity on Rarotonga and Aitutaki. Bicycles can be rented on both islands, and also on Mauke. The distances are short, roads are pretty flat, and a bicycle enables you not only to get around but also to get right off the beaten track, and to see the islands at an island pace.

Caving

Atiu, Mauke, Mitiaro and Mangaia all have interesting caves to explore. See the individual chapters for details.

In 1997 we met Paul Tobin, an intrepid Aussie cave-diving enthusiast fresh back on Rarotonga after a cave-diving trip to Mauke. He told us the following:

Cave diving can be done in all the islands of Nga Pu Toru (Atiu, Mauke and Mitiaro), *if* you're a certified cave diver and *if* you bring all your own specialised cave-diving gear. You must get permission from the island council before cave diving, and you must also get permission from the individual land owner in order to enter each cave.

All of these islands have many caves, and not all the people know about all of the caves. Some people know about some caves, others know about others. To visit all the caves on an island, you'll probably have to do a lot of asking around, and get several people to take you to caves that they know. We met a fellow on Mauke who took us to a cave that even most locals don't know about.

Tumunu

Though the missionaries managed to stamp out the practice on most of the other Cook Islands, *tumunu*, or bush beer-drinking schools, are still held on the island of Atiu. Related to the *kava*-drinking ceremonies of Fiji and some other Pacific islands, this is about the last place in the Cooks where you'll be able to experience this custom.

Visiting Marae

History and archaeology buffs will enjoy visiting the historic *marae* on many of the Cook Islands. Rarotonga and Aitutaki have some particularly impressive marae, but they are found in some form on all the islands. Traditional religious meeting places associated with particular chiefs, high priests or clans, the marae are still very significant in some aspects of culture on Rarotonga and on many other islands. Although the carved wooden figures on the marae were destroyed, burned or taken away by the zealous British missionaries, the stones of many of the ancient marae are still there.

Dancing

Cook Islands dancing is some of the most famous and beautiful in the Pacific, so you should be sure to see at least one performance while you're here. Don't forget that dancing is not only performance – it is also a popular activity that you can participate in. Friday night is the big night for going out dancing, especially on Rarotonga and Aitutaki. Even the smaller islands of Atiu and Mangaia manage to have a Friday night dance. Dancing in the Cooks is fun, with lots

of swaying hips, quivering knees and plenty of enthusiasm.

Sports

Tennis is a popular sport on several islands. On Rarotonga you can hire racquets at the two large resort hotels and play on their courts. There are many other courts around the island which you can play on if you have your own tennis gear. Atiu has a remarkable number of tennis courts, Mangaia has courts, and in fact, if you have your own gear, you can probably play tennis one way or another on most of the islands.

On Rarotonga you can join the Hash House Harriers, Hussies & Hoffspring for an easy fun run every Monday afternoon.

Rarotonga has a golf course, and there's also a smaller, much more basic golf course on Aitutaki. Visitors are welcome to try their hand at lawn bowling at the Rarotonga Bowling Club. Horse riding is also available on Rarotonga. For aerobics and body building you can go to the Topshape Health & Fitness Centre in Rarotonga.

The two major sports in the Cooks are rugby, which is played with all-out passion in tournaments from May to August, and cricket, played over the summer months, particularly from January to April. Each village has a team vying against the others in tournaments, and it's all great fun. Even the seniors compete in 'Golden Oldies' rugby and cricket tournaments! Though the tournaments are played by organised teams, there's always a chance of coming upon a casual game – don't be shy to ask if you want to play. Both games are played not only in tournaments, but also just for fun, all year round.

Netball is another popular sport, played in tournaments by women at the same time as the men are playing rugby. Soccer, hockey and volleyball are other sports played in the Cooks.

WORK

Tourists are prohibited from working in the Cook Islands. The government makes a concerted effort to ensure that jobs that can be done by locals, go to locals. If you get caught working on a visitor's (tourist) permit, you'll be in big trouble.

You will see a number of foreigners working, though, especially on Rarotonga. These people often have Cook Islands permanent resident status – many are married to Cook Islanders – and often they have skills to perform jobs which could not be filled by locals and thus were granted special work permits. Others are here on various volunteer programs – Australian Volunteers, the World Health Organisation and the United Nations Volunteer Program all send volunteers to the Cooks.

In order to work legally in the Cook Islands you must obtain a work permit from the Ministry of Foreign Affairs & Immigration, in the big white three-storey government building behind the Banana Court in Avarua. Contact this office (☎ 29-347, fax 21-247; PO Box 105, Avarua, Rarotonga, Cook Islands) to find out the current requirements for getting a work permit.

Work permits are not easy to obtain. You may have to go back to your country of origin, apply for a work permit from there, and wait for it to be granted before you can return. You may have to come up with an employment sponsor in the Cooks, who must convince the government that the job could not be done by a local. Or you could always volunteer with one of the volunteer programs.

ACCOMMODATION

Although there is no visa requirement to enter the Cooks, there is one stipulation for all visitors: you are supposed to have booked accommodation when you arrive.

Up until recently, this was an iron-clad rule and if you did not have booked accommodation, the immigration people at the airport had every right to turn you away and put you back on the airplane without ever setting foot outside the airport. One traveller wrote to tell us he saw this happen to a couple who had written simply 'hostel' on their arrival form.

Recently, enforcement of this rule has become a little more relaxed. Most of the places to stay have someone at the airport to meet every flight, and nowadays if you have not booked a place to stay, you may be ushered to an area where you can get information about your options and be introduced to the representative of the hotel you pick. Nevertheless, the prior booking rule is still officially on the books, and you will do best to have a booking when you arrive.

The prior booking rule isn't quite as totalitarian as it sounds. For a start, they don't say how long you have to book for – conceivably you could book for the first night only. Secondly, there's nothing to stop you changing your mind as soon as you see the place you've booked into and go looking elsewhere – some people do change their minds quite legitimately. And thirdly, often nobody really checks – you could easily walk out of the airport saying you'd booked into Hotel A or Z when you'd done nothing of the sort.

'Prior booking' is the law, however, and you will be asked to fill in a blank on your arrival form stating where you are booked to stay.

This rule is supposedly to stop people sleeping on beaches, camping out or staying with local people. It's also done to try to make sure that every visitor has a place to stay. Some of the more popular hotels on Rarotonga are routinely booked up months in advance; if you simply arrive and expect to find a room at these places, you will be sadly disappointed. Other hotels are not so busy, but there are increasing numbers of tourists arriving on Rarotonga and only a limited number of hotel rooms.

People staying long-term often rent houses locally. You can get quite a reasonable place, fully furnished with everything you need including linen and kitchenware, for around NZ$100 to NZ$200 a week. No doubt some people stay with locals, although it's not very common on Rarotonga.

Rarotonga is far and away the major attraction and it has by far the most places to stay. Aitutaki also has an increasing number of places to stay, and there's organised

Top: Canoes (*vaka*) on the beach, Mangaia
Bottom: Te Rua Manga ('The Needle') as seen on the Cross-Island Trek, Rarotonga

NANCY KELLER

NANCY KELLER

NANCY KELLER

Top: Hammock under the palms, Aitutaki
Bottom Left: Baby sea turtles & starfish in tank at Ministry of Marine Resources, Aitutaki
Bottom Right: Canoes (*vaka*) in the Cook Islands are christened not with a bottle of
champagne, but a coconut

accommodation on all the other southern group islands that have air services.

In the northern group, Manihiki and Penrhyn now have guest houses. On other northern group islands where accommodation is very limited you may have to stay with local people. On some islands this is organised, arranged and prices are firmly set. On others, where visitors are few and far between, arrangements are likely to be very informal. In such a case, make certain that you do not take advantage of Polynesian hospitality – be sure to pay your way. Bringing along an ample supply of food, not only for yourself but also to share, is always appreciated.

On Rarotonga there are two major resort hotels, some hostel-style accommodation and pretty much everything else is motel-style, closely related to the motels in New Zealand. This is no bad thing in one way – nearly every place has some sort of kitchen or cooking facilities. On the other hand it's a disappointment that most of the accommodation makes so little reference to the Pacific. The average Rarotongan motel could easily be in Newcastle, Australia or Palmerston North, New Zealand. A few places are trying to cultivate more of a South Pacific atmosphere.

FOOD

Rarotonga has a number of good restaurants, Aitutaki has a few, and Mangaia and Atiu each have a couple. Elsewhere in the islands the choice of places to eat is much more limited.

Fortunately most accommodation has kitchen facilities so you can fix your own food and save some money along the way. The catch here is that a lot of food is imported and is consequently expensive. There are a couple of ways of improving this situation. First of all, look for local produce. There's little in the way of local packaged food, apart from the expensive Frangi fruit juices and the Vaiora soft drinks; virtually all other packaged food is imported (usually from New Zealand) and very expensive. The price

tags on anything from packaged cereal to yoghurt can be astonishing.

There are, however, plenty of locally grown fruits and vegetables. The trick is finding them – you might do better looking for them in local shops, at the Punanga Nui open market, one of the Wigmore's stores on Rarotonga, at the Orongo Centre by the wharf in Aitutaki, or even buying direct from the locals rather than from big supermarkets. Locally grown fruits and vegetables can be very reasonably priced, but in the supermarkets you often find the vegetables have come straight from New Zealand and cost several times the New Zealand or Australian prices. Bread and doughnuts are baked locally on most of the islands and are reasonably priced.

The second way of economising on food is to bring some supplies with you. All food imports must be declared on arrival and although fresh produce is prohibited, you'll have no problem with packaged goods.

Remember that just as costs on Rarotonga are higher than in New Zealand, Australia or North America, costs are also higher again on the outer islands than on Rarotonga. If you are going to the outer islands you would be wise to bring some food supplies with you. If you're going to a place with no formal accommodation it's only polite to supply as much food as you eat and some more besides.

Local Food

You won't find too much local food on the restaurant menus but at 'island night' buffets or at barbecues you'll often find interesting local dishes. An *umukai* is a traditional feast cooked in an underground oven: food is *kai*, underground is *umu*.

Some dishes you might come across include:

arrowroot – also called manioc, manioca or tapioca, the starchy root of this plant is a common food

breadfruit/kuru – spherical fruit which grows on trees to grapefruit size or larger. It is more like a vegetable than a fruit and can be cooked in various ways (eg like french fries).

eke – octopus

ika mata – raw fish, marinated in lemon or lime juice then mixed with coconut cream and other ingredients

kumara – sweet potato

poke – pawpaw or banana pudding, mixed with coconut sauce and arrowroot starch to give it a gummy texture

puaka – suckling pig

rukau – taro leaves cooked and mixed with coconut sauce and onion that look and taste much like spinach

taro – all-purpose tuber vegetable. The roots are prepared rather like potato.

DRINKS
Nonalcoholic Drinks

The truly local drink is coconut water and for some reason Cook Islands coconuts are especially tasty. The young coconuts (*nu*) are the drinking nuts; the older nuts are used for their meat.

Try the Atiu Island Coffee, grown and processed on Atiu. If you visit Atiu you can take a tour of the coffee plantation and factory. The coffee is sold in bags at various places around Rarotonga, and served in some restaurants.

The Frangi juice factory, on the main road near the Rarotonga international airport, makes a variety of fresh juices including orange, mango-orange, passionfruit-orange and pineapple. Frangi juices are sold at the factory outlet, called The Cold Shop, and at some of the small shops around the island, but not in the supermarkets.

The local soft drink bottling company is called Vaiora, and they make soft drinks in orange, pineapple, lemonade, cola and other flavours.

Alcoholic Drinks

Cook's Lager, Rarotonga's own beer, is quite good as well as being the least expensive beer in the Cooks. Free tours are given of the Rarotonga Brewery in Avarua, followed by a free beer.

A wide variety of New Zealand beers are also available, Steinlager being the favourite, plus Fosters (Australian), San Miguel (Philippines), Heineken (Dutch), Hinano (Tahitian) and Viamo (Samoan). They cost around NZ$2 to NZ$3 a can in bars and are cheaper from shops, where a large bottle of Steinlager costs around NZ$4.

Until independence Cook Islanders were strictly forbidden western alcohol which was, however, permitted to *papa'a* (Europeans and other foreigners). Perhaps as a result beer is a problem in the Cook Islands: far too much money gets spent on it and drunkenness is a social problem.

Liqueurs made from local products (coconut, pineapple, banana, mango and Atiu coffee) are made on Rarotonga and sold at The Perfume Factory on the back road in Avarua, and at Perfumes of Rarotonga with outlets in Avarua and Matavera. They are strong (40% alcohol) and taste good either straight or mixed with juice or coffee.

Imported liquors are available in the Cooks, but are heavily taxed and thus quite expensive. The widest selection is found at the CITC Liquor Centre near Avatiu Harbour on Rarotonga.

If you go to Atiu, check out a tumunu, or bush beer-drinking session. Tumunu are also held on Mauke but although there is a bar named the Tumunu on Rarotonga the ceremonies are really only performed on Atiu and Mauke. Nowadays the tall, hollowed-out coconut tree stump (the tumunu) from which the home brew used to be served has been replaced by plastic drums; you can see a couple of really old tumunu at the Cook Islands Library & Museum Society museum in Avarua. The old ritual kava ceremonies, to which the tumunu is related, were stamped out by the missionaries and were no longer found in any form.

ENTERTAINMENT

Cook Islands dancing is considered to be some of the best dancing in the Pacific and there are plenty of chances to see it at the 'island nights' held around Rarotonga most nights of the week. The 'island nights' start off with a buffet dinner of local foods, followed by a floor show of dance, music and song. The grand finale is when the performers come out into the audience, choose unsuspecting partners and take them up on stage to have a go at Cook Islands dance. It's good fun and definitely worth doing sometime during your stay. The Cook Islands Cultural Village on Rarotonga is another good place to see Cook Islands dancing, along with many other elements of Cook Islands culture. 'Island nights' are also held on Aitutaki.

Then there's going out dancing yourself. Cook Islanders love to dance and Friday night is the popular night. Rarotonga and Aitutaki both have venues, and even Atiu and Mangaia manage to have a dance on Friday night. Hips sway and shake and knees quiver like they never do back home! It's good fun.

The Empire Cinema in Avarua is the only one in the Cook Islands. It has two sides (Cinema 1 and Cinema 2) and each presents two films each evening (no shows on Sunday). Check the *Cook Islands News* for the daily schedule.

SPECTATOR SPORT

Sport is popular in the Cooks and there are plenty of chances to see a variety of sports, with everything from sedate lawn bowls to rousing rugby or cricket games, to sailing races. Anytime there's a game, you're welcome to go and watch. See the *Cook Islands News* for announcements of upcoming games. There are also a number of sports you can engage in yourself. See the Activities section earlier in this chapter for more details.

THINGS TO BUY

There are many things that you can buy as souvenirs of the Cooks, ranging from unique, very high quality handicrafts to cheap tourist products. Several islands in the Cooks have their own handicraft specialities. Most of them can be bought on Rarotonga, but if you take a trip to the outer islands you may find things you haven't seen on Rarotonga, and they'll probably cost less.

Tangaroa Figures

Tangaroa is the squat, ugly but well-endowed figure you find on the Cook Islands' one dollar coin. Traditional god of the sea and fertility, Tangaroa is a beloved

figure for Cook Islanders and he has become the symbol of the Cooks. It's been a long-term rehabilitation though because the early missionaries, in their zeal to wipe out all traces of heathenism, did a thorough job of destroying traditional gods wherever they found them. Tangaroa, along with the rest of the old gods, was banned. When the Cook Islanders did start carving Tangaroa figures again they were often sexless, but now they're fully endowed once again. You can get Tangaroa figures ranging from key ring figures a couple of centimetres high up to huge ones standing 1m high or more, and just about requiring a crane to move them. A figure about 25cm high will cost around NZ$40.

Tangaroa, god of fertility and the sea

Other Wooden & Stone Products

Carved wooden slit drums (*pate*) are a Polynesian speciality; you can find them in most of the crafts shops. Ukeleles, made of wood and coconut shells, are another good souvenir.

Traditional Mangaian ceremonial stone adzes with intricately carved wooden handles or stands and sennit binding (museum pieces in some of the world's major museums) are still made on Mangaia. You can take a look at them in the museums on Rarotonga, and visit the craftspeople on Mangaia to buy one if you like, and you might find them for sale on Rarotonga. Stone taro pounders are also still made and used on Mangaia.

Rito Hats

The beautiful hats which the women wear to church on Sunday are a Cook Islands speciality. These *rito* hats are woven of fine, bleached pandanus leaves and the best ones come from the islands of Rakahanga and Penrhyn. Prices start at about NZ$50, so they're not cheap, but they're even more expensive in Tahiti.

Baskets & Woven Pandanus Products

Some good-quality basket work is still done but look out for plastic carton strapping and other man-made materials creeping into use. Traditional baskets of excellent quality are still made on Mangaia, where you can buy them directly from the women who make them, and on several other of the outer islands.

Traditional woven pandanus products such as mats, purses and fans are now rarely made on Rarotonga, since the pandanus which used to grow on this island has mostly died off, but you can find them in the arts and crafts shops. On most of the other islands of the southern group, with the exception of Atiu where there is also less pandanus now than there used to be, all the traditional pandanus items are still made for everyday use. If you visit the outer islands, you'll see pandanus products everywhere.

Pearls

Pearls, an important Cook Islands product, are farmed on the northern group islands of Manihiki and Penrhyn and sold on Rarotonga. Black pearls, golden pearls, white pearls, pearls embedded in their mother-of-pearl shells, and mother-of-pearl products are all available on Rarotonga. Black pearls, very rare in the world, are a speciality of the Cooks.

Shells & Shell Jewellery

The tiny Shells & Craft shop in Muri on Rarotonga has a wide selection of unusual shells.

A lot of shell jewellery is produced as well as larger items like shell lamps. Some of this work is imported, principally from the Philippines, but some fine shell work is produced locally. *Pupu* eis, long necklaces made of tiny yellow or white pupu shells collected on the makatea of Mangaia, are a sought-after item; you can buy these necklaces individually or by the dozen on Rarotonga and on Mangaia, where they are less expensive.

Before you rush off to buy shells remember that something has to be evicted to provide the shell, and conservationists are worried about some species being collected to extinction.

Tivaevae

These colourful and intricately sewn appliqué works are traditionally made as burial shrouds, but are also used as bedspreads, and smaller ones for cushion covers. They're rarely seen for sale on most islands; if you do find a full-size tivaevae for sale, you'll find they cost several hundred dollars due to the enormous amount of time required to make them. Smaller wall hangings, cushion covers, or clothing using tivaevae-inspired patterns are cheaper.

The Atiu Fibre Arts Studio on Atiu is the only place in the Cook Islands where tivaevae are commercially produced and always available. If you stop by the Tivaivai Cafe on Atiu you can see a selection of tivaevae, wall hangings, clothing and more; tivaevae are on sale there or you can special order one, choosing the pattern and colour scheme you prefer. Tivaevae are also sold at a few places on Rarotonga.

Other Souvenirs

There's a multitude of other things you can buy as souvenirs of the Cooks. Pure coconut oils and coconut oil-based soaps come either in their natural state or scented with local flowers, including *tiare maori* (gardenia), frangipani, starfruit flower and jasmine. The Perfume Factory and Perfumes of Rarotonga, both on Rarotonga, sell quality perfumes made from these local flowers for about NZ$20 a bottle, for both men and women.

Colourful pareu come in many styles and thicknesses; original tie-dyed ones of very thin material, costing about NZ$12, are the most popular and the best for the warm climate. You can also find a multitude of T-shirts in the shops around Rarotonga with logos saying Cook Islands, Rarotonga, South Pacific etc.

A kilogram or two of Atiu Island Coffee is another good souvenir. Liqueurs made from local fruits and coffee beans are also a popular souvenir and can be tasted and bought at The Perfume Factory and Perfumes of Rarotonga, both with outlets in Avarua. Tangaroa-shaped ceramic bottles are also sold there, to put the liqueur in, if you like.

Rarotonga has a couple of resident artists and their paintings and other artwork are on sale, often at very reasonable prices.

At the low end of the spectrum, Tangaroa figures with spring-loaded, pop-up penises are about the most tasteless but there are plenty more where that came from. More insidious are the Cook Islands handicraft souvenirs that don't originate from the Cooks at all. A lot of the shell jewellery and wooden bowls were born in the Philippines! There are also plenty of New Zealand Maori items which the unscrupulous might try to pass off as Cook Islands Maori. In fact you might be suspicious of anything which could conceivably be made overseas – even supposedly indigenous items like Tangaroa figures. Fortunately the craft shops do seem to be remarkably honest and if you ask if a piece is local or made elsewhere you'll usually be given a straight answer.

Getting There & Away

Occasionally a cruise ship might call on the Cooks, and some yachts pass through, although the Cooks are nowhere near as popular for yachties as Tahiti, Fiji or Tonga. Usually, however, getting to the Cooks means flying, and since Rarotonga is the only island with an international airport, that's where you'll land. Yachties can enter the Cooks at a couple of other islands.

AIR
Airports & Airlines
The Rarotonga international airport is a rather simple airport, by international standards. When the plane lands, a set of stairs on wheels is rolled up to the plane, and you get off and walk across the tarmac to the airport building. Music will be playing to greet you, and there's a festive feeling in the air.

Unless you're a Cook Islander you'll be given a free 31-day visitor's permit upon arrival, which can later be extended (see the Facts for the Visitor chapter for details). You'll be asked to fill in an arrival form, including a blank for where you'll be staying. This is a vitally important blank, because the Cook Islands has a 'prior booking requirement' and technically you

can be turned away and sent back to the airplane if you haven't booked a place to stay, at least for the first night of your visit (see the Accommodation section in the Facts for the Visitor chapter for details). You'll also be asked to show an onward or return ticket.

After you've picked up your bags and passed through customs, you'll be greeted and asked where you're staying. A fleet of mini-buses and taxis meets each flight, and you will be directed to the one going to your place of stay. See the Getting Around section in the Rarotonga chapter for more on airport-transport options.

The Westpac bank at the airport is open for all arriving and departing flights. If you have New Zealand dollars you won't need to change money, as New Zealand and Cook Islands money is used interchangeably in the Cooks. If you need to change money, however, you can do it here.

Buying Tickets
Air New Zealand is the only international airline serving the Cook Islands. Even though there is only one airline, it still pays to take the time to do some research and compare prices and stopover options when buying your ticket. Travel agents often work

---

Aviation History
Aviation in the Cook Islands has had quite an interesting history. During WWII, airstrips were built on Penrhyn, Aitutaki and Rarotonga, and in 1945 a DC3 service operated every two weeks on a Fiji-Tonga-Western Samoa-Aitutaki-Rarotonga route. This service by New Zealand National Airways Corporation was dropped in 1952, but Tasman Empire Airways Limited (TEAL) had meanwhile started a monthly Solent flying-boat service on the 'Coral Route' from Auckland to Papeete via Fiji and Aitutaki. See the Aitutaki chapter for more about this route.

The Solent service was increased to once every two weeks and continued until 1960. For a time there were no flights at all to the Cooks apart from infrequent New Zealand Air Force flights. In 1963 Polynesian Airways started a service from Apia in Western Samoa to Rarotonga but this was stopped in 1966 due to new regulations banning small aircraft making such long-distance flights over water. Once again the Cook Islands were left without international connections, and it was not until the new Rarotonga international airport was opened in 1974 and big jets could fly into Rarotonga that flights resumed. ■

out special package deals (air fare plus accommodation) that cost the same or even less than what you'd pay for the air fare alone.

It's possible to visit the Cooks as a destination by itself, as a stopover when you're travelling across the Pacific, or as part of a Round-the-World or Circle Pacific ticket. Depending where you're coming from, it may not cost much more to visit the Cooks in combination with other destinations than it would to visit the Cooks, or the other destinations, alone.

High and low-season air fares apply when flying to the Cooks, but the high and low seasons are variable, depending where you're coming from. Check your dates and options carefully when you book your ticket; going just a day or two earlier or later can make a big difference in the cost. Special deals such as two-for-one companion tickets and youth or senior travel incentives are more likely to be offered at off-peak times.

There are more Cook Islanders living in New Zealand than there are in the Cook Islands themselves, and many of them come home for the Christmas and summer school holiday period, beginning in mid-December and ending in January. This means there's an extra heavy demand for air seats coming from New Zealand to the Cooks in December, and going in the other direction in January. Keep this in mind when making your travel plans; if you're travelling at this time you may find many flights are full, so it's a good idea to reserve your seats as far in advance as possible. It may not be easy to change your dates if you're flying around this busy time.

Travellers with Special Needs

If you have special needs of any sort – if you've broken a leg, you're vegetarian, travelling in a wheelchair, taking the baby, terrified of flying – you should let the airline know as soon as possible so that they can make arrangements accordingly. You should remind them when you reconfirm your

booking (at least 72 hours before departure) and again when you check in at the airport. It may also be worth ringing the airline before you make your booking to find out how they can handle your particular needs.

Airports and airlines can be surprisingly helpful, but they do need advance warning. Most international airports will provide escorts from check-in desk to plane where needed, and there should be ramps, lifts, wheelchair-accessible toilets and reachable phones. Note, however, that the Rarotonga international airport has none of these things, so plan accordingly. Aircraft toilets are likely to present a problem; travellers should discuss this with the airline at an early stage and, if necessary, with their doctor.

Guide dogs for the blind will often have to travel in a specially pressurised baggage compartment with other animals, away from their owner; though smaller guide dogs may be allowed in the cabin. All guide dogs will be subject to the same quarantine laws (six months in isolation etc) as any other animal when entering or returning to countries currently free of rabies, such as Britain and Australia.

Deaf travellers can ask for airport and in-flight announcements to be written down.

Children under two travel for 10% of the standard fare, as long as they don't occupy a seat. They don't get a baggage allowance either. 'Skycots' will be provided by the airline if requested in advance; these will take a child weighing up to about 10kg. Children between two and 12 can usually occupy a seat for half to two-thirds of the full fare, and do get a baggage allowance. Push chairs (strollers) can often be taken as hand luggage.

Bicycles can travel by air. You *can* take them to pieces and put them in a bike bag or box, but it's much easier simply to wheel your bike to the check-in desk, where it should be treated as a piece of baggage. You may have to remove the pedals and turn the handlebars sideways so that it takes up less space in the aircraft's hold; check all this with the airline well in advance, preferably before you pay for your ticket.

New Zealand

Air New Zealand has three direct flights weekly between Auckland and Rarotonga; return fares are NZ$1055/1295 in low/high season for a one-year ticket. High season is from around July to October, and the whole month of December; low season is any other time.

If you want to visit other places around the Pacific, check out the airline's many stopover options – you can include Rarotonga as a stopover in combination with other destinations.

For example, Air New Zealand's flights between Auckland and Los Angeles offer stopover options of Fiji, Tonga, Samoa, Rarotonga, Tahiti and Hawaii. Typically one free stopover is allowed, with an additional charge of NZ$100 for each additional stopover, but options vary. Airline-quoted fares vary from around NZ$2000 to NZ$3000, depending on a variety of factors including date of travel (high or low season), length of validity (three-month, six-month and one-year tickets are available), advance purchase (seven, 14 or 21-day advance purchase) and the number of stopovers.

Remember that costs can be less if you buy through a discount ticket agency. STA and Flight Centres International are popular discount travel agents. STA has offices in Auckland, Christchurch and Wellington; Flight Centres have dozens of offices throughout New Zealand. Skytrain in Auckland is another good agency to try.

Also be sure to check around with various travel agents to see what package-holiday options are on offer; numerous travel agents in New Zealand offer very attractive prices in package holidays (air fare plus accommodation) to Rarotonga which can work out even cheaper than the air fare alone. Or you can get a package to include a number of Pacific destinations.

Other Pacific Islands

Apart from New Zealand, the only Pacific islands with direct flight connections to Rarotonga are Fiji, Tahiti and Hawaii. If you want to visit any other island, you'll have to fly via one of these.

Australia

There are no direct flights between Australia and Rarotonga; all of Air New Zealand's flights are routed through Auckland.

A basic low-season return air fare between Australia and Rarotonga, valid for four months, costs around A$1170 from Sydney, A$1210 from Brisbane or A$1400 from Melbourne.

As always, air fare costs may be cheaper from discount travel agencies. STA and Flight Centres International are major dealers in cheap air fares; both have offices in all the major cities including Sydney, Melbourne, Brisbane, Adelaide, Canberra, Cairns, Darwin and Perth.

Be sure to check around with various travel agents for package deals – one that was recently available included two weeks of accommodation, with air fare included, for less than the air fare alone would have cost. Check the travel agents' ads in the Yellow Pages and ring around, because each seems to have its own particular deal.

Asia

As in New Zealand and Australia, package holidays can be the most economical way of visiting Rarotonga if you're starting from Asia or Japan, or you may want to include the Cooks as a stopover if you're visiting other places in the Pacific.

Ticket discounting is widespread in Asia, particularly in Hong Kong, Singapore and Bangkok; Hong Kong is probably the discount air-ticket capital of the region. There are a lot of fly-by-night operators in the Asian ticketing scene so a little care is required. STA, which is reliable, has branches in Hong Kong, Tokyo, Singapore, Bangkok and Kuala Lumpur.

The USA

Air New Zealand's flights from the continental USA into the Pacific depart from Los Angeles. All flights between Los Angeles and Rarotonga are routed through either

Honolulu or Tahiti; you can make a stopover in either place if you want. If you're coming from another city, you can connect with Air New Zealand's flights in either Los Angeles or Honolulu; most major American cities have direct flights to either one. There's no extra charge to depart from San Francisco – Air New Zealand will throw in a connecting flight on another airline to take you from San Francisco to Los Angeles.

On low-season prices, a basic one-month return ticket Los Angeles-Rarotonga-Los Angeles costs US$848. A three-month ticket, allowing a free stopover in Honolulu or Tahiti, costs US$998 to US$1058. Flights departing from Honolulu cost around US$200 less than the ones from Los Angeles. See the 'Pacifica' Fares section below for more about options on Air New Zealand flights.

You may be able to do better than these straightforward fares with travel agents; ask about discounted air fares as well as about package holidays (air fare plus accommodation).

Two of the most reputable discount travel agencies in the USA are STA and CIEE/ Council Travel. STA has offices in Los Angeles, Santa Monica, San Francisco, Berkeley, Seattle, Chicago, Boston, Cambridge, Philadelphia, New York, Washington DC, Miami, Gainesville and Tampa. Council Travel has 52 offices throughout the USA.

Two other reputable agencies specialise in travel in the South Pacific region; both do a lot of nationwide business and they can mail tickets to you wherever you are. Island Adventures, 574 Mills Way, Goleta CA 93117 (☎ (805) 685-9230, toll-free (800) 289-4957, fax (805) 685-0960) specialises in personal service; owner Rob Jenneve is very helpful and knowledgeable about all kinds of options for travel in the South Pacific region, a great resource for trip planning. Discover Wholesale Travel, 2192 Dupont Drive, Suite 105, Irvine, CA 92715 (toll-free (800) 576-7770 in California, (800) 759-7330 elsewhere, fax (714) 833-1176) specialises in discounted fares – it's worth checking with them.

The Sunday travel sections of papers like the *Los Angeles Times*, the *San Francisco Examiner*, the *Chicago Tribune* and the *New York Times* always have plenty of ads for cheap airline tickets and there are often good deals on flights across the Pacific, especially in the west coast papers. Even if you don't live in these areas, you can have the tickets sent to you by mail. The magazine *Travel Unlimited* (PO Box 1058, Allston, MA 02134) publishes details of the cheapest air fares and courier possibilities for destinations all over the world from the USA.

'Pacifica' Fares Air New Zealand's flights between Los Angeles and New Zealand have some excellent stopover options, including Rarotonga. The basic one-month return Los Angeles-Auckland-Los Angeles flight is US$925 if you fly direct with no stopovers. Or, you can get a three-month Los Angeles-Auckland-Los Angeles ticket with one stopover for US$1048 to US$1108, and add additional stopovers for US$135 each. Six-month tickets are US$1198 with the same stopover options; one-year tickets, allowing six free stopovers, cost US$1758. (All these are low-season fares; add US$200 for shoulder season, or US$400 for high-season travel. Low-season prices apply from mid-April to the end of August, high-season prices apply from December to February, and the shoulder-season prices apply during the rest of the year.)

Stopover options include Honolulu, Tahiti, Rarotonga, Samoa, Tonga and Fiji. You can also continue on from Auckland to Australia for an extra US$103 as another stopover option. You can ask for as many or as few stopovers as you like, with a few restrictions on how you can organise your routing (eg there's no direct flight between Honolulu and Tahiti). There's no limit on how long you can stay at any stopover point, as long as you finish your entire trip by the specified time.

Air New Zealand also has arrangements with other airlines whereby you can add the Solomon Islands, Vanuatu, Papua New Guinea and New Caledonia as further

Air Travel Glossary

Apex Apex, or 'advance purchase excursion', is a discounted ticket which must be paid for in advance. There are penalties if you wish to change it.

Baggage Allowance This will be written on your ticket: usually one or two items to go in the hold, with a total weight not to exceed 20kg, plus one item of hand luggage. If your route goes through the USA, however, the baggage allowance is greater – usually two pieces of checked luggage, each piece not to exceed 32kg, plus one item of hand luggage. Be sure to check with the airline if you're in doubt, as the fees charged for overweight or excess baggage can be amazingly high.

Bucket Shop An unbonded travel agency specialising in discounted airline tickets.

Bumped Just because you have a confirmed seat doesn't mean you're going to get on the plane – see Overbooking.

Cancellation Penalties If you have to cancel or change an Apex ticket there are often heavy penalties involved. Insurance can sometimes be taken out against these penalties. Some airlines impose penalties on regular tickets as well, particularly against 'no show' passengers.

Check In Airlines ask you to check in a certain time ahead of the flight departure (usually 1½ hours on international flights). If you fail to check in on time and the flight is overbooked, the airline can cancel your booking and give your seat to somebody else.

Confirmation Having a ticket written out with the flight and date you want doesn't mean you have a seat until the agent has checked with the airline that your status is 'OK' or confirmed. Meanwhile you could just be 'on request'.

Discounted Tickets There are two types of discounted fares – officially discounted (see Promotional Fares) and unofficially discounted. The lowest prices often impose drawbacks like flying with unpopular airlines, inconvenient schedules, or unpleasant routes and connections. A discounted ticket can save you other things than money – you may be able to pay Apex prices without the associated Apex advance booking and other requirements. Discounted tickets only exist where there is fierce competition.

Full Fares Airlines traditionally offer first-class (coded F), business-class (coded J) and economy-class (coded Y) tickets. These days there are so many promotional and discounted fares available from the regular economy class that few passengers pay full economy fare.

Lost Tickets If you lose your airline ticket an airline will usually treat it like a travellers cheque and, after inquiries, issue you with another one. Legally, however, an airline is entitled to treat it like cash and if you lose it, it's gone forever. So, take good care of your tickets.

No Shows No shows are passengers who fail to show up for their flight, sometimes due to unexpected delays or disasters, sometimes due to simply forgetting, sometimes because they made more than one booking and didn't bother to cancel the one they didn't want. Full-fare passengers who fail to turn up are sometimes entitled to travel on a later flight. The rest of us are penalised (see Cancellation Penalties).

On Request An unconfirmed booking for a flight, see Confirmation.

---

options for stopovers. Check with Air New Zealand for details on these, as these fares are outside their basic Pacifica fare structure. If you want to do more island-hopping, check with travel agents about international air passes: Air Pacific and Polynesian Airlines both offer attractively priced air passes for travel in the Pacific region.

Canada

Air New Zealand quotes return fares to Rarotonga of C$1289/1693 in low/high season starting from Vancouver, and C$1652/2057 starting from Toronto.

As when coming from other countries, you can get better deals on air fares by buying from discount travel agencies; also check around for package deals offered by various travel agents.

Travel CUTS/Voyages Campus, a reputable discount and student travel agency, has 46 offices all over Canada. The *Globe & Mail* and the *Vancouver Sun* carry travel agents' ads. The magazine *Great Expeditions* (PO Box 8000-411, Abbotsford BC V2S 6H1) is also useful.

Flights between Canada and Rarotonga are usually routed through Hawaii. See the

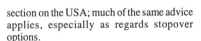

Open Jaws A return ticket where you fly out to one place but return from another. If available, this can save you backtracking to your arrival point.

Overbooking Airlines hate to fly with empty seats and since every flight has some passengers who fail to show up (see No Shows) airlines often book more passengers than they have seats. Usually the excess passengers balance those who fail to show up but occasionally somebody gets bumped. If this happens guess who it is most likely to be? The passengers who check in late.

Promotional Fares Officially discounted fares like Apex fares which are available from travel agents or direct from the airline.

Reconfirmation At least 72 hours prior to departure time of an onward or return flight you must contact the airline and 'reconfirm' that you intend to be on the flight. If you don't do this the airline can delete your name from the passenger list and you could lose your seat. You don't have to reconfirm the first flight on your itinerary or if your stopover is less than 72 hours. It doesn't hurt to reconfirm more than once.

Restrictions Discounted tickets often have various restrictions on them – advance purchase is the most usual one (see Apex). Others are restrictions on the minimum and maximum period you must be away, such as a minimum of 14 days or a maximum of one year. See Cancellation Penalties.

Standby A discounted ticket where you only fly if there is a seat free at the last moment. Standby fares are usually only available on domestic routes.

Tickets Out An entry requirement for many countries – including the Cook Islands – is that you have an onward or return ticket, in other words, a ticket out of the country. If you're not sure what you intend to do next, the easiest solution is to buy the cheapest onward ticket to a neighbouring country or a ticket from a reliable airline which can later be refunded if you do not use it.

Transferred Tickets Airline tickets cannot be transferred from one person to another. Travellers sometimes try to sell the return half of their ticket, but officials can ask you to prove that you are the person named on the ticket. This is unlikely to happen on domestic flights, but on an international flight tickets can easily be compared with passports.

Travel Agencies Travel agencies vary widely and you should ensure you use one that suits your needs. Some simply handle tours while full-service agencies handle everything from tours and tickets to car rental and hotel bookings. A good one will do all these things and can save you a lot of money but if all you want is a ticket at the lowest possible price, then you really need an agency specialising in discounted tickets. A discounted ticket agency, however, may not be useful for other things, like hotel bookings.

Travel Periods Some officially discounted fares, Apex fares in particular, vary with the time of year. There is often a low (off-peak) season and a high (peak) season. Sometimes there's an intermediate, or shoulder season, as well. At peak times, when everyone wants to fly, not only will the officially discounted fares be higher but so will unofficially discounted fares or there may simply be no discounted tickets available. Usually the fare depends on your outward flight – if you depart in the high season and return in the low season, you pay the high-season fare. ■

---

section on the USA; much of the same advice applies, especially as regards stopover options.

South America

The Lan Chile airline has three flights a week between Papeete (Tahiti) and Santiago (Chile), with a stop at Easter Island on the way. Connections are easy between Papeete and Rarotonga, a 1½-hour flight on Air New Zealand.

The UK

Rarotonga is about as far away as you can get from the UK, so most travellers coming this far also visit other destinations. Compare air fares carefully; travelling great distances like this is when Round-the-World air fares become especially economical.

Air New Zealand has a direct flight between London and Los Angeles, with connections from there to the rest of the Pacific (see the USA section).

A straightforward economy return air fare from London to Rarotonga with Air New Zealand costs £920 from February to June, £1249 from July to January. As always, though, you can get air fares cheaper from discount ticket agencies, known as 'bucket shops' in UK parlance.

There has always been cut-throat competition among London's many bucket shops; London is an important European centre for cheap fares. There are plenty of bucket shops in London and although there are always some untrustworthy operators, most of them are fine. Their prices are well advertised in publications such as *Time Out* and the *Evening Standard*, both widely available in London. The best choice is in *TNT*, London's free weekly entertainment, travel and employment magazine, available at some London underground stations or ring ☎ (0181) 244-6529 for details of the nearest pick-up points. The *Sunday Times* has the best choice of the national newspapers. The Globetrotters Club (BCM Roving, London WC1N 3XX) publishes a newsletter called *Globe* which covers obscure destinations and can help in finding travelling companions. Before you buy a ticket, note whether the ticket vendor is 'bonded' (ie affiliated with ABTA, ATOL or AITO), which gives you protection if they go bankrupt.

Two good, reliable low-fare specialists are Trailfinders in west London, which produces a lavishly illustrated brochure including air fare details, and STA with a number of branches in London and around the UK. Trailfinders has regional branches in Manchester, Bristol, Glasgow, Birmingham and Dublin.

Continental Europe

Air New Zealand has a direct flight between Frankfurt and Los Angeles, with connections from there to the rest of the Pacific (see the USA section). A straightforward Frankfurt/Rarotonga return air fare varies from around DM2000 to DM3000, depending on the season. April to June can be the best time to fly; Air New Zealand often offers a range of special discounted fares at this time, such as two-for-one companion tickets and special youth or senior travel incentives.

Air New Zealand also offers a number of competitive 'pex/superpex' air fares in combination with airlines of various European countries. One of the most successful combinations is the World Navigator fare, which combines the networks of nine airlines for prices starting at around f3100, allowing for a combination of destinations including Europe, the USA, the South Pacific, New Zealand, Australia, Asia and/or South Africa, all on one ticket.

As usual, you can get better fares from the discount ticket agencies; also check with travel agents and compare the options on package holidays. Also compare the options for Round-the-World fares, which could work out favourably, and compare stopover options if you want to also visit other places in the Pacific or elsewhere.

There are many bucket shops where you can buy discounted air tickets. STA and Council Travel, the two worldwide discount and student travel agencies, have a number of offices in various European countries. Any of their offices can give you the details on which office might be nearest you. In Amsterdam, NBBS is a popular travel agent.

Round-the-World Tickets

Round-the-World (RTW) tickets have become very popular in the last few years. The airline RTW tickets are often real bargains, and can work out no more expensive or even cheaper than an ordinary return ticket. Prices start at about UK£850, A$1800 or US$1300, with many variables, including which airlines are involved and seasons of travel.

The official airline RTW tickets are usually put together by a combination of two airlines, and permit you to fly anywhere you want on their route systems so long as you do not backtrack. Other restrictions are that you (usually) must book the first sector in advance and cancellation penalties then apply. There may be restrictions on how many stops you are permitted and usually the tickets are valid for 90 days up to a year. An alternative type of RTW ticket is one put together by a travel agent using a combination of discounted tickets.

Circle Pacific Tickets

Circle Pacific tickets use a combination of airlines to circle the Pacific, combining Australia, New Zealand, North America and Asia, with a variety of stopover options in and around the Pacific. As with RTW tickets there are advance-purchase restrictions and limits on how many stopovers you can make. These fares are likely to be around 15% cheaper than RTW tickets.

Other types of tickets also allow you to visit a number of destinations in the Pacific. Air New Zealand has the 'Pacifica' fares if you're coming from the USA, which you can also connect with if you're coming from Canada, the UK or mainland Europe (see the USA section).

SEA

The only regularly scheduled passenger ship connecting the Cook Islands with the outside world is the small *World Discoverer* cruise ship (read on). The occasional luxury liner cruise ship passes through, stopping for only a day or two, but this is very infrequent. Otherwise, if you're coming by sea, it usually means you'll be coming on a private yacht.

The Cook Islands are not a major Pacific yachting destination like French Polynesia, Tonga or Fiji. Nevertheless, a steady trickle of yachts do pass through the islands, except during the November-to-March hurricane season. Official entry points are Rarotonga and Aitutaki in the southern group and Penrhyn and Pukapuka in the northern group. Many yachties only visit the practically uninhabited atoll of Suwarrow – illegally if they haven't already officially entered the country. Yachties are under the same entry and exit regulations, including the departure tax, as those who arrive and depart by air.

It doesn't happen often but there's a remote chance that you might be able to catch a yacht sailing from the Cooks to other nearby destinations like Tonga, Samoa, Fiji, French Polynesia or New Zealand. Check with the Ports Authority at Avatiu Harbour on Rarotonga, and on its downstairs bulletin board, as yachties sometimes use this as a message board.

In the unlikely event that a yacht is looking for crew, of course they'd prefer to take on experienced crew members. However, it's not very likely that fully qualified and experienced crew members are hanging around the Cook Islands waiting for a yacht to happen by and pick them up. Being able to pay for your own food and even part of the passage costs, being personable, flexible, uncomplaining, a fast learner, an eager worker, a good cook and so on, are all assets in your favour. But if you're really serious about catching a yacht you'll do better to try your luck at some of the other Pacific islands more on the main sailing routes.

Passenger Cruise Ship

The *World Discoverer* is a small 138-passenger cruise ship which includes the Cook Islands in its South Seas itineraries each year from approximately March to October. The ship has seven decks, 71 cabins (all with lower beds) and amenities including a swimming pool, fitness centre/sauna, dining room and two lounge bars.

All of the cruises travel between Rarotonga at one end and Tahiti at the other, or vice versa. Stops include Rarotonga, Aitutaki and Atiu in the Cook Islands, and Tahiti, Huahine, Raiatea, Bora Bora and Mopelia in French Polynesia. (Plans are in the works for expansion into Fiji and Samoa, as well.) Prices include return air fare to/from Los Angeles at either end and lots of activities including land tours, diving and snorkelling. A number of cruises are made each season, each lasting from nine to 17 days; prices start at US$1995 to US$2995 per person in the most economical cabins.

Some of the cruises offer the option of spending an extra week in the Cook Islands at the end of the cruise, or a combination of the Cook Islands and Fiji, for an extra cost.

The only way you can come on the *World Discoverer* is if you come via Los Angeles; you can't just see the ship in the harbour somewhere along its journey and jump on. Contact: Society Expeditions Inc, 2001

Western Ave, Suite 300, Seattle, WA 98121 USA (☎ (206) 728-9400, toll-free ☎ (800) 548-8669, fax (206) 728-2301, societyexp@aol.com).

DEPARTURE TAX

There's a NZ$25 departure tax when you fly out of Rarotonga; for children aged two to 12 it's NZ$10, and it's free for children under two. You can pay it at the airport, or at the Westpac bank in Avarua. Westpac bank has a branch at the airport, open for all arriving and departing flights.

WARNING

The information in this chapter is particularly vulnerable to change: prices for international travel are volatile, routes are introduced and cancelled, schedules change, special deals come and go, and rules and visa requirements are amended. Airlines and governments seem to take a perverse pleasure in making price structures and regulations as complicated as possible. You should check directly with the airline or a travel agent to make sure you understand how a fare (and ticket you may buy) works. In addition, the travel industry is highly competitive and there are many lurks and perks.

The upshot of this is that you should get opinions, quotes and advice from as many airlines and travel agents as possible before you part with your hard-earned cash. The details given in this chapter should be regarded as pointers and are not a substitute for your own careful, up-to-date research.

Getting Around

There are basically just two ways of getting from island to island around the Cooks (unless you have a yacht). In the southern group you can fly with Air Rarotonga or you can take the interisland passenger freighter ships. If you want to go to the northern islands, Manihiki, Penrhyn and Pukapuka are the only ones with airstrips, and the flights are long and expensive. Otherwise the only way to reach the northern group islands is by sea.

AIR

Air Rarotonga, with two 18-passenger Bandeirante turbo-prop planes, is the only commercial interisland air service in the Cooks. Flights go several times a day between Rarotonga and Aitutaki, several times a week between Rarotonga and the other southern group islands, and only once a week between Rarotonga and the northern islands of Manihiki and Penrhyn. There are no flights on Sunday on any of Air Rarotonga's routes.

One-way fares (double for return) are:

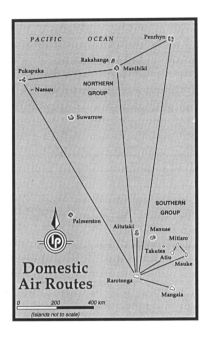

Route	Cost	Flying Time
Rarotonga-Aitutaki	NZ$142	50 minutes
Rarotonga-Mangaia	NZ$127	40 minutes
Rarotonga-Atiu	NZ$127	45 minutes
Rarotonga-Mitiaro	NZ$142	50 minutes
Rarotonga-Mauke	NZ$142	50 minutes
Rarotonga-Manihiki	NZ$475	3½ hours
Rarotonga-Penrhyn	NZ$525	4 hours
Rarotonga-Pukapuka	NZ$525	4¼ hours
Manihiki-Pukapuka	NZ$159	1½ hours
Manihiki-Penrhyn	NZ$139	1 hour

If you're going to more than one of the southern group islands, you can get a 30-day 'Paradise Island Pass' for NZ$96 per sector. Note that there are no direct flights between Atiu and Mauke, so if you want to fly between those two islands it requires two sectors (Atiu to Mitiaro, then Mitiaro to Mauke, or vice versa).

A special 'Super Saver' fare is offered on flights between Rarotonga and Aitutaki (NZ$118 one way, NZ$190 return), with certain conditions: it applies only on the last flight of the day from Rarotonga to Aitutaki, the first flight of the day from Aitutaki to Rarotonga, and is available only if you book and purchase your ticket locally, in cash, within 14 days of travel.

Day tours to Aitutaki depart from Rarotonga airport at 8 am and return to Rarotonga by about 6.30 pm, every day except Sunday; see the Aitutaki chapter for details. These tours can be booked through any travel agent or directly with Air Rarotonga.

All the Rarotonga travel agents offer package tours to the southern group islands which include air fare plus accommodation.

Flying in the Cooks

Flying among the various Cook Islands is done in 18-passenger Bandeirante turbo-prop planes. With people travelling back and forth among the islands for many different reasons, there's often quite a motley collection of passengers on any flight.

Around December and January large numbers of people fly to and from the outer islands, as relations living in Rarotonga, New Zealand, Australia and other places overseas return to the outer islands to spend the Christmas holidays at home. If you're travelling at this time, book a seat as early as possible; despite additional scheduled flights, finding an available seat can still be difficult.

The tradition of giving *eis* whenever people arrive and depart is alive and well in the outer islands. It's still practised on Rarotonga too, but much more so in the outer islands where, to many people, it would be inconceivable for a guest to arrive or depart without being garlanded with flowers. Sometimes, as in the case of important figures, so many eis are draped around the neck that the recipient seems to be practically buried in flowers. The small airplanes sometimes feel like mobile florist shops, and the aroma can be almost overpowering! ■

You can visit just one island this way, or several; a popular combination is to visit Atiu, Mitiaro and Mauke all in one go.

Packages are also offered to the northern islands of Manihiki and Penrhyn. Note, however, that flights to these islands are scheduled only once a week, and adverse circumstances, such as bad weather, limited fuel supplies and too few bookings, can sometimes cause them not to operate. Rarotonga travel agents recommend travel insurance covering unavoidable delays if you are depending on these flights. Flights to Pukapuka operate not on any particular schedule, but only as needed.

Another option is to charter a plane through Air Rarotonga, but of course this works out to be more expensive than going on the scheduled flights. You can charter a plane to any licensed airport in the Cook Islands, including the islands of the northern group, and even internationally. The normal charter fare includes the pilot, but if you have a pilot's licence, you can bring in your logbook and see about flying the plane yourself if you wish. Ask Air Rarotonga for details.

Air Rarotonga has an office at the Rarotonga international airport (☎ 22-888, fax 20-979, PO Box 79, bookings@airraro.co.ck) where tickets are sold and bookings are made. The administration office (☎ 22-890) is off to one side.

BOAT

Shipping services have had a colourful history in the Cooks: companies have come and gone, ships have run onto reefs, fortunes have been made but more often lost. Despite the increasing use of air services, shipping is still vital to the islands. Most of the northern islands can only be served by ship and throughout the islands, ships are necessary to bring in commodities and export produce.

Shipping services in the islands face two major problems. Firstly, there are simply too few people and they're too widely scattered to be easily and economically serviced. From the ship owners' point of view, shipping between the islands is only feasible with a government subsidy. From the islanders' point of view, it's difficult to produce export crops if you can't be certain a ship will be coming by at the appropriate time to collect them.

The second problem is that the islands generally have terrible harbours. The south sea image of drifting through a wide passage in the reef into the clear sheltered waters of the lagoon doesn't seem to apply to the Cooks. In the northern atolls the reef passages are generally too narrow or shallow to allow large ships to enter. In the southern volcanic islands the passages through the fringing reefs are usually too small to let a ship enter and dock. Even Rarotonga's main harbour, Avatiu, is too small for large ships

– or even too many small ones. All this means that ships have to anchor outside the reef and transfer passengers and freight to shore by lighters. At some of the islands even getting the lighters through the narrow reef passages is a considerable feat. Unless conditions are ideal it's not even possible to anchor offshore at some of the Cook Islands, and freighters have to be under way constantly, even while loading and unloading.

If you plan to explore the outer islands by ship you need to be flexible and hardy. Schedules are hard to pinpoint and unlikely to be kept to – weather, breakdowns, loading difficulties or unexpected demands can all put a kink in the plans. At each island visited, the ship usually stays just long enough to discharge and take on cargo. Travellers get the chance to spend a few hours visiting each island before taking off again. Outside of Rarotonga, only the northernmost island of Penrhyn has a wharf; at all the others, you have to go ashore by lighter or barge.

On board the ships, conditions are adequate, but these are not luxury cruise liners. They're also small and the seas in this region are often rough. If you're at all prone to seasickness you'll definitely spend some time hanging your head over the side. See the Health section in the Facts for the Visitor chapter for suggestions on what to do for motion sickness.

Despite the discomforts travelling by ship through the Cook Islands does have its romantic aspects. This may be one of the last places in the world that you can sleep out on the deck of a South Pacific island freighter, savouring the wide horizon, chatting with your fellow passengers and the captain and crew, watching the moon rise up out of the ocean and the stars above you in the velvety-warm air.

Fortunately the distances are not too far; travel throughout the southern islands usually involves setting off in the late afternoon or early evening, sleeping on the way and arriving at the next island early in the morning. Trips from Rarotonga to the northern islands naturally take longer; travel time can be about three days to reach the northern group but the round-trip time may be extended by visiting several islands, or by taking longer to load and unload cargo, since sailings to the northern islands are less frequent than around the southern group. Typically, a northern group trip, departing Rarotonga and visiting a couple of the northern islands, often with a stop at Aitutaki on the way, might take about 10 days or so before getting back to Rarotonga.

Interisland Ships

Two ships, the *Maunga Roa* and *Te Koumaru*, provide interisland passenger and

---

Why the Shipping Services Don't Run to Schedule

In Aitutaki we met a group of marine geologists from Fiji, a woman off to Manihiki to research musical instruments and other artefacts, and a man off on a loop around the northern islands. Supposedly two days out from Rarotonga towards Manihiki, the ship was already four days behind schedule.

Day one was lost at Mauke when it was too rough and they had to wait for conditions to improve before unloading. Day two was lost because although the ship was not supposed to be going to Aitutaki in the first place it had been diverted there because of the marine geologists and all their equipment. Then because of the day lost at Mauke the ship arrived at Aitutaki on a Sunday instead of a Saturday. Since no work gets done on a Sunday they couldn't unload and another day was lost. On Sunday night a ferocious wind blew up (some yachties told us the next morning they recorded wind speeds of 50 knots) and continued all day Monday – so again there was no unloading. The marine geologists spent the day climbing hills to see if they could spot the ship, with their equipment, offshore. It had moved round to the other side of the island to shelter from the wind.

On Tuesday we flew back to Rarotonga, leaving them all wondering whether they would get their gear off that day and if the ship would be continuing north that night.

Tony Wheeler

Cook Islands' Interisland Shipping Services

Deck/cabin prices on the *Maunga Roa* are as follows:

	Deck (one way)	Deck (return)	Cabin (one way)	Cabin (return)
From Rarotonga to:				
Atiu	NZ$50	NZ$100	NZ$100	NZ$150
Mauke	NZ$50	NZ$100	NZ$100	NZ$150
Mitiaro	NZ$50	NZ$100	NZ$100	NZ$150
Mangaia	NZ$50	NZ$100	NZ$100	NZ$150
Aitutaki	NZ$50	NZ$100	NZ$100	NZ$150
Palmerston	NZ$95	NZ$150	NZ$195	NZ$250
Manihiki	NZ$280	NZ$560	NZ$380	NZ$760
Rakahanga	NZ$280	NZ$560	NZ$380	NZ$760
Nassau	NZ$280	NZ$560	NZ$380	NZ$760
Pukapuka	NZ$280	NZ$560	NZ$380	NZ$760
Penrhyn	NZ$350	NZ$600	NZ$500	NZ$815
Between Atiu, Mauke, Mitiaro or Mangaia:				
	NZ$50	NZ$100	NZ$100	NZ$150
From Manihiki to:				
Rakahanga	NZ$30	NZ$50	NZ$60	NZ$70
Penrhyn	NZ$40	NZ$60	NZ$75	NZ$95
Pukapuka	NZ$35	NZ$55	NZ$65	NZ$75
From Rakahanga to:				
Manihiki	NZ$30	NZ$50	NZ$60	NZ$70
Penrhyn	NZ$40	NZ$60	NZ$75	NZ$95
Pukapuka	NZ$35	NZ$55	NZ$65	NZ$75

cargo services for the Cooks. Both are good, modern ships brought over from Norway in 1996 and now based at Rarotonga's Avatiu Harbour. Information, schedules and bookings services are available at the office of Taio Shipping Ltd, downstairs in the Ports Authority building at Avatiu Harbour in Avarua (☎ 24-905, 20-535, fax 24-906, PO Box 2001).

Both ships offer two classes of passenger service: cabin and deck. Deck passengers sleep out on decks, which can be covered for protection from sun and rain. They normally bring their own food, but they can eat aboard at a specified cost per meal. Meals are included in the prices for cabin passengers.

The 36m (119-foot) *Maunga Roa* has two cabins, each with six bunks. The larger, 48m (157-foot) *Te Koumaru* has five cabins – three with two bunks, one with four bunks and one with nine. Fresh-water showers and toilets are available to all passengers.

Prices are given in the accompanying table.

HITCHING

Hitching is never entirely safe in any country in the world, and we don't recommend it. Travellers who decide to hitch should understand that they are taking a small but potentially serious risk. However, many people do choose to hitch, and the advice that follows should help make their journeys as fast and safe as possible.

	Deck (one way)	Deck (return)	Cabin (one way)	Cabin (return)
From Pukapuka to:				
Nassau	NZ$20	NZ$30	NZ$40	NZ$50
Manihiki	NZ$35	NZ$55	NZ$65	NZ$75
Rakahanga	NZ$35	NZ$55	NZ$65	NZ$75
Penrhyn	NZ$55	NZ$65	NZ$90	NZ$110
From Penrhyn to:				
Pukapuka	NZ$55	NZ$65	NZ$90	NZ$110
Manihiki	NZ$40	NZ$60	NZ$75	NZ$95
Rakahanga	NZ$40	NZ$60	NZ$75	NZ$95
Nassau	NZ$55	NZ$65	NZ$90	NZ$110

Prices are a little higher on the *Te Koumaru*:

	Deck (one way)	Deck (return)	Cabin (one way)	Cabin (return)
From Rarotonga to:				
Atiu	NZ$70	NZ$140	NZ$150	NZ$300
Mauke	NZ$70	NZ$140	NZ$150	NZ$300
Mitiaro	NZ$70	NZ$140	NZ$150	NZ$300
Mangaia	NZ$70	NZ$140	NZ$150	NZ$300
Aitutaki	NZ$70	NZ$140	NZ$150	NZ$300
Palmerston	NZ$120	NZ$240	NZ$195	NZ$300
Manihiki	NZ$280	NZ$560	NZ$450	NZ$900
Rakahanga	NZ$280	NZ$560	NZ$450	NZ$900
Nassau	NZ$280	NZ$560	NZ$450	NZ$900
Pukapuka	NZ$280	NZ$560	NZ$450	NZ$900
Penrhyn	NZ$280	NZ$560	NZ$450	NZ$900

Between Atiu, Mauke, Mitiaro or Mangaia:				
	NZ$70	NZ$140	NZ$150	NZ$300

Hitchhiking is not the custom in the Cooks and it's quite likely you'll never see anyone do it. If you do see someone hitching, it will be a foreigner, not a local. However, it's not illegal, only rather cheeky, and if you do hitchhike you'll probably get a ride in short order. You may have better luck if you flag down a vehicle rather than sticking your thumb out pointing skyward, which can be interpreted as a rude gesture in the Cooks.

LOCAL TRANSPORT

On Rarotonga there's a bus service, taxis, and you can hire cars, Jeeps, mini-buses, motorcycles and bicycles. Aitutaki has rental cars, Jeeps, motorcycles and bicycles. Atiu has rental motorcycles, and a taxi service. On Mauke and Mitiaro the guesthouses rent motorcycles and bicycles. Mangaia has only one pick-up truck and a few motorcycles for rent. Elsewhere you can walk. See the individual island chapters for more information.

Vaka (canoes), the traditional form of inter-island transport

ORGANISED TOURS

There are various interesting tours you can take in the Cooks. On Rarotonga the 'Circle Island' tours provide a good introduction to the island and its history, culture, people, agriculture, economy and more. Circle island tours are also offered on Aitutaki, Atiu, Mauke and Mangaia. More specialised tours (cave tours, etc) are mentioned in the individual island chapters.

Day tours are available from Rarotonga to Aitutaki. Rarotonga travel agents also organise one-island or multi-island package tours. See the Air section above.

The Southern Group

Rarotonga

Population: 11,100
Area: 67.1 sq km

Rarotonga is not only the major island and population centre of the Cook Islands – it's also virtually synonymous with the whole island chain, like Tahiti is to French Polynesia.

Rarotonga is extravagantly beautiful – it's spectacularly mountainous and lush green. The interior is rugged, virtually unpopulated and untouched – the narrow valleys and steep hills are simply too precipitous and overgrown for easy settlement. In contrast, the coastal region is fertile, evenly populated and neat, clean and pretty – like some South Pacific Switzerland. You almost feel somebody zips round the island every morning making sure the roads have all been swept clean and the flowers all neatly arranged and watered. Fringing this whole Arcadian vision is an almost continuous, clean, white beach with clear, shallow lagoons and, marked by those ever-crashing waves, a protective outer reef.

HIGHLIGHTS

- Enjoying traditional dance, music and delicious local cuisine at an 'island night'
- Relaxing on pristine, white-sand beaches
- Learning about the Cook Island's culture, environment, and history at the Cultural Village
- Snorkelling in beautiful lagoons or diving beyond the reef
- Taking one of the Circle Island Tours
- Trekking across the island and discovering the interior's mountains, streams and valleys

History

Numerous legends touch upon the early existence of Rarotonga, which was clearly one of the best known and most important of the Polynesian islands.

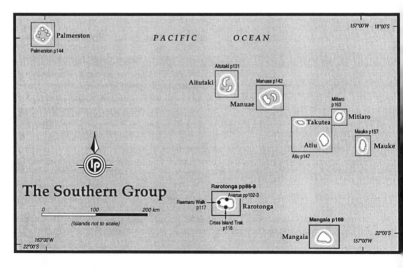

The Southern Group

Ancient oral histories relate that the first person to discover the island was Io Teitei, also called Io Tangaroa, who was from Nuku Hiva in the Marquesas Islands, now part of French Polynesia. He came by canoe about 1400 years ago, but didn't stay; he went back to Nuku Hiva and never returned to Rarotonga.

Back in Nuku Hiva, Io Tangaroa's younger brother, Tongaiti, followed Io Tangaroa's directions and came to Rarotonga. Later, Io Tangaroa's eldest son, To'u Ariki, came. They too both went back to Nuku Hiva and never returned to Rarotonga, but To'u Ariki's first-born son, Tumutoa, who had been with his father when they came to Rarotonga and returned to Nuku Hiva, later did return to Rarotonga.

The Ara Metua inland road, also called Te Ara Nui O Toi ('The Great Road of Toi') was built around the 11th century, though no one today knows precisely who Toi was. History often states that the definite, permanent settlement of the island occurred in the early or mid-13th century, when Tangiia arrived from Tahiti and Karika arrived from Samoa, both bringing settlers to establish communities on the island. Tangiia settled in the area that still bears his name, Ngatangiia; Karika settled where Avarua is today. Even though Tangiia and Karika were probably not the island's first settlers – in one version of history, Kainuku Ariki and his tribe were already living in Ngatangiia when Tangiia arrived – their arrival to establish communities on the island was an important event in the history of the island's settlement.

In one version of history it was Tongaiti who gave the island its first name: Te Ou Enua O Tumutevarovaro. Tumutevarovaro means 'source of the echo' (*tumu* means source; *te* means the; *varovaro* means echo); the entire name means something like 'the misty land of Tumutevarovaro' or 'the mist rising from Tumutevarovaro' (*te* means the; *ou* means mist; *enua* means land; *o* means of). In another version, it was Tu-te-rangi-narama who named the island Tumutevarovaro; other traditions say it could have been others who gave the island its name.

There are also various stories relating to how the island got its present name of Rarotonga. *Raro* means under or down; *tonga* means south, so the name means something like 'down south' or 'under the south'. In yet another version, *raro* in the ancient language of eastern Polynesia meant the direction the tradewinds came from, that is, west; so Rarotonga could then mean 'south-west'. From the point of view of the early discoverers and navigators from the Marquesas and Society Islands, Rarotonga was certainly to the south-west. The giving of the name Rarotonga has been credited to a number of the early figures in the island's history including Tongaiti, Iro from Tahiti, Tangiia and Karika.

Eventually the island was settled and the land divided among six tribes, each headed by a tribal king, or *ariki*. There were three districts on the island which still remain today: Te Au O Tonga on the north side of the island, Takitumu on the east and south-east side and Puaikura on the west. Conflicts and wars over land and other issues were frequent among the tribes, and the people did not live on the low coastal plain as they do today; they lived at the higher elevations where they could better defend themselves from attack, only venturing down to the sea in armed groups, for fishing. Inland they practiced agriculture and raised livestock, including pigs.

Around 1350 AD, Rarotonga was the island from which the canoes departed on the 'great migration' to settle New Zealand. Fourteen canoes, coming from various Polynesian islands including Rarotonga itself, assembled at Avana Harbour in Ngatangiia and took off from there to sail to New Zealand or, as it was known to them in those days, Aotearoa ('land of the long white cloud'). They followed the sailing directions of Kupe, an early Polynesian navigator who had discovered and named Aotearoa around 900 AD, explored it, then returned and told about the land and how to get there. Seven of the 14 canoes completed the trip. The people on these canoes became the great ancestors of several New Zealand Maori tribes, with the tribes taking the names of the

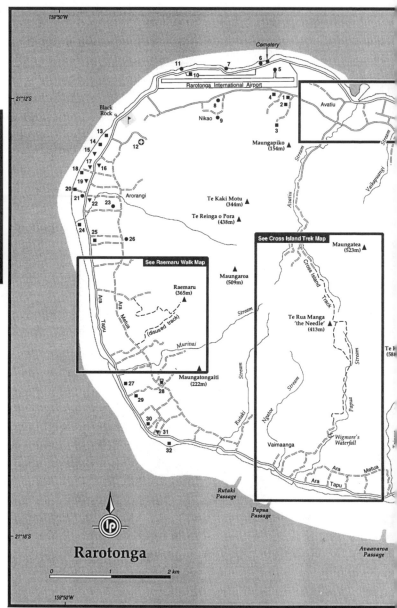

159°50'W

21°12'S

Cemetery

11
10
7
6
5

Rarotonga International Airport

4 1
2
3

Avatiu

8
Nikao 9

Maungapiko
(154m)

Avatiu Stream

Vaikapuangi Stream

Black
Rock

13
14
15
17
18 16
19
20
21 22 23
24
25
26

Arorangi

Te Kaki Motu
(344m)

Te Reinga o Pora
(438m)

See Cross Island Trek Map

Maungatea
(523m)

See Raemaru Walk Map

Ara Tapu
Ara Metua

Raemaru
(365m)

(disused track)

Murivai

Maungaroa
(509m)

Stream

Cross Island Track

Te Rua Manga
'the Needle'
(413m)

Te M
(58

Maungatongaiti
(222m)

27
28
29
30
31
32

Rutaki Stream

Ngatoe Stream

Papua Stream

Vaimaanga

Wigmore's
Waterfall

Ara Metua
Ara Tapu

Rutaki
Passage

Papua
Passage

21°16'S

Rarotonga

0   1   2 km

159°50'W

Avaavaroa
Passage

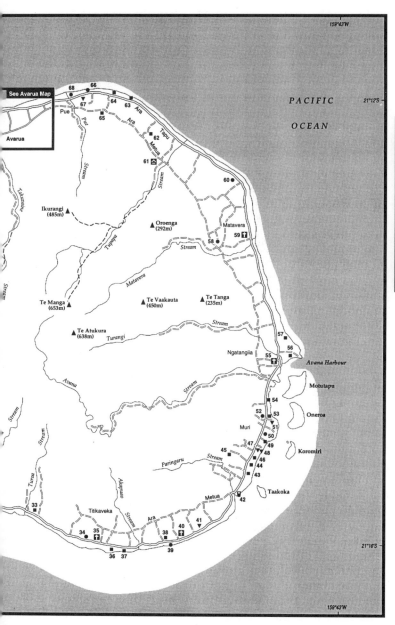

PLACES TO STAY
1 Tiare Village Dive Hostel
2 Wild Palms
3 Matareka Hostel
4 May's Apartments
10 Airport Lodge
13 Oasis Village; Oasis Restaurant & Hopsing's Chinese Wok
14 Rarotongan Sunset Motel
18 Edgewater Resort
20 Aunty Noo's Beach Lodge
24 Manuia Beach Hotel
25 Are-Renga Motel
27 Puaikura Reef Lodge
29 Backpackers International Hostel
30 Lagoon Lodges
32 Rarotongan Beach Resort
33 Beach Lodge; Official Residence of Queen's Representative
36 Moana Sands Hotel
37 Little Polynesian
38 Raina Beach Apartments
43 Aremango Guesthouse
44 Vara's Beach House
45 Vara's Beach House Villa
46 Muri Beachcomber
49 Pacific Resort
53 Sokala Villas
54 Aroko Bungalows
56 Avana Marina Condos
57 Sunrise Beach Motel
62 Ariana Bungalows & Hostel
63 Kii Kii Motel
64 Club Raro
65 Sea View Lodge

PLACES TO EAT
15 Alberto's Steakhouse & Bar
16 PJ's Sports Cafe

17 Spaghetti House
19 Tumunu Restaurant & Bar
22 The Flamboyant Place
31 Kaena Restaurant
41 Fruits of Rarotonga
47 Emil's Cafe
48 Rarotonga Sailing Club Sails; Boardwalk Cafe
51 Flame Tree
67 Just Burgers

OTHER
5 Airport Terminal
6 RSA & Citizens Club
7 Parliament
8 Tereora College
9 National Stadium
11 Meteorological Station
12 Hospital
21 Dive Rarotonga
23 Cook Island Divers
26 Cook Islands Cultural Village
28 Local Homestead Bar
34 Kent Hall
35 Titikaveka CICC Church
39 Beach Cargo
40 Roman Catholic Church
42 Reef Runner Bar
50 Shells & Craft
52 Pacific Divers
55 Ngatangiia CICC Church
58 The Gallery
59 Matavera CICC Church
60 Perfumes of Rarotonga; Pottery Studio
61 Arai-Te-Tonga
66 Kenwall Gallery
68 Outpatient Clinic

canoes the ancestors arrived on as their tribal names (eg the Tainui tribe, the Te Arawa tribe).

European Contact Surprisingly, considering its historic importance and also that it is the largest and most populous of the Cook Islands, Rarotonga was one of the later islands to be found by Europeans. The first European sighting can probably be credited to the mutineers on the *Bounty*, who happened upon Rarotonga after they had returned to Tahiti and were searching for a remote island where they could hide from the British navy. This was probably some time in late 1789 but, hardly surprisingly, the mutineers didn't come forward to tell abou their important discovery.

In any case, the mutineers did not set foc upon Rarotonga; nor did the crew of Captai Theodore Walker's *Endeavour* who sighte the island in 1813. A piece of sandalwoo floating in the sea, however, was picked u by the *Endeavour* and taken to Australia. Th idea that the island might have sandalwoo – a valuable commodity – led to the forma tion of a sandalwood company in Austral and to the next European visitor. Phili Goodenough, captain of the *Cumberland* showed up in 1814 and spent three month on Rarotonga – three less than harmoniou and peaceful months. Unable to find an sandalwood the crew of the *Cumberlan* decided to take back *nono* wood instead. This was an unsuccessful gamble as nono wood turned out to be of negligible value.

During their stay at Ngatangiia the crew managed to get themselves involved in some local squabbles which resulted in the deaths of a number of the crew – including Goodenough's female companion, Ann Butcher (the first European woman to come to the island), and also numerous Rarotongans. Eventually the *Cumberland* left Rarotonga with some haste, but two local women and a man were taken with them and left at their next stop, Aitutaki. William Gill later described the *Cumberland's* visit to Rarotonga as a 'continued series of rapine, cruelty, vice and bloodshed'. Understandably, Goodenough did not go into great detail about his adventures so Rarotonga remained comparatively unknown. In the following years a number of vessels visited Rarotonga but only stayed for short periods.

In 1821 Papeiha, the Polynesian missionary, or 'teacher', from Raiatea in the Society Islands, was landed on Aitutaki by the English missionary John Williams. In 1823 Williams returned to Aitutaki to see how successful he had been. Papeiha had done remarkably well so Williams and Papeiha set off to convert Rarotonga, leaving two other Polynesian missionaries on Aitutaki to carry on the work. They took with them the three Rarotongans whom Goodenough had left on Aitutaki nine years earlier, together with two Rarotongan fishermen whose canoe had blown off course when they had gone fishing from Rarotonga and so had made for Aitutaki.

Despite having Rarotongan passengers on board, the island proved elusive, and after a week's futile search they gave up and made for the island of Mangaia instead, which had been charted by Captain James Cook. The Mangaians did not rush out to greet the arrival of Christianity with open arms; on the day the mission ship arrived, Papeiha and some other missionaries who had gone ashore were attacked and felt lucky to have escaped with their lives, so the missionaries hastily sailed on.

Their next stop was Atiu, the main island of the group known as Nga Pu Toru ('The Three Roots') which also includes Mauke and Mitiaro. Here Williams, Papeiha and Tamatoa Ariki, an Aitutakian ariki (chief) who was also with them, convinced Rongomatane, a notorious cannibal king, to embrace Christianity. This was achieved in a remarkably short time and the neighbouring islands of Mauke and Mitiaro were converted with equally amazing speed due to Rongomatane's assistance. As a finale Rongomatane, who had never been to Rarotonga, gave Williams sailing directions which turned out to be spot on.

As he had been on Aitutaki, Papeiha was left on Rarotonga to convince the islanders to give up their religion and take on the new one. And, as on Aitutaki, he succeeded with thoroughness and surprising speed. Four months later, additional Polynesian missionaries were landed to assist Papeiha and in little more than a year after his arrival Christianity had taken firm hold.

The first permanent London Missionary Society (LMS) missionaries were Charles Pitman and John Williams who came to Rarotonga in 1827, followed a year later by Aaron Buzacott. These three men translated the entire Bible into Maori, and Buzacott also established the village of Arorangi which was to be a model for new villages on the island. The missionaries wished to gather the previously scattered population together in order to speed the propagation of Christianity.

Cannibalism may have been stamped out, but the arrival of Christianity was not all peace and light. The indigenous culture was all but destroyed and missionaries also introduced previously unknown diseases: dysentery, whooping cough, mumps and measles were just some of them. At the time of European arrival on Rarotonga the estimated population was between 6000 and 7000 people, but by 1848 it had fallen to 2800, and 20 years later it was less than 2000. Although the missionaries tried to exclude other Europeans from settling, more and more whalers and traders visited the island.

In 1850 to 1851 more than 20 trading ships and 60 whalers paused at Rarotonga, and Buzacott's wife lamented that men of 'some wealth and little religious principle' were settling on the island. The Rarotongans had been firmly warned to beware of the French, however, who had taken over Tahiti in 1843. The dangers of papism were a major worry for the LMS!

In 1865 a Rarotongan ariki, frightened by rumours of French expansionism in the Pacific, requested British protection for the first time. This request was turned down. In the following years the missionaries' once absolute power declined as more Europeans came to the island and trade grew. Finally in 1888 a British protectorate was formally declared over the southern islands and Rarotonga became the unofficial capital of the group.

What to do with the islands next was a subject of some controversy but eventually in 1901 they were annexed to newly independent New Zealand and the close relationship between the two countries, that continues to this day, was established.

Geography

Rarotonga is the only high volcanic island in the Cook Islands. The inland area is mountainous with steep valleys, razorback ridges and swift-flowing streams. Most of this area is covered with dense jungle. Rarotonga is the youngest of the Cook Islands: the volcanic activity which thrust it above sea level occurred about two million years ago, more recently than on any of the other islands. The island's major mountains are the remains of the outer rim of the cone. The cone is open on the north side and Maungatea rises in the centre.

The narrow coastal plain with its swampy area close to the hills is somewhat like the raised outer coral fringe, or *makatea*, of several other islands in the southern group, though on Rarotonga the coastal plain is fertile, sandy loam rather than the jagged razor-sharp coral of true makatea. On Rarotonga the plains are far more fertile than on islands like Mitiaro, Mauke, Atiu or Mangaia.

The lagoon within Rarotonga's outer reef is narrow around most of the island but it widens out around the south side where the beaches are also best. Muri lagoon, fringed by four *motu*, or small islands – three sand cays and one volcanic islet – is the widest part of the lagoon, although even here it is very shallow in most places. There are few natural passages through the reef and the main harbour at Avatiu has been artificially enlarged. Yachts also anchor at Avarua and at Avana Harbour.

Orientation

Finding your way around Rarotonga is admirably easy – there's a coastal road (the Ara Tapu), another road about 500m inland (the Ara Metua) going most of the way around the island, and a lot of mountains in the middle. Basically it's that simple. A number of roads connect the Ara Tapu to the Ara Metua and a few roads lead into inland valleys. If you want to get all the way into the middle, or cross the island from one side to the other, you must do it on foot.

Maps New Zealand's Department of Lands & Survey produces excellent 1:25,000 topographical maps of each of the Cook Islands. The Rarotonga map shows all the roads, a number of walking trails, the reefs and the villages, with a separate enlargement of Avarua. These maps are available for about NZ$8.50 at many shops in Avarua – check at the post office, CITC, Bounty Bookshop, Island Craft Ltd, Pacific Supplies, Kenwall Gallery, Joyce Peyroux Garments and even at some of the rental car companies and travel agents. You can buy them a little cheaper at the Cook Islands Survey Department office (☎ 29-433, fax 27-433) near the golf course in Arorangi.

The tourist office in Avarua hands out a couple of free publications containing good maps: *Jason's* has a large fold-out map of Rarotonga and Aitutaki, and the *What's On* booklet also contains maps. *Rarotonga's Mountain Tracks and Plants* by Gerald

McCormack & Judith Künzle contains detailed maps for a number of walking tracks.

Information

Tourist Office The Cook Islands Tourist Authority (☎ 29-435, fax 21-435, PO Box 4, tourism@cookislands.gov.ck) has an office right in the middle of Avarua – look for the 'i' sign (for 'information') out on the street. They have the usual sort of tourist information and can help you with everything from accommodation, nightspots and island nights' to interisland shipping services and flights. They also give out free copies of *What's On in the Cook Islands*, an excellent annually produced information-and-adverts booklet guide to Rarotonga and Aitutaki, and *Jason's*, a fold-out advertisement sheet with good maps of both islands. The office is open weekdays from 8 am to 4 pm, Saturday 8 am to noon.

Money The two principal banks on Rarotonga, Westpac and ANZ, are both in Avarua. Westpac is easy to spot on the main road, beside the Foodland supermarket; ANZ is tucked away in the rear of the big, white, three-storey building between Foodland and the police station. They're both open weekdays from 9 am to 3 pm; Westpac also opens Saturday, 9 to 11 am. Travellers cheques and major currencies in cash can be changed at either bank. They also give cash advances on Visa, MasterCard and Bankcard, and do telegraphic transfers.

Travellers cheques and major currencies in cash can also be changed at some of the larger hotels, but the banks give a better rate of exchange. Most of the larger stores, hotels and rental-car companies accept Visa, MasterCard and Bankcard.

Post & Communications The post office, just inland from the traffic circle in central Avarua, is open weekdays from 8 am to 4 pm. Poste restante is handled here; they will receive and hold mail for you for 30 days. It should be addressed to you, c/o Poste Restante, Avarua, Rarotonga, Cook Islands.

There are also postal 'depots' at several small shops around the island, where you can buy stamps, and post and receive letters.

Local, interisland and international telephone, telegram, telex and fax services are available at the Telecom office on Tutakimoa Rd in Avarua, a couple of blocks inland from Cook's Corner. You can make an international collect phone call from any phone on the island, but if you want to pay for the call yourself, you must either find someone who will allow you to do it on their telephone, use a card phone or come in and place it here. You can also receive faxes here. The office is open 24 hours every day.

Phonecards costing NZ$10, NZ$20 or NZ$50 can be purchased at the post office, Telecom, CITC or Island Craft Ltd. Local, interisland and international phone calls can all be made on the card phone. A card-operated public telephone is outside the post office in Avarua; others are on the grassy strip separating the lanes of the coast road opposite the police station, and on the outside wall of the CITC Shopping Centre, opposite Cook's Corner.

Email and Internet connections are available at Polyaccess (republic@banana.co.ck), in the Perfumes of Rarotonga shop beside the Banana Court. Email is NZ$2 per message to send or receive. Internet connection is NZ$26.40 per hour or NZ$0.40 per minute, with a 10-minute (NZ$4.40) minimum.

Travel Agencies Rarotonga travel agencies include:

Cook Islands Tours & Travel
    Airport (☎ 28-270, after hours ☎ 20-270, fax 27-270, PO Box 611, raroinfo@citours.co.ck)
    Pacific Resort tour desk (☎ 20-427)
Hugh Henry & Associates
    Betela (☎ 25-320, fax 25-420, PO Box 440, hhenry@gatepoly.co.ck)
Island Hopper Vacations
    Avarua (☎ 22-026, fax 22-036, PO Box 240, travel@islandhopper.co.ck)
Matina Travel
    Avarua (☎ 21-780, fax 24-780, PO Box 54)
Stars Travel
    Avarua (☎ 23-669, 23-683, fax 21-569, PO Box 75, holidays@starstravel.co.ck)

Bookshops The largest selection of books about the Cook Islands – history, literature, legends, poetry, arts and crafts, politics and culture etc – are found at three places in Avarua: the University of the South Pacific (USP) centre, the Cook Islands Library & Museum Society opposite USP, and the CITC department store. The USP centre sells all the books published by USP at prices much lower than anywhere else – check here first, there's a great selection. CITC has a wide selection of other general-interest paperback books as well, including children's books.

The Bounty Bookshop in the large white three-storey building between Foodland and the police station has a good selection of foreign magazines, the *New Zealand Herald* and local newspapers, and a variety of books, including books on the Cook Islands and other Pacific destinations. Island Craft Ltd and Pacific Supplies also have books about the Cook Islands.

You can access all the books at the Cook Islands Library & Museum Society, including the Pacific Collection, by simply signing up for a Temporary Borrower's Card. The National Library also allows visitors to borrow books. At both you pay a refundable deposit and a small library fee.

Cultural Centre The Alliance Française de Rarotonga (☎ 22-741, fax 28-018, Private Bag 1, french@alliance-francaise.org.ck) is a friendly group whose aim is to promote French cultural activities and language. Its office is in Avarua, in the building between Cook's Corner and the Energy Centre petrol station. The group holds a weekly lunchtime get-together which visitors are welcome to attend, offers classes in French, and other activities.

Laundry Snowbird Laundromat (☎ 21-952) in Avarua charges NZ$3.50 per washload, including soap and softener, and NZ$5 for every 10 minutes to dry. Wash-dry-fold is NZ$9/17/24 for one/two/three loads. It's open weekdays 8 am to 4 pm, Saturday 8 am to noon.

Photography Cocophoto (☎ 29-295) at the CITC Pharmacy in Avarua sells colour print, slide and video film and offers same-day colour print processing.

Medical Services Rarotonga's hospital (☎ 22-664) is on a hill up behind the golf course, west of the airport. A sign on the main road marks the turn-off. There's also an out-patient clinic (☎ 20-065) on the main road at Tupapa, about 1km east of Avarua. You can go to either one. Several private doctors also practice on Rarotonga; see 'Doctors – Private' in the telephone directory.

Emergency Emergency phone numbers are

Police ☎ 999
Ambulance & Hospital ☎ 998
Fire ☎ 996

The National Police Headquarters (☎ 22-499) is on the main road in the centre of Avarua.

Activities

Walking & Climbing You don't have to get very far into the interior of Rarotonga to realise the population is almost entirely concentrated along the narrow coastal fringe. The mountainous interior is virtually deserted and can be reached only by walking tracks and trails.

Rarotonga's Mountain Tracks and Plants by Gerald McCormack & Judith Künzl (Cook Islands Natural Heritage Project, 1994) is an excellent booklet that is very useful if you plan to walk any of the mountain tracks. The same authors also publish a separate colour-illustrated booklet, *Rarotonga's Cross-Island Walk* (Cook Islands Natural Heritage Project, 1991) about the cross-island walk alone. These booklets give much more interesting detail about each walk, together with its geology, plants, animals and other natural features, than we have space to include here. Much of what follows is based on these authors' detailed knowledge of the inland areas.

The valley walks are easy strolls suitable even for older people or young children and the scaling of the hill behind the hospital is also easy and short, although a bit steep. Most of the mountain walks are hard work, often involving difficult scrambling over rocky sections.

Apart from the cross-island track by the Needle and the ascent of Raemaru behind Arorangi village, both of which we've included directions for here, most of the mountain walks are a cross between scaling Everest and hacking your way through the Amazon jungle.

The interior of Rarotonga is surprisingly mountainous with some steep slopes and sheer drops. Keep an eye out for these drops, as you can stumble across them quite suddenly. Although the trails are often difficult to follow, Rarotonga is too small for you to get really lost. You can generally see where you're going or where you've come from. If you do get lost, the best thing to do is to walk towards the coast on a ridge crest. Streams often have sprawling hibiscus branches, making progress very slow.

Walking will generally be easier if you follow the ridges rather than trying to beat your way across the often heavily overgrown slopes. Rarotonga has no wild animals, snakes or poisonous insects (except for centipedes, wasps and annoying red ants) but the valleys and bushy inland areas do have plenty of very persistent mosquitoes, so bring repellent. Shorts are cool and easy for walking, but you may want to wear some sort of leg or ankle protection as you can easily get badly scratched if you lose the track and have to force your way through fern or scrub. Wear adequate walking shoes or boots, not thongs or sandals, as the trails can often be challenging. They can also be quite muddy and slippery after rain; don't underestimate the danger of this when you're on a steep incline. Carry plenty of drinking water with you; hiking on Rarotonga can be thirsty work.

Most important, be sure to observe the basic tramping safety rules of letting someone know where you're going and when you expect to return, and *don't go alone*. There have been numerous instances of trampers getting injured or lost in the mountains. If you slip and injure yourself it could be a very long time before anyone finds you. Don't be paranoid, but do take sensible precautions.

Walking times quoted are for a complete trip from the nearest road access point and do not allow for getting lost – which on most trails is a distinct possibility.

Organised Walks The popular Cross-Island Trek is organised through local travel agents and private guides. Guided walks across the island include hotel transfers at both ends and a light lunch along the way. They only go in fine weather, as the track is very slippery when wet. If you'll only be staying on the island for a short time and you want to do a cross-island walk, it's sensible to do it as soon as you can upon arriving, so you don't find yourself planning to do it on your last day and then it turns out to be raining.

Pa (☎ 21-079), a big, friendly dreadlocked fellow, leads a group most days of the week for NZ$35 per person. For the same price Pa also leads a less strenuous Earth Garden Walk up the Matavera stream, introducing you to fauna, flora and medicinal plants of the island, and will guide other walks by arrangement.

Tangaroa Tours (see Organised Tours) leads the Cross-Island Trek on Sunday for NZ$25 (children NZ$10), or at other times by arrangement.

Water Sports Muri lagoon is the best place for a variety of water sports including windsurfing, sailing and kayaking, and of course it's also good for swimming. Sailing races are held every Saturday at 1 pm from the Sailing Club on Muri beach. Muri beach is also the departure point for glass-bottom boat tours (read on).

Watersports equipment can be hired at two places on Muri beach: Aquasports (☎ 27-350, fax 20-932) at the Rarotonga Sailing Club, and Captain Tama's Beach Hut at the Pacific Resort (☎ 20-427, fax 21-427). Both hire snorkelling gear, reef shoes, kayaks, windsurfing boards, Sunbursts (dinghies with sail), small catamarans etc. They also give sailing and windsurfing lessons.

Prices are about the same at either place, though it never hurts to compare. Ask Aquasports about their all-day adult, child and family passes, which include unlimited use of all gear plus a lagoon tour and discounts on lessons and food. Aquasports also arranges hotel transfers.

The Rarotongan Beach Resort also has water sports equipment including snorkelling gear, kayaks and outrigger canoes. Anytime you have a meal in the restaurant, or even a drink in the bar, you are considered a guest for the time you are there, and you're welcome to use all the watersports equipment and the swimming pool. The only stipulation is that if a paying hotel guest wants to use something and there is only one, they get priority.

Snorkelling Snorkelling is wonderful in the lagoon, with lots of colourful coral and tropical fish. The lagoon is shallow all the way around but the south side, from the Rarotongan Beach Resort to Muri lagoon, has the best snorkelling. The lagoon roughly in front of the Raina Beach Apartments, the Little Polynesian Motel and Moana Sands Hotel has the best snorkelling on the island.

Snorkelling gear can be rented from the two watersports places on Muri beach, or from any dive shop. Aquasports offers one-hour snorkelling trips in the lagoon either alone (NZ$10) or as part of an all-day activities pass. The glass-bottom boat tours include snorkelling on their trips too. A few accommodation places have snorkelling gear available for their guests, so be sure to ask at the place you're staying before you spend money to hire it. If you want to buy your own gear, try The Dive Shop in Avarua.

All the diving operators will take snorkel-

lers along on their diving trips outside the reef if there's room on the boat for around NZ$20, equipment included.

Diving Diving is good outside the reef. There's coral, canyons, caves and tunnels and the reef drop-off goes from 20 to 30m right down to 4000m! Most diving is done at 3 to 30m, where visibility is 30 to 60m (100 to 200 feet) depending on weather and wind conditions; it's seldom less than 30m.

In addition to the brilliant visibility, other special features of diving on Rarotonga include shipwrecks, the largely unspoiled reef with several varieties of colourful living coral, and the very short boat trip to reach the diving grounds. The fact that Rarotonga is a small, round island means that regardless of where the wind is coming from there's practically guaranteed to be good diving somewhere around the island. For the novice diver, the sheltered lagoon makes an excellent learning and practising ground.

Rarotonga has three diving operators. Cook Island Divers (☎ 22-483, fax 22-484, PO Box 1002, gwilson@gatepoly.co.ck), Pacific Divers (☎/fax 22-450, PO Box 110, dive@pacificdivers.co.ck) and Dive Rarotonga (☎ 21-873, fax 21-878, PO Box 38, jacqui@gatepoly.co.ck).

All offer morning and afternoon diving trips outside the reef for certified divers. Dives cost around NZ$60, with discounts for multiple dives, two dives in one day, or if you have your own gear. Snorkellers can go along for around NZ$20, including gear, if there's enough room in the boat.

Cook Island Divers and Pacific Divers offer 3½-day diving courses leading to internationally recognised PADI or NAUI certification for NZ$425. They also offer PADI-approved resort courses – two-hour Discover Scuba courses designed to give an initial feel for diving – in the lagoon for NZ$60. Ask about night dives.

Deep-Sea Fishing Deep-sea fishing is excellent right off the reef and with the steep drop-off there's no long distance to travel out to the fishing grounds – within two minutes

NANCY KELLER

NANCY KELLER

NANCY KELLER

Top Left: Piri Puruto III and his coconut crab from Atiu, Piri Puruto show, Rarotonga
Top Right: Making maire *eis*, Mauke
Bottom: Mitiaro women having a good time

Top Left: Taro leaves (*rukau*), Punanga Nui market, Rarotonga
Top Right: Stand with typical Rarotongan foods at Punanga Nui market, Rarotonga
Bottom Left: Preparing the *umukai* (Polynesian feast), Rarotonga
Bottom Right: Coconut grater at The Hut handicrafts shop, Atiu

of leaving the dock, you're already in deep water and you can start fishing. World-class catches are made of many fish including tuna, mahi mahi, wahoo, barracouta, sailfish and marlin. Yellowfin tuna, dogtooth tuna, big eye tuna and mahi mahi are found in Rarotonga's waters all year round; seasonal catches include wahoo and barracouta (July to November), marlin and sailfish (November to March) and skipjack tuna (December to May).

Several boats are available to take you deep-sea fishing; prices vary so it pays to compare. Ask if lunch is included, and if you can keep your fish; on some boats the fish is divided among the passengers but on others the boat operators keep the fish themselves, or sell your fish back to you at a per-kilogram rate.

Motorised yachts making deep-sea fishing trips include the MV *Seafari* (☎ 20-328) and Pacific Marine Charters (☎ 21-237, fax 25-237). They can take four to six passengers; cost is around NZ$85 to NZ$95 per person for a five-hour trip. They provide lunch, but any fish you catch stays with the boat.

Another motorised vessel, the *Angela II*, costs NZ$70 per person for a three to four-hour trip. It's operated by the folks at Metua's Cafe, who say 'if you hook it, we cook it' – they'll cook you a fine meal out of any fish you catch. Contact Bill Kavana at Metua's Cafe (☎ 20-850).

Brent's Fishing Tours (☎ 23-356) goes on a three to four-hour tour around the island on an 8m (26-foot) catamaran, fishing as you go, so it's a scenic tour as well as a fishing trip. The cost is NZ$60 per person; there's a maximum of four or five passengers and any fish caught are shared among the passengers. Beco Game Fishing Charters (☎ 21-525, 24-125) also does catamaran fishing tours; a four-hour trip is NZ$85 per person, lunch included, and if you catch any fish they stay with the boat.

Oki Come Fishing (☎/fax 28-144) is a newer operator doing fishing trips; it charges NZ$100 per person, or four people for NZ$300.

The Cook Islands Game Fishing Club (☎ 21-419) is a popular hangout for fishing folk; they can help you to arrange fishing trips.

Surfing Surfing on Rarotonga isn't exactly world class, but you may see a scattering of surfers trying their luck on the waves at Avarua, right in front of the traffic circle. Other surfing spots include Avana Harbour, Black Rock and Matavera (near the Matavera School). Ollies Surf Gear (☎ 20-558, 27-999, fax 20-202), in the same building as Stars Travel and the ANZ Bank in Avarua, sells surfing supplies and a map of Rarotonga's best surfing spots.

Reef Walking Walking on the reef to see the colourful coral, crabs, shells, starfish and other creatures is always fascinating but make sure you wear strong shoes as the coral is very sharp; coral cuts can be nasty and take a long time to heal. An old pair of running shoes is much better than thongs. Listen for the clicking sounds made by tiny hermit crabs as they clamber and fall across the rocks. Walk gently, try not to damage the coral, and if you turn anything over to see what is beneath remember to turn it back again.

Whale Watching Humpback whales visit the Cook Islands each year from July to October; you might be able see them just outside the reef. Pacific Divers (see Diving) offers whale-watching trips in season.

Glass-Bottom Boat Tours The two watersports places on Muri beach – Aquasports and Captain Tama's – both operate glass-bottom boat tours of the lagoon. The tours cruise out to some fine snorkelling spots (snorkelling gear is provided) and then to Koromiri island in Muri lagoon for a barbecue lunch and entertainment. The tours last from 11 am to 3.30 pm and go every day except Sunday; Aquasports occasionally operates Sunday tours too. The cost is NZ$35.

Aquasports offers the combination of the glass-bottom boat tour with other activities on an all-day pass, or doing the tour alone, without the barbecue (1½ hours, NZ$15). Captain Tama's goes to a prettier spot on Koromiri, and Captain Tama and the boys offer good entertainment; they also offer a barbecue on Wednesday night on Koromiri with music and entertainment, short sunset or other lagoon cruises, and weddings (see the Weddings section). Contact Captain Tama (☎ 20-810, (☎/fax 23-810) for more information.

Reef Runner You can hire a Reef Runner – a self-drive small boat with a clear floor allowing you to see the coral below, like a glass-bottom boat – at Reef Runner (☎ 26-780) in Paringaru, beside the Paringaru stream on the south end of Muri lagoon. The cost is NZ$35, including snorkelling gear.

Reef Sub The Reef Sub (☎ 25-837, 20-427) is a semisubmersible viewing vessel that goes outside the reef, viewing coral formations, shipwrecks and fish, sharks, whales and whatever else might be outside the reef. Cruises lasting 1½ to two hours depart twice a day from Avatiu Harbour; cost is NZ$35.

Horse Riding Horse riding tours are offered by Aroa Pony Trek (☎ 21-415), just inland from the Kaena Restaurant, near the Rarotongan Beach Resort. Two-hour morning and afternoon rides go down the beach, inland up to Wigmore's Waterfall for a swim, then back again. The cost is NZ$30 (children NZ$15), and bookings are essential.

Fun Runs The Hash House Harriers meet every Monday at 5.30 pm for an easy fun run somewhere around the island. Look for the announcement on the sports page of the *Cook Islands News* each Monday, or phone David Lobb (work ☎ 22-055, home ☎ 27-002) to find out where the run will be. In the Cooks the Hash House Harriers have a couple of other branches – Hash House Harriers, Hussies and Hoffspring!

Gymnasium The Topshape Health & Fitness Centre (☎ 21-254) has aerobics classes each weekday, a weights room, a massage clinic and beauty salon. It's open weekdays 6.30 am to 8.30 pm, Saturday 8 am to noon. Visitors are welcome.

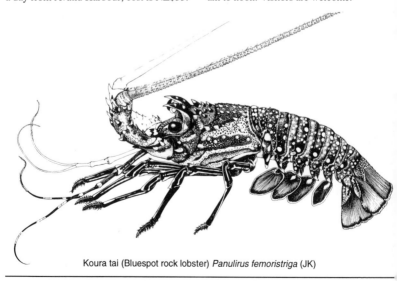

Koura tai (Bluespot rock lobster) *Panulirus femoristriga* (JK)

Other Sports There are **tennis** courts and rental gear are available at the Edgewater and Rarotongan Beach resorts (phone for reservations); many public tennis courts dotted around the island can be used for free if you have your own gear. You can usually find a **volleyball** game on the beach at the Rarotongan Beach Resort, especially on Sunday. **Lawn bowling** is held at the Rarotonga Bowling Club in Avarua most Saturdays and there's an annual tournament. There's a nine-hole **golf** course just south of the airport.

Scenic Flights Scenic flights are great for working out exactly where those mountain trails go and where the good diving spots are. A 20-minute flight is NZ$49 per person (minimum two passengers, maximum three). They'll take you up any day, 8.30 am to 3.30 pm; contact Air Rarotonga (☎ 22-888).

Weddings Captain Tama's Island Paradise Weddings (☎ 20-810, (☎/fax 23-810, PO Box 45) organises any type of wedding you can think of. Most popular are the beach weddings on Koromiri, the most beautiful island in Muri lagoon, but they'll help you to do whatever you want. Music, photos, video, flowers and food can all be arranged.

May Kavana (☎ 21-877, fax 23-088, PO Box 856) of May's Apartments (see Places to Stay) also arranges weddings.

Organised Tours
Do a Circle Island Tour sometime during your stay on Rarotonga. Several interesting and informative tours are offered, and they provide insight into many aspects of Rarotongan history and culture, both ancient and modern, that you'll never learn if you simply go around on your own.

The Cook Islands Cultural Village operates a Circle Island Tour which starts off with an island-style lunch and a show of legends, song and dance; see the separate entry.

Raro Tours (☎ 25-325, 25-324, fax 25-326, rarotour@gatepoly.co.ck) does a 3½-hour Circle Island & Historical Tour each weekday (NZ$25).

Raro Safari Tours (☎ 23-629, after hours 22-627) does an inland 4WD Jeep expedition every day of the week. It gets right off the beaten track, going on the back roads, up inland valleys and up the mountains for good views (NZ$45, children under 10 free).

Tangaroa Tours (☎ 29-968, 21-060, fax 28-070) offers a variety of tours including a 3½ hour Circle Island Historical Tour (NZ$23), a three-hour Horticulture & Agriculture Tour (NZ$19), a three-hour Black Pearl Tour (NZ$19), a three-hour Factory Tour (NZ$19), a four-hour Friday Nightlife Tour (NZ$19) and a four-hour Cross-Island Walk (NZ$25).

Cook Islands Tours & Travel (☎ 20-427, 20-270, fax 27-270, raroinfo@citours.co.ck) offers personalised three-to-four-hour island orientation tours for just two to four passengers. The cost is NZ$30 per person and they'll go anytime, at your own convenience.

Getting There & Away
See the earlier Getting There & Away chapter for information on getting to Rarotonga from overseas and the Getting Around chapter for interisland transport within the Cooks.

Getting Around
The Airport Most hotels, motels and hostels send vans to the airport to meet incoming international flights; independent taxis also meet incoming flights. If you've booked your accommodation, you'll probably be met by a van from your hotel. If you opt for a taxi you'll be efficiently organised into parties going in various directions, funnelled into waiting taxi mini-buses and shot off – all for a fare of NZ$10 per person.

If on the other hand you're a real shoestringer and think NZ$10 per person is pretty outrageous for travelling, say, 5km to Arorangi, you can get together a group and check the taxis, or even just stand on the main road in front of the airport and wait for the public bus; it costs NZ$2 to anywhere on the island's coast road. Unfortunately, most international flights arrive at ungodly hours when the public bus doesn't operate.

Bus A round-the-island bus service runs right round the coast road in both directions. The bus is a good way of getting around, and an easy way to do a complete round-the-island circle to get an initial feel for the place. The complete trip takes 50 minutes.

The bus departs on the hour and the half-hour from the bus stop at Cook's Corner in Avarua. Buses going clockwise round the island depart every hour on the hour from 7 am to 4 pm weekdays, 8 am to 1 pm Saturday. Buses going round the island in an anticlockwise direction depart every hour on the half-hour, 8.30 am to 4.30 pm, weekdays only. There are no buses on Sunday. The service seems to run pretty much on time so you can work out relevant arrival times around the island; you can flag the bus down anywhere along its route.

The bus fare is NZ$2 for one ride, NZ$3 for a return trip (two rides) or NZ$15 for a 10-ride ticket. There's also a NZ$5 all-day bus pass, good for a whole day from 7 am to 4.30 pm.

The same buses operate at night, but on a more limited schedule. Most go around the island in a clockwise direction. Departure times from Cook's Corner are at 6, 9 and 10 pm Monday to Saturday, with additional late-night buses departing at midnight and 1.30 am on Friday night. The cost is NZ$4 return.

Bus timetables are printed in the *What's On* tourist booklet available free from the tourist office; the bus drivers also have time-tables. Or ring Cook's Island Bus (☎ 25-512, after hours 20-349) for information.

Car & Motorcycle Before you can rent a car or motorcycle you must obtain a local driving licence from the police station in Avarua. It's a straightforward operation taking only a few minutes and costing NZ$10. Even an international driving permit is not good enough for the Cooks and if your home licence does not include the type of vehicle you'll be driving on Rarotonga –

motorcycles, for example – you'll have to pay another NZ$5 and take a practical driving test. The test seems to consist of riding down the road from the police station, round the traffic circle outside the Banana Court and back again, without falling off. You can get your licence any weekday from 8 am to 3 pm, weekends 8 am to noon. You must present your home driving licence or passport as identification when you apply for your licence.

You don't need to hire anything very big on Rarotonga – the farthest place you can possibly drive to is half an hour away. It's worth phoning around to check the prices, as every company seems to have some sort of special deal going. Be sure to ask if insurance and the 12.5% VAT tax are included in the stated cost.

At one extreme are the big international rental car companies, Budget and Avis, with the widest selection of cars. Their rates are around NZ$60/73/85 per day for a small/medium/large car, NZ$85 per day for a Jeep or NZ$100 per day for a nine-seater van, with discounts for three to five-day rentals and even further discounts for rentals of a week or more.

Locally owned TPA Rentals has the cheapest cars on the island, for NZ$35 per day. Several other locally owned companies hire cars at prices somewhere between TPA and the 'big boys'.

Small motorcycles are the principal mode of transport on Rarotonga and there are lots of motorcycles to hire, mostly 80cc to 100cc models. All of the car-rental agencies rent motorcycles; ring round to find the best deal. Lowest rates are about NZ$20 per day, NZ$90 per week. Many hotels also rent motorcycles; ask at the place you're staying, and compare prices. Most places offer discounts for weekly rentals.

Rarotonga rental car companies include:

Avis Rental Cars
    Avarua (☎ 22-833, fax 21-702); Airport (☎ 21-039).
BT Bike Hire
    Arorangi (☎ 23-586).

Budget Rent-A-Car & Polynesian Bike Hire
Avarua (☎ 20-895, fax 20-888); Edgewater Resort (☎ 21-026); Rarotongan Beach Resort (☎ 20-838); Airport (☎ 21-036).
Hogan's Service Centre
Arorangi (☎ 22-632, fax 23-632).
Rarotonga Rentals
Avatiu (☎ 22-326, fax 22-739).
Tipani Rentals
Avarua (☎ 21-617, fax 25-611); Arorangi, opposite Edgewater Resort (☎ 22-328).
TPA Rental Cars
Arorangi (☎ 20-611, 20-610).

There are few surprises for drivers on Rarotonga. The driving is reasonably sane (except late on Friday and Saturday, the two nights when there's heavy drinking) and there's no reason to go fast as there's not far to go wherever you're going. The speed limit is 30km/h (20mph) in town, 40km/h (25mph) out of town. You drive on the left – like in New Zealand, Australia, Japan and much of the Pacific and South-East Asia.

There are two rental car rules: don't leave windows open, not because of the risk of theft but because of the chances of an unexpected tropical downpour leaving the car awash; and don't park under coconut palms, because a falling coconut can positively flatten a tiny Japanese car.

Bicycle Bicycles are readily available for hire and generally cost around NZ$5 to NZ$10 a day for mountain bikes, with discounts for weekly rentals. The island is compact enough and the traffic is light enough to make riding a pleasure, particularly on the inland roads.

Avis, BT Bike Hire, Hogan's Service Centre, Polynesian Bike Hire and Tipani Rentals (see the Car & Motorcycle section above) all rent bicycles; so does Vaine's Rental Bikes (☎ 20-331) opposite Vara's Beach House in Muri. Many hotels also rent bicycles.

Taxi Taxis are radio-controlled so you can phone for them. Taxi operators include A's Taxis in Pue (☎ 27-021), BK Taxis in Ruatonga (☎ 20-019), JP Taxis in Arorangi (☎ 26-572), Muri Beach Taxis in Muri

(☎ 21-625) and Ngatangiia Taxis in Ngatangiia (☎ 22-238). Rates are around NZ$1.50 per kilometre, so it will cost around NZ$20 to go from Muri to the airport.

AVARUA

Avarua, the capital of the Cook Islands and Rarotonga's principal town, lies in the middle of the north coast, about 2km east of the airport. Until quite recently it was just a sleepy little port, very much the image of a south seas trading centre. The town had quite a facelift to spruce it up for the international Maire Nui festival in October 1992. It's now more attractive and has more businesses, but its relaxed, friendly ambience still remains.

Avarua doesn't demand a lot of your time but it does have all the basic services (post office, banks, supermarket, shops and restaurants) and some interesting places to visit. If you're looking for nightlife, Avarua is probably where you'll find it.

Orientation

Finding your way around Avarua is no problem; there's only one main road, the Ara Maire Nui, and it's right along the waterfront, with a grassy strip down the middle with plenty of shady trees.

An obvious landmark you can use to orient yourself is the traffic circle, on the main road near the Takuvaine stream and the Avarua Harbour entrance.

Standing at the traffic circle, to your east you'll see a group of seven tall coconut trees arranged in a circle – this is the 'Seven-in-One Coconut Tree'. Look inland and you'll see the post office on the right side of the road; the Philatelic Bureau and the New Zealand High Commission are in the two-storey building next door. Heading inland down this road past the post office brings you to the turn-off for Rarotonga Breweries and, farther on, to the Papeiha Stone and then the road heading up the Takuvaine Valley.

A number of interesting sights are in the couple of blocks to the east of the traffic circle. They include the Para O Tane Palace, the Beachcomber Gallery, the Avarua CICC church with its distinctive surrounding

THE SOUTHERN GROUP

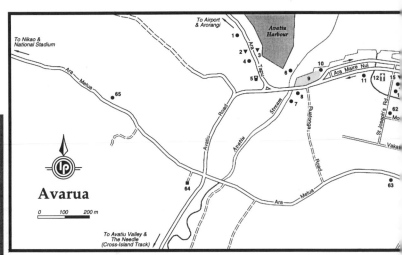

Avarua

graveyard, and just inland from the church, the University of the South Pacific (USP) centre and opposite it the Cook Islands Library & Museum Society. From this corner where the University and the Library & Museum Society face each other, one block

inland is the Takamoa Theological College and one block to the east is the Sir Geoffrey Henry National Culture Centre with the National Auditorium, National Library and National Museum.

The commercial centre of town is just west

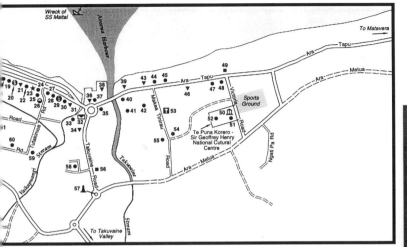

23	Police Station	41	Snowbird Laundromat
24	The Energy Centre Petrol Station	42	Para O Tane Palace
		44	Beachcomber Gallery
25	The Pearl Shop; Alliance Française de Rarotonga	45	The Bakery
		47	Are Tiki Shop
26	Cooks Corner Arcade; Cook's Corner Cafe; Simone's Bistro; Bus Stop	48	Vakatini Palace
		50	National Museum
27	CITC Shopping Centre – CITC Department Store; Pharmacy & Duty-Free; Cocophotos	51	National Library
		52	National Auditorium
		53	Avarua CICC Church
28	Avis Rent-A-Car; Pearl Factory, Matina Travel	54	University of the South Pacific (USP)
		55	Cook Islands Library & Museum Society
29	Tourist Office		
30	Pearl Hut; Perfumes of Rarotonga Dr Wolfgang Losacker	57	Papeiha Stone
		58	Rarotonga Breweries
32	Post Office; Philatelic Bureau; New Zealand High Commission	59	Telecom
		60	Prime Minister's Office
33	Government Building – Ministry of Foreign Affairs & Immigration	61	Rarotonga Bowling Club
		62	Petrol Station
35	Seven-in-One Coconut Tree	63	The Perfume Factory
37	T-Shirt Factory	65	Michael Taveoni's Studio
40	Empire Theatre		

of the traffic circle. The Banana Court Bar which you can see from the traffic circle, with the Blue Note Cafe on the verandah, is a Rarotongan landmark. A few little shops line the east side of the Banana Court, and just past those is the Tourist Authority visitor information office, with an 'i' sign hanging out front on the footpath. The large CITC department store is on the corner, there's a petrol station on the opposite corner, and just a few doors inland from this corner is Cook's Corner Arcade, where the bus stops. Keep heading inland down this road to reach the Telecom office and the Perfume Factory.

West on the main road are the police station, banks, supermarket, shops and cafes. A couple of long blocks down, on the seaward side of the road, is the Punanga Nui open-air market with fruit and vegetable stalls, arts and crafts, and takeaway food caravans. Just past this is Avatiu Harbour, where the interisland passenger freighter ships are based. The airport is 1km or so farther west.

Information

For information about Avarua see the Rarotonga Information section at the beginning of this chapter.

Seven-in-One Coconut Tree

Just to the east of the traffic circle is a group of seven tall coconut trees growing in a perfect circle. Tradition has it that they are really all one tree! Supposedly in the distant past an amazing coconut with seven sprouts was found on the island of Takutea, near Atiu, and brought here to be planted.

Papa Tangaroa Kainuku, oral historian of Rarotonga and *tumu korero* (speaker) of Kainuku Ariki, tells a different story about the trees, however. Apparently his grandfather, Frederick Goodwin, brought seven coconuts (not one) from Manihiki when he returned to Rarotonga sometime around 1900, and planted the seven trees in a circle here to commemorate the birth of his daughter, Papa Tangaroa's mother, Te Ariki Vaine Akakino Ia E Te Vaa Tangata I Taputapuatea, who was born on 6 November 1898 while Goodwin was away in Manihiki. The circle of trees marked the boundary between Kaviri on the east, belonging to Makea Nui Ariki, and Tura'i on the west, belonging to Karika Ariki.

Philatelic Bureau

Cook Islands stamps, coins and bank notes are all international collector's items. The Cook Islands Philatelic Bureau (☎ 29-336), next door to the post office, sells uncirculated mint and proof sets of coins and

bank notes, plus collector editions of Cook Islands stamps. It's open weekdays, 8 am to 4 pm.

Rarotonga Breweries

Rarotonga Breweries (☎ 21-084) produces the Cook Islands' own beer – Cook's Lager. Free 15-minute brewery tours operate Monday, Wednesday and Thursday at 2 pm, followed by a free glass of the amber liquid. To get to the brewery, take the road heading inland from the traffic circle past the post office, take the first right turn where you see the sign and continue around to the large two-storey warehouse-style building.

Papeiha Stone

A block further inland, the stone upon which Papeiha stood in 1823 when he preached the gospel in Rarotonga for the first time sits atop a raised traffic circle.

Stones are very important in traditional Cook Islands culture, and this one has an interesting history. It lay ignominiously in the bush near its present location for many years, until 1945 when it was moved to the Avarua CICC church. In 1996 Prime Minister Geoffrey Henry had the stone moved back here, near its original site, and given a place of honour.

Para O Tane Palace

Half a block east of the traffic circle on the inland side of the main road are the Para O Tane Palace and Taputapuatea, the palace area of Makea Takau. She was the ariki, or chief, of this district in 1888 when the LMS withdrew to the sidelines and the British government officially took control of the Cook Islands (or at least the southern group), forestalling any possibility of a French takeover from Tahiti. The palace, once a grand edifice, was destroyed in the hurricane of 1942 and remained a ruin for many years. It was restored in the early 1990s and renamed the Para O Tane Palace, though its original name was Beritani (Rarotongan for 'Britannia'). It is the residence of Makea Takau's descendent, Makea Nui Teremoana Ariki, and is not open to the public.

This whole area where the church and palace were built was once the site of the largest and most sacred *marae* (religious meeting ground) on Rarotonga. The missionaries wanted to take over and replace the old religion so they destroyed the old marae; today nothing remains of it.

Beachcomber Gallery

One long block east of the traffic circle on the sea side of the main road, facing the CICC church, the Beachcomber Gallery (☎ 21-939) occupies a building constructed in 1845 by the LMS for their Sunday school. The building, which had been worn down to a ruin, was restored in 1992 and converted into a gallery for Cook Islands arts, crafts, jewellery, pearls and other items of interest. You can visit the workshop in the back to see how the black pearl jewellery and shell carvings are made.

Avarua also has several other galleries; see Arts & Crafts in the Things to Buy section, a little further on.

CICC Church

The CICC church in Avarua is a fine, old, white painted building made of coral, much in the same mould as other CICC churches in the Cooks. It was built in 1853 when Aaron Buzacott was the resident missionary. The interesting graveyard around the church is worth a leisurely browse. At the front you'll find a monument to the pioneering Polynesian 'teacher' Papeiha. Just to the left (as you face the church) is the grave of Albert Henry, the first prime minister of the independent Cook Islands. You can't miss it – it's the one with a life-size bronze bust wearing a pair of spectacles! Other well-known people buried here include author Robert Dean Frisbie.

You're welcome to attend services; the main service of the week, as at all of Rarotonga's CICC churches, is Sunday at 10 am. See the Religion section in the Facts about the Country chapter for advice about attending a CICC church.

Library & Museum Society

Inland behind the Para O Tane Palace, the small Cook Islands Library & Museum Society (☎ 26-468), with its friendly staff, houses a collection of rare books and literature on the Pacific. If you inquire, you may be able to inspect and read the collection, but only on the premises. You can borrow books from the extensive Pacific collection, as well as other books of general interest. You can get borrowing privileges even if you're only visiting the island: visitors staying up to three months can get a library card for NZ$15 plus a NZ$10 deposit which is refunded when you go. If you stay for over three months the cost is just NZ$10 for a year's membership.

The small museum has an interesting collection of ancient and modern artefacts – basketry, weaving, musical instruments, wooden statues of various old gods, adzes, shells and shell fishhooks, spears, tools and other historical items, a beautiful old outrigger canoe, one of the original missionaries' printing presses and a collection of historical photographs. Admission is NZ$2. The library and museum are open Monday to Saturday from 9 am to 1 pm, and Tuesday from 4 to 8 pm.

If you're going to Atiu, check out the large *tumunu* pots here in the museum. You can read more about tumunu ceremonies in the Bush Beer Schools aside in the Atiu chapter, and attend a modern tumunu if you visit that island. But the only place you'll see a real tumunu pot is right here.

And no, the large iron pot on the verandah wasn't used in cannibal rites – it's an old whaling pot, used for boiling down blubber to make whale oil. When people were eaten in the Cooks, they were baked in ovens.

University of the South Pacific (USP)

The University of the South Pacific (USP) (☎ 29-415), based in Suva, Fiji, has its Cook Islands Centre in the building opposite the library. Most classes are taught externally from the main campus. A wide selection of books on the Cook Islands and other parts of the Pacific, published by the university, are on sale in the office. If you're planning a lengthy stay in the Cooks, you can ask here about classes for learning the Cook Islands Maori language.

Takamoa Theological College

Just inland from the Library & Museum Society and USP is Takamoa Theological College, built in 1842. One of the earliest mission compounds on the island, it is in its original condition and still in use. It was established to train locals for the ministry and from here missionaries were sent out to many parts of the Pacific. It still educates CICC ministers today.

National Culture Centre

One block inland from the Paradise Inn is the large Sir Geoffrey Henry National Culture Centre. Conceived by Prime Minister Sir Geoffrey Henry, the complex was formally opened on 14 October 1992. The centre is home to the National Auditorium, the National Museum, the National Library, the Conservatory & National Archives and the Ministry of Cultural Development.

The National Auditorium is the venue for large-scale concerts and other events.

The National Museum is a small museum with a selection of Cook Islands and South Pacific artefacts. It's open weekdays from 8 am to 4 pm; admission is free, with donations appreciated.

The small National Library is open weekdays from 9 am to 4 pm, later (until 8 pm) on Monday and Wednesday. Visitors can get borrowing privileges by paying a NZ$50 refundable bond plus a monthly NZ$5 library fee.

Wreck of the *Maitai*

West of the traffic circle and directly offshore from the centre of Avarua is the wreck of the SS *Maitai*, a 3393-ton Union Steam Ship vessel which used to trade between the Cook Islands and Tahiti. She ran onto the reef, fortunately without loss of life, on 24 December 1916. Her cargo included a number of Model T Fords. All that remains today is her rusted boiler, just off the edge of

the fringing reef. In the 1950s a couple of enterprising New Zealanders brought up one of the ship's bronze propellers.

The Perfume Factory

The Perfume Factory is easy to spot on the Ara Metua road just behind town, heading west. Here you can buy perfumes, colognes and pure coconut oil, all scented with local flowers including frangipani, gardenia and jasmine. Handmade coconut-oil soap, lotions, shampoos, and many imported French and other perfumes are also available. You can also taste and buy some locally produced liqueurs made from various combinations of coconut, pineapple and Atiu coffee. The Perfume Factory has been enormously successful since its opening in 1981 and now exports its products. It's open Monday to Saturday from 8 am to 4.30 pm, Sunday 10 am to 2 pm.

Punanga Nui Outdoor Market

On the main road and beside the waterfront near Avatiu Harbour, Punanga Nui is an outdoor market with a collection of stalls selling fresh fruits and vegetables, clothing, handicrafts and takeaway foods. Saturday morning is its busiest time.

Avatiu Harbour

This small harbour on the west end of Avarua is Rarotonga's principal harbour. An international freighter or two, the two interisland passenger freighters, a collection of fishing boats and yachts and the occasional visiting ship of one kind or another are all often seen here.

Places to Stay

The *Central Motel* (☎ 25-735, fax 25-740, PO Box 183, stopover@central.co.ck), half a block inland from the post office, is a favourite with visiting businesspeople. It's spotless, new and very well kept, with 14 units, three of which can be interconnected. Rates are NZ$95 per night.

The *Paradise Inn* (☎ 20-544, fax 22-544, PO Box 674, paradise@gatepoly.co.ck) is the next closest hotel to the centre of town, just a short walk east on the main road. Although the beach is rocky and shallow here, not good for swimming, the amenities are good, with a large lounge area, video movies, board games, library, informal bar and a barbecue area on the seafront patio. Most of the units are townhouse-style and spacious, with a double bed in the ample sleeping loft and sitting room, kitchen, bath areas downstairs. Singles/doubles/triples cost NZ$73/80/93. A larger family unit sleeping five is NZ$99, though they don't accept children under 12; a couple of budget single rooms are NZ$47.

Atupa Orchid Units (☎ 28-543, fax 28-546, PO Box 64), about 500m inland from Avatiu Harbour, is quiet and peaceful, yet close to town. It's operated by Ingrid Caffery, an ebullient German lady who speaks English, German, Swiss-German, French and Dutch. The five spotless new bungalows each have one, two or three bedrooms, well-equipped kitchen, sitting room, bath and verandah. The cost is NZ$18 per person to share, or if you want a whole bungalow to yourself it's NZ$45 for one or two people, NZ$65 for three, NZ$75 for four. Bicycles and motorcycles are available for hire.

Places to Eat

Restaurants *Trader Jack's* (☎ 26-464, 25-464), on the seafront near the traffic circle, is one of Rarotonga's most popular bar-and-grill restaurants. The indoor tables, as well as those out on the deck over the sea, all have a great sea view. The lunch and dinner menus are ample and varied; specialities include seafood, pastas and charcoal-grilled steaks. Lunch is served Monday to Saturday, dinner every night. The bar, popular with Rarotonga's upmarket crowd, features live music every night.

A couple of doors east of Trader Jack's, *Metua's Cafe* (☎ 20-850), hidden away in Browne's Arcade, is also pleasantly situated on the waterfront. It's a good, inexpensive open-air restaurant/bar with some tables under cover and others out in the open. The food is good and varied, with plenty of selections for all meals. Friday and Saturday nights there's a live band under the stars. It's open Monday to Saturday, starting at 7.30 am and staying open until 10 pm Monday to Thursday, until 2 am Friday and until midnight Saturday. Food is served straight through, from opening till closing time.

A little farther east, the *Staircase Restaurant/Bar* (☎ 22-254) is upstairs behind the Topshape Health & Fitness Centre. It's a family restaurant specialising in quality food at low prices, with a NZ$10 dinner special changing every night plus an à la carte menu, and live music nightly. It's open Tuesday to Friday from 6.30 pm; dinner reservations are preferred.

Across the road is *Portofino* (☎ 26-480), one of the best restaurants on the island. The menu is eclectic and international; the fresh fish of the day, the big fisherman's platter, the pasta and pizzas are all very good and so are the desserts. There's an indoor air-conditioned section and an outdoor patio dining area, all with romantic candlelight, and a bar with an extensive and reasonably priced wine list. It's open for dinner Monday to Saturday, 6.30 to 9.30 pm, and until midnight on Friday when there's a special on pizza slices and beer. They deliver pizzas and other foods around the island at set times in the evenings; ring to arrange it. Dinner reservations are recommended.

On the airport side of Avarua, *Ronnie's* (☎ 20-824) is a pleasant restaurant-bar-cafe with a moderately fancy indoor restaurant plus a garden cafe and bar. There's quite a variety on the menu, with reasonably priced meals and bar snacks. You can dress up or come as you are. On Friday night Ronnie's is very crowded, having become the 'in' place to go, and there's a lot of back-and-forth between it and the First Club disco in the rear; the rest of the time it's quite peaceful. It's open Monday to Saturday, 11 am to midnight.

Snacks & Takeaways *Mama's Cafe*, beside the Foodland supermarket in central Avarua, is a popular cafe with inexpensive meals and snacks, plus an ice-cream counter. On the other side of Foodland, a few doors down in

THE SOUTHERN GROUP

the Mana Court, *Courtney's Cafe* is a simple little place with picnic tables in the courtyard and an enthusiastic clientele of locals.

Cook's Corner Cafe in Cook's Corner, where the bus stops, is another popular hangout with basic cafe food; a separate bar and beer garden is off to one side. Outdoors in the patio of the Cook's Corner Arcade, *Simone's Bistro* specialises in pizzas and steaks.

The *Blue Note Cafe* on the verandah of the Banana Court, near the traffic circle, is a fine place to catch the breeze, have a coffee, lunch or snack and watch the world go by.

Nearby on the beach side of the traffic circle, the *Breez'n Cafe* serves basic take-aways like burgers and fish and chips, and is probably most notable for its long opening hours: Monday to Thursday 7 am to 10 pm, Friday 7 am to 3 am, Saturday 7 am to midnight. On the inland side of the traffic circle just past the post office, *Southern Fried Chicken* is a KFC clone, open Monday to Saturday, 8 am to 10 pm.

Nearby, *Metua's Cafe* is an open-air seaside restaurant (see Restaurants) but in the daytime it's also a pleasant hideaway for an inexpensive meal or snack or for lingering over a coffee or beer.

On the west side of Avarua, Punanga Nui, the outdoor market, has a couple of caravans selling basic takeaways, with picnic tables where you can relax and eat. Fresh fruits and vegetables are sold in the marketplace stalls.

Palace Takeaways at Avatiu Harbour is a popular takeaway with some picnic tables out front; try the legendary Palace Burger. Across the road, another *Southern Fried Chicken* has fried and roast chicken and the usual extras (corn, coleslaw etc). Both places are open long hours: weekdays 8 am to 1 am (4 am on Friday night), Saturday 8 am to 2 am, Sunday noon to 10 pm.

Markets & Supermarkets The Foodland supermarket in the centre of Avarua has a good selection of foods. If you have a lot of food shopping to do, it can be worth taking a trip into town to do it here. Packaged and imported food is often cheaper here than at the tiny local grocery shops dotted around the island; for produce, you may find a better selection elsewhere, especially at the Punanga Nui open-air market stalls. Other large supermarkets in Avarua include Meatco, a few doors inland from Budget Rent-A-Car, and the CITC Wholesale Store opposite Avatiu Harbour.

The Punanga Nui open-air market has many stalls with a selection of fresh fruits and vegetables. Early in the morning you can often buy whole fresh fish. There are also some takeaway food caravans, and stalls selling *pareu* (sarongs), clothing and handicrafts. Punanga Nui is open every day except Sunday; the biggest market day is on Saturday morning, when it's quite festive.

Entertainment

Cinema The *Empire Theatre* shows films every night except Sunday, usually with double features. The cost is NZ$5 (children NZ$2.50).

Bars There's quite a selection of places where you can go out on Rarotonga, especially on Friday night when most of the places mentioned here are quite crowded. Once you get into town you can easily walk from one to another. They tend to attract different crowds – one place might attract young people in their early 20s, another an older and more upmarket crowd. Popularity of watering holes changes rapidly; the place that 'everybody' ·was going to last month may be eclipsed by some new place this month, or the crowd may simply walk around from one place to another.

Though Friday night is the big partying night, most of the places mentioned have entertainment on both Friday and Saturday nights; a couple have music every night. Typically they stay open until around midnight most nights, till around 2 am on Friday night. On Saturday night they shut bang on midnight so as not to be revelling on Sunday.

Lots of people start Friday night off with the 'island night' performance at *Club Raro*, then drift into town hitting the Staircase, then Trader Jack's, then Ronnie's, Tere's Bar and onwards, as they make their way on a 'pub crawl' around the island.

Trader Jack's, on the waterfront near the traffic circle, is a restaurant/bar very popular with the upmarket set, with live music in the bar every night. Nearby, *Metua's Cafe* in Browne's Arcade is another popular restaurant/bar, with a live band on the patio on Friday and Saturday nights. Also nearby, *TJ's Nightclub*, a disco with super-loud music and flashing lights, is popular with the 18-to-25 age group on Friday and Saturday nights.

The *Staircase* restaurant/bar, upstairs in the rear of the Topshape Health & Fitness Centre building, is a smaller family bar, with live music Tuesday to Friday nights. Another small, intimate bar, the *Hideaway Bar*, is in the Cook's Corner Arcade in the centre of Avarua; it has live music on Wednesday and Friday nights.

Ronnie's is another popular drinking spot, especially on Friday night, when its large garden patio is packed with drinkers. *The First Club*, immediately behind Ronnie's, has a disco for teenagers (aged 13 up to around 20) on Friday night from about 7 pm to midnight. There's a lot of people going back and forth between Ronnie's and the First Club on Friday night. The rest of the time, Ronnie's is quieter.

The *Banana Court Bar* near the traffic circle in Avarua was once the best-known drinking hole and dance hall in the Cook Islands, indeed in the whole South Pacific. It's still a major landmark but nowadays it only opens for special events and functions.

Tere's Bar at Avatiu Harbour is another popular nightspot, with tables outdoors or under cover, and a live band on the patio on Friday and Saturday nights.

Things to Buy
Arts & Crafts Island Craft Ltd (☎ 22-009) has an excellent selection of very good Cook Islands arts and crafts, including an impressive collection of masks and spears from around the Cook Islands and the Pacific, with plenty of dramatic examples from Papua

New Guinea. Both the prices and the quality here are some of the highest on the island.

The Beachcomber Gallery (☎ 21-939) also has a wide selection of excellent local handicrafts and artwork of all kinds, including weavings, *tivaevae*, paintings, jewellery and plenty more. You can visit the workshop in the back to see shell carvings and black pearl jewellery being made.

Local artists' works are also displayed at the Arasena Gallery (☎ 23-476), tucked behind the Blue Note Cafe in the Banana Court. Beside the Banana Court, paintings and prints by Rick Welland, a long-time Rarotongan resident, are displayed and sold in the tiny Perfumes of Rarotonga shop. A variety of local artists' works, mostly paintings, are also available at the Kenwall Gallery (☎ 25-527), next to Pacific Supplies.

Island handicrafts are available at several stalls in the Punanga Nui open-air market. Rosie's Are Crafts, here in the market, specialises in women's handicrafts from the outer islands, especially the northern group.

Several artists on Rarotonga have private studios where you can come and see their work. Michael Taveoni, one of the Cook Islands' most skillful and renowned carvers, shows a wide variety of top-quality wood and stone carvings at his studio on the Ara Metua in Atupa, going out towards the airport from Avarua; stop where you see the thatch hut and the big stone carvings out on the lawn. He may be opening a shop at Punanga Nui too. Some of Michael's large stone carvings grace the area in front and to the side of the Sir Geoffrey Henry National Culture Centre.

Exham Wichman (☎ 21-180), another fine Cook Islands carver, has a shop behind his house in Arorangi where he displays all types of carved wooden handicrafts; see the Arorangi section.

Jillian Sobieska (☎ 21-079) has a studio called The Gallery on a back road in Matavera; follow the signs. You're welcome to stop by and see her paintings.

Judith Kunzlé (☎ 20-959) sells watercolours of local land and seascapes, and drawings and paintings of Cook Islands dancers, from her home studio. She is one of the Cook Islands' best artists; her drawings appear in many books and posters in the Cook Islands.

Pearls & Jewellery Pearls are a speciality of the Cook Islands. The northern group islands of Manihiki and Penrhyn are important producers of black pearls (which are among the rarest pearls in the world) but pearls in other colours, including golden ones and white ones, are also produced in the Cooks and sold on Rarotonga. Being on Rarotonga gives you the chance to see a fine selection of pearls and buy them at much better prices than you'll find elsewhere in the world.

Several shops in Avarua sell pearls – loose pearls, pearl jewellery, pearls still embedded in their shells, mother-of-pearl shells and many other innovative creations. Check out The Pearl Shop in the Cook's Corner Arcade, The Pearl Hut near the Banana Court Bar, the Beachcomber Gallery and June's Pearls, among others – pearl shops are springing up all the time.

Black-lip pearl oyster

Shells & Shell Products Shell jewellery is also popular in the Cooks, and you'll find it at many of the arts and crafts places mentioned in this section.

Necklaces, handbags, fans, wind chimes, statues, jewellery boxes and many other items are sold at a number of places in Avarua including Island Craft Ltd, the Beachcomber Gallery, Rosies Are Crafts and at the Punanga Nui open-air market. The Shells & Craft shop in Muri also has shells.

Perfumes, Soaps & Coconut Oil Locally made perfumes and soaps made from pure coconut oil are sold direct from the manufacturers at The Perfume Factory and at Perfumes of Rarotonga, which has a small shop beside the Banana Court and another shop on the main road in Matavera village. For more information see the preceding The Perfume Factory section.

Pure coconut oil, good for skin and hair, is sold at many places around Avarua including Island Craft Ltd, the CITC Pharmacy, the Punanga Nui open-air market, Rosie's Are Crafts and at both of the perfume shops. You can buy it plain or scented with various local flowers and herbs. Mauke Miracle Oil contains a special medicinal herb (*pi*) which gives protection from the sun and is good for healing cuts.

Pareu The most common clothing on Rarotonga is, of course, the pareu, worn by men, women and children. A pareu is simply a length of fabric, which you wrap around yourself. It can be tied in a variety of ways – a book has even been published showing some of the many ways of tying pareu. Called by different names in different countries, the pareu serves as the general all-purpose garment of the Pacific islands.

Rarotonga has several distinctive styles of pareu. Most popular are tie-dyed pareu, often with overlays of breadfruit leaves and other designs. Printed pareu are also popular. Pareu are sold for around NZ$15 at many places around Rarotonga. At least a dozen shops in Avarua sell them; circle around the island on the coast road and you'll see many other places selling pareu.

Tattooing Tattooing is a traditional Polynesian art form. Michael Taveoni (see Arts & Crafts under Things to Buy in the Avarua section) does tattooing at his studio in Atupa. Or there's T's Tatts (☎ 23-576) operated by

Tetini Pekepo ('T'), inland from the Kaena Restaurant. Both offer traditional Polynesian tattooing, contemporary and custom designs.

Other Clothing T-shirts and singlets (tank tops) emblazoned with logos including the words Rarotonga and Cook Islands are sold in many shops around Avarua and in the Punanga Nui open-air market. Linmar's, the T-Shirt Factory and the Punanga Nui all have wide selections and good prices. There's a lot of competition so shop around before you buy.

A number of boutiques, such as Joyce Peyroux Garments, June's Boutique, Tav and Tuki's Pareu sell locally manufactured clothing, including distinctive Cook Islands *muu-muus* and Mother Hubbard dresses. Prices tend to be quite high – NZ$100 for a dress is not uncommon. Much of the clothing is exported to New Zealand.

Duty-Free There are a number of duty-free shops around Avarua and though prices aren't bad, Rarotonga is definitely not Hong Kong or Singapore for shopping. Don't make duty-free shopping a reason for coming to Rarotonga.

AROUND THE ISLAND

Most island attractions are on or near the coastal road that encircles Rarotonga. The coast road, the Ara Tapu ('Sacred Road') is a wide, well-surfaced route, paralleled by a second road, the Ara Metua ('Ancient Road') which is slightly inland.

This second road, the Ara Metua – called 'the back road' by locals – follows the path of an ancient road originally built of coral blocks around 1050 AD. Historically it was known as Te Ara Nui O Toi ('The Great Road of Toi'), although who, exactly, Toi was has been lost in history. None of the old road remains in an original state; most of it was surfaced or built over during WWII and a road improvement campaign in the early 1990s took care of the rest.

Prior to the arrival of missionaries the Rarotongans lived inland near the planta-

tions and gardens they tended. The missionaries moved them down to the coast and concentrated them in villages centred around churches to make them easier to control. If you hire a vehicle or take a circle-island tour and go around the island on the Ara Metua, you'll see another side to the island – swamp taro fields, white goats and black pigs grazing in pawpaw patches, citrus groves, men on ancient tractors or even digging out entire fields with shovels, and graves of the ancestors off to one side of the houses.

The following description moves around the island anticlockwise, starting from Avarua; distances in kilometres from the centre of Avarua running anticlockwise are indicated.

Airport (2.5km)

The Rarotonga international airport was officially opened in 1974 and tourism in the Cooks really started at that time.

Behind the airport is the National Stadium, where many of Rarotonga's big sporting events are held. The first international stadium to be built in the Cook Islands, it was constructed in 1985 for the South Pacific Mini Games. Beside it is Tereora College.

Cemetery (2.5km)

Opposite the airport terminal is a small graveyard known locally as the 'brickyard'. A controversial Australian cancer-cure specialist Milan Brych (pronounced 'brick') set himself up on Rarotonga after being chucked out of Australia. When his patron, Prime Minister Sir Albert Henry, was run out of office in 1978, Brych was soon run out of the country as well. Cancer patients who died despite his treatment are buried in the graveyard.

Tom Neale, the hermit of Suwarrow atoll, is also buried opposite the airport. He died in 1977 and his grave is in the front corner of the Retired Servicemen's Association (RSA) cemetery, with its 'Lest We Forget' sign. You can enter to see his grave.

Parliament (3.5km)

The Cook Islands Parliament is opposite the Air Rarotonga terminal. The building was erected in 1973 and 1974 as a hostel for the New Zealand workers that came to work on the construction of the airport. The prime minister's and other ministers' offices are in the former bedrooms, with a few walls rearranged.

Parliament meets at various times throughout the year, according to need; it's usually in session from around August to January, but there is no fixed schedule. Stop by or ring the parliament building (☎ 26-500) to find out when Parliament will be in session. You are welcome to watch the proceedings from the public gallery, so long as you're properly dressed; taking photos is not permitted. If you happen to wander in when Parliament is not in session, one of the staff will give you a short tour of the building.

Golf Course (5.5km)

The Rarotonga Golf Club (☎ 27-360, 20-621) welcomes visitors to play on its nine-hole course. A round costs NZ$12 for the green fee and you can hire a set of clubs for another NZ$12. The golf course is open weekdays from 8 am to 4 pm; Saturday is for members only and it's closed on Sunday.

Black Rock (6.5km)

Just beyond the golf course and down on the beach is Black Rock, where the missionary Papeiha is supposed to have swum ashore, clasping the Bible over his head. Actually he was rowed ashore in a small boat! This is also the departure point from where the spirits of the dead are supposed to commence their voyage back to the legendary homeland of Avaiki. If you follow the road up behind the hospital there are good views (see the Mountain Tracks section later in this chapter).

Arorangi (8km)

On Rarotonga's west coast, Arorangi was the first missionary-built village and was conceived of as a model village for all the others on the island.

The main place of interest in Arorangi is the 1849 CICC church – a large white building which still plays an important role in village life. The missionary Papeiha, the first to preach the Christian gospel on Rarotonga, is buried here, right in the centre front of the church; a huge monument to him has been raised by his many descendants.

To the left of the church is the old Tinomana Palace, built for the last local ruler by the British. The name of the palace is *Au Maru*, meaning 'the peace brought by Christianity'.

Interestingly, Tinomana, the chief who first accepted the message of Christianity from Papeiha, is not buried in the church graveyard although he is honoured by a memorial plaque inside the church, which is built on land he gave to the missionaries. He later became Papeiha's father-in-law when the missionary married one of his daughters. Tinomana is buried on the hill behind Arorangi, near his old marae. Did he have second thoughts about his adopted religion?

Rising up behind Arorangi is the flat-topped peak of Raemaru. See the Walking & Climbing section for details of the climb to the top, and the Aitutaki chapter for the story of why the mountain is flat-topped and what happened to the rest of it!

Exham Wichman (☎ 21-180) is a fine Cook Islands carver, and he has a shop out behind his house in Arorangi where he displays all types of carved wooden handicrafts; look for the sign pointing inland to Maria's Housekeeping Apartments & Backpackers, Woodcarving & Crafts, opposite Bunny's Diner.

A number of popular places to stay and eat are in Arorangi. Along the road are numerous small shops, and a branch of the Snowbird Laundromat.

Cultural Village (7km)

The Cook Islands Cultural Village on Arorangi's back road is a delightful experience; you'll learn more about traditional Cook Islands culture in one day here than you probably will for the rest of your stay.

Guided tours through the village, beginning weekdays at 10 am, visit a number of traditional huts and include information and demonstrations of many aspects of Cook Islands culture, including history, Maori medicine, ancient fishing techniques, weaving, coconut husking, woodcarving, traditional firemaking and cooking, costume making and dancing. The tour is followed by a feast of traditional foods, with your tour hosts and the people from the various huts all getting together for a rousing show of traditional music, dance and chants, lasting until about 1.30 pm.

In the afternoon, the Cultural Village offers a Circle Island Tour around Rarotonga featuring history, agriculture, culture and many other aspects of Rarotongan life, ending around 5 pm. You can take the tour by itself with the lunch, show and transfers included (NZ$25), or do a combined visit to the Cultural Village and the Circle Island Tour, either all in one day (NZ$60) or on two separate days (NZ$64), transfers included.

The morning village tour alone costs NZ$39, including the lunch and show, plus NZ$4 for transport if you need it, with discounts for children 11 years and under. Ring (☎ 21-314, fax 25-557) to make bookings and to arrange transport.

Highland Paradise (9km)
High atop a slope up behind Arorangi, Highland Paradise is on the site of the original village of the Tinomana people, where they lived before the arrival of Christianity. Raymond Pirangi, a descendant of Tinomana Ariki, takes visitors on a two-hour tour of the site, with its marae, other historical places, and an extensive botanical garden, telling stories of the old days followed by a traditional *umukai* (underground oven feast) lunch. It's open weekdays, 9.30 am to 4 pm; tours start at 10 am and cost $30, with lunch included. Bookings are essential (☎ 20-610, 20-611).

South Coast (from 12km)
The south coast of Rarotonga, from the Rarotongan Beach Resort right around to Muri lagoon, has the best beach and the best swimming and snorkelling possibilities. The reef is much farther out and the sea bottom

is relatively free from rocks and sandier than the other beaches. There are lots of good places to stop for a swim, particularly from around the 16 to 20km mark. At 16.5km you can pull off the road beside the beach and park – the beach is very fine here.

Wigmore's Waterfall (15km)
On the eastern edge of the Sheraton Resort complex, a road leads inland to Wigmore's waterfall, a lovely little waterfall dropping into a fresh, cool, natural swimming pool. You can drive all the way up to the waterfall, though the last stretch of road is quite rugged and is probably most suitable for 4WD vehicles or sturdy motorbikes. Otherwise it makes a pleasant walk from the coast road up to the waterfall and back. If you do the Cross-Island Trek you will come to the waterfall near the end of your journey.

Titikaveka (19km)
There's another picturesque CICC church at Titikaveka with some interesting old headstones in the graveyard. The church was built in 1841 of coral slabs, hewn by hand from the reef at Tikioki and passed to the site at Titikaveka hand-to-hand in a human chain.

Muri (22 to 25km)
Muri beach, on Muri lagoon on the southeast side of the island, is particularly beautiful. The shallow water has a sandy bottom dotted with countless sea cucumbers and some coral formations making it interesting for snorkelling. Out towards the reef are four small islands, or motu: Taakoka, Koromiri, Oneroa and Motutapu. Taakoka is volcanic, the other three are sand cays.

The Rarotonga Sailing Club (☎ 27-349) on Muri beach welcomes visitors. The *Sails* restaurant/bar upstairs and the *Boardwalk Cafe* downstairs have a great view of the lagoon. A few doors down, the Pacific Resort also has restaurants. Watersports equipment and lagoon cruises are available from both places; see the Water Sports & Activities section earlier in this chapter.

The beach between the Pacific Resort and the Rarotonga Sailing Club is especially

THE SOUTHERN GROUP

Matu Rori

Sea cucumbers (bêches-de-mer) are an Asian delicacy and many people around Muri find their lagoon's abundant sea cucumbers (rori) delicious. The creature's innards look rather like spaghetti and around here a reference to eating spaghetti probably means rori rather than pasta. Matu rori are best cooked with butter, garlic and spices but the locals are equally happy to eat them raw. It's not uncommon to see someone pick one up in the lagoon, tear the skin open, squeeze the guts out as if from a tube of toothpaste, toss the black skin away and eat the 'spaghetti' on the spot. Surprisingly, the animal survives – a couple of weeks later, the same animal can yield the same harvest of 'spaghetti' all over again.

Rarotonga's lagoon is home to several species of rori, but only two are eaten: the matu rori ('fat rori') and the somewhat less popular rori toto ('blood rori'). Matu rori can be eaten raw or cooked, but if you want to eat rori toto, you'll have to cook it first. Bon appetit. ■

popular; at low tide you can easily wade out to Koromiri motu.

Shells & Craft (☎ 22-275), a small shop by the main road in Muri, is the pet project of a retired shell collector, Mr Terry Lambert. There's a remarkable array of shells for sale, with everything from tiny, intricate shells to amazingly large ones. Most of the giant-size ones come from the northern group islands, where the lagoons are large and the water is warm.

Avana (Ngatangiia) Harbour (25km)

Beside Motutapu, the northernmost of the four Muri lagoon islands, is the comparatively wide and deep reef passage into Avana Harbour, also sometimes called Ngatangiia Harbour since it's in Ngatangiia. It's a popular mooring spot for visiting yachts and small fishing boats.

This harbour is historically significant as

the departure point for the Maori canoes which set off around 1350 AD on the great voyage ('the great migration') which resulted in the Maori settlement of New Zealand. In the grassy park opposite the big white Ngatangiia CICC church, a circle of seven stones with a historical plaque commemorates this event. Each of the seven stones stands for one of the canoes that completed the journey. On the point of land to your left as you gaze out through the harbour passage is the large, well-preserved marae where the mariners were given their blessing for the journey and where human sacrifices were made to the gods.

Matavera (27.5km)

The old CICC church at Matavera, also made of coral, is beautiful at any time, but especially lovely at night when the outside is all lit up. The scenery inland of the stretch of road between Matavera and Avarua is particularly fine.

Perfumes of Rarotonga (☎ 25-238), on the main road in Matavera, makes its own perfumes and colognes from local flowers; liqueurs from local mangoes, bananas and coffee; coconut oil soap from the local coconuts and other products. They also have an outlet in Avarua, beside the Banana Court Bar. There's a pottery shop at the rear.

Jillian Sobieska (☎ 21-079) has a studio called The Gallery on a back road in Matavera; follow the signs. You're welcome to stop by and see her paintings.

Arai-Te-Tonga (30km)

Just before you arrive back in Avarua a small sign points off the road to the most important marae site on the island. Marae were the religious ceremonial gathering places of pre-Christian Polynesian society; the koutu, similar in appearance, were political meeting grounds where ariki, the great chiefs of pre-missionary Rarotonga, held court. The ceremonial offerings to the ancient gods were collected on the koutu before being placed upon the marae.

A small sign on the coast road marks the turn-off for Arai-Te-Tonga. A great marae is on your right as you go down the small road heading inland towards Arai-Te-Tonga. When you meet the Ara Metua there's a stone-marked koutu site in front of you; walk down the Ara Metua to your left and you'll see on your right (the inland side) yet another ceremonial ground. This whole area was a gathering place and the remains of the marae, the koutu and other meeting grounds are still here.

Arai-Te-Tonga has the remains of an oblong platform 4m long that was at one time over 2m high. At one end stands the 'investiture pillar', a square basalt column 2m high which extends an equal distance down into the ground. Don't walk on the marae; it's still a sacred site.

Inland Drives

Two inland drives on the north side of the island give you an opportunity to see the lush fertile valleys of Rarotonga, with mountains towering above on every side. Both drives follow streams and are in areas which were populated by the Rarotongan people before the missionaries came.

The drive along Avatiu stream begins at Avatiu Harbour – just turn inland at the harbour and keep going straight ahead. The road extends about 3.5km inland; at the end is the beginning of the Cross-Island Trek, which must be continued on foot past this point.

The other drive is up into the Takuvaine Valley, reached by going inland on the road past the post office in Avarua and continuing inland. It's a wonderfully peaceful place. The Happy Valley Road extends inland for about 2km; a walking track continues inland and climbs up to the summit of Te Ko'u mountain.

Cross-Island Trek (three to four hours)

The trek across the island, via the 413m Te Rua Manga ('the Needle'), is the most popular walk on the island. It can also be done as a shorter walk from the north end to the Needle and back again, rather than continuing all the way to the south coast. It's

important that you do the walk in a north-south direction, as the chances of taking a wrong turn are greater if you try it from the other direction. Be sure to wear adequate shoes and to take enough drinking water with you. There are several places on this walk that get extremely slippery, and therefore dangerous, when there's been wet weather.

The road to the starting point runs south from Avatiu Harbour. If you're driving, continue on the road up the Avatiu Valley until you reach a prominent sign stating that this is the beginning of the walk and that vehicles cannot be taken past this point. After this point a private vehicle road continues for about 1km.

A footpath takes off from the end of the vehicle road. It is fairly level for about 10 minutes, then it drops down and crosses a small stream. Avoid following the white plastic power cable track up the valley; instead pick up the track beside the massive boulder on the ridge on your left, after the stream crossing.

From here the track climbs steeply and steadily all the way to the Needle, about a 45-minute walk. If it wasn't for the tangled stairway of tree roots the path would be very slippery in the wet (which it often is). The roots make the climb easy but also tiring. At the first sight of the Needle there's a convenient boulder right in the middle of the path, where you can rest and admire the view.

A little farther on is a very obvious T-junction. Te Rua Manga ('the Needle') is a 10-minute walk to the right; Wigmore's Waterfall is a 90-minute walk to the left. Up to now you've been ascending a ridge running in a north-south direction; at this junction it intersects with another ridge, running in an east-west direction. This is an important junction and you will return to it after you visit the Needle.

Actually climbing the Needle is strictly for very serious rock climbers – it's high and sheer. You can, however, scramble round the north side to a sheer drop and a breathtaking view from its north-western corner. From here you can look back down the valley you've ascended or look across north-west to the flat peak of Raemaru. You can also see the south coast from the Needle and there are fine views across to Maungatea and Te Ko'u to the east. Take care on this climb: the ledge is very narrow and there's a long and unprotected drop which would be fatal if you slipped. Do *not* try to climb round to the southern side of the Needle, as there is no view from that side and it's extremely dangerous.

Retrace your steps back to the T-junction, from where the left fork takes off heading east. Just before you reach the T-junction you'll come to a path leading off to the right

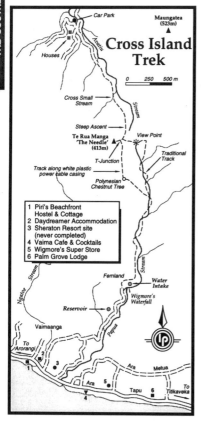

Cross Island Trek

0   250   500 m

1 Piri's Beachfront Hostel & Cottage
2 Daydreamer Accommodation
3 Sheraton Resort site (never completed)
4 Vaima Cafe & Cocktails
5 Wigmore's Super Store
6 Palm Grove Lodge

(south), following a white plastic electric cable casing which was put there around 1990. Some guides take this way, as the traditional track is slightly more difficult. If you take this way, however, you will miss the most spectacular view of the Needle on the entire track, visible from the peak just east of the T-junction.

From the T-junction, the traditional track drops slightly, then climbs to a small peak that gives you the best view of the Needle. From here the track leads down a long, slippery ridge for about half an hour's walking time. Despite the helpful tree roots, this long descent can be annoyingly slippery, and positively treacherous in wet weather.

After about 30 minutes the track meets the Papua stream and follows it down the hill, zigzagging back and forth across the stream several times. After about 45 minutes of following the stream, the track emerges into fernland. Here the track veers away from the stream to the right, passing clearly through the fernland. Be sure to stick to the main track; there are several places where newer, minor tracks seem to take off towards the stream but don't take these, as they will bring you out at dangerous spots upstream from the waterfall. After about 15 minutes the main track turns back towards the stream, bringing you to the bottom of the beautiful Wigmore's Waterfall. If you're hot, sweaty and muddy by this time, the pool under the fall is a real delight.

A rough dirt road comes from the south coast up to Wigmore's Waterfall. Walking down this road brings you to the coast road in about 15 minutes, passing alongside the eastern edge of the large Sheraton Resort site.

The public bus will drop you at Avatiu Harbour, from where you can begin the walk inland, and you can flag the bus down when you reach the coast road again at the end of the track. Note, however, that on Saturday the last daytime bus departs from Avarua at 1 pm, and there are no more buses until the night bus schedule starts at 6 pm. There is no public bus on Sunday. If you come on an organised trek across the island, hotel trans-

'ers are provided at both ends; see Organised Walks, earlier in this chapter.

Mountain Tracks

There are several other good mountain tracks on Rarotonga. Instructions for the easier ones are given here, but look for the *Rarotonga's Mountain Tracks and Plants* book by Gerald McCormack & Judith Künzle if you want to do some real mountain trekking. The Cook Islands Natural Heritage Project, publisher of the book, is working in concert with the Cook Islands Conservation Service to upgrade and maintain Rarotonga's inland tracks. Several tracks which were once overgrown are being cleared and consistently maintained, so you can now actually find them. A few signs are also being posted, to clarify the routes. Particularly difficult spots – going up vertical rock faces, for example – are being made safer with the help of ropes, as there's not much point in having

a steady stream of hikers injured in the same predictable places on the tracks.

Raemaru Raemaru (365m) is the flat-topped peak rising directly behind Arorangi village on Rarotonga's west coast. From the coast road you can see the route to the top running up the northern ridge line, before it crosses to the southern ridge to approach the rock face on the south-west side of the summit. You ascend this rock face to reach the summit. See the Aitutaki chapter for the legend explaining why this mountain, unlike all the others on Rarotonga, is flat-topped.

Turn off the coast road onto Akaoa Road, about 200m south of the Arorangi CICC church, and then turn right (south) onto the Ara Metua. There is a small road immediately on the left; park on the Ara Metua and walk up this small road, passing the gate leading to the house on the hill to your right, veering to the right and then following the road as it makes a sharp left turn.

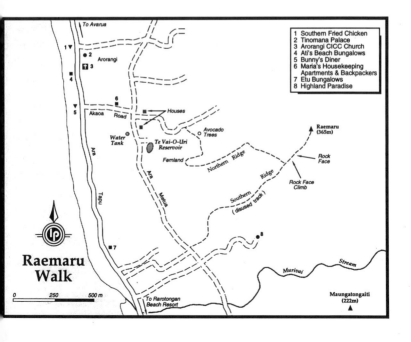

1 Southern Fried Chicken
2 Tinomana Palace
3 Arorangi CICC Church
4 Ati's Beach Bungalows
5 Bunny's Diner
6 Maria's Housekeeping Apartments & Backpackers
7 Etu Bungalows
8 Highland Paradise

Raemaru Walk

About 50m past this turn, find the walking track leading off to the right, then walk uphill through a grove of avocado trees. The track then veers off to the right, into fernland, and doubles back and forth across the hill a couple of times as it heads uphill. The clay is very slippery when wet – be careful.

Before long the track meets the ridge and proceeds uphill very clearly along the spine of the ridge. Be careful, as the steeper sections can be slippery even in dry weather; they are positively hazardous when wet.

At the top of the ridge the track veers to the right (south) and crosses over to the southern ridge, then turns left and follows this ridge uphill to the rock face. The place where you scale the rock face is about 15m high. Safety equipment has been installed on the rock face, but you must still be careful.

Finally you emerge onto an open grassy area which slopes gently to the top. From the far end you can look down across a valley to Maungaroa (509m) and Te Rua Manga (413m), the easily recognised peak known as 'the Needle'. Looking back you can see along the coast all the way from south of Arorangi to the airport runway in the north.

The return walk takes around two to 2½ hours.

Maungatea Bluff Maungatea (523m) is the peak behind that impressively sheer cliff face directly overlooking Avarua. The climb brings you to the top of the 340m bluff at the top of the cliff face, not to the top of the mountain itself, which is very difficult to reach and affords no great view once you get there. The bluff, on the other hand, offers a great view over Avarua and the north coast. The track is muddy and extremely slippery when wet. The track begins from the Ara Metua (the inland road) behind Avarua, beside the Tauvae Store. The return walk takes three to four hours.

Te Ko'u Te Ko'u (588m) is more or less in the centre of the island and is interesting because there is a volcanic crater at the top which you can traverse. The walk offers spectacular views of Rarotonga's inland

mountains and of the south coast. It starts off with an easy one-hour walk up the Takuvaine Valley behind Avarua, followed by a more challenging 1½-hour, steep climb up the mountain which is treacherous when wet. The return walk takes about five hours.

Ikurangi The ascent of Ikurangi (485m) is a vigorous walk to a spectacular view of the north coast, Avarua and the Takuvaine Valley. It's easier than the Te Ko'u walk. The track starts from the Ara Metua just to the east of Arai Te Tonga and takes about four hours return – a half-hour walk up the Tupapa Valley following the Tupapa stream followed by a 1½-hour ascent of the mountain. A couple of small rock faces are encountered on the way to the summit.

Te Manga Rarotonga's highest mountain Te Manga (653m) is probably the most difficult climb on the island – the long, strenuous climb has several sections which are difficult and very steep. Starting at the same place as the Ikurangi walk, the return walk to Te Manga takes about six hours, with a one-hour walk up the valley following the Tupapa stream followed by a two-hour ascent up the mountain.

Hospital Hill About the easiest way to climb up to a good viewpoint is to drive up the hill to the hospital, just behind the golf course, park in the parking lot there and continue on foot. It's an easy walk which even children and elderly people can do without a struggle. For those in good shape, the walk to the top takes about five minutes. The view from the top is beautiful and unobstructed, with the airport on one side, a lush agricultural valley stretching inland from there between mountain ridges and, on the other side, the village of Arorangi, pushing from the coast up to the sides of the mountains. The different colours of water in the lagoon, much deeper blue out past the reef, the wide vista of ocean stretching off into the distance and the fresh breezes all make it a refreshing change from the lowlands.

Valley & Beach Walks The mountain walks on Rarotonga are hard work. If you want something easier consider the valley walks, such as the stroll along the Avana stream from Ngatangiia. You can drive quite a distance up the road beside the stream and then follow the trail, repeatedly crossing the stream until you reach a pleasant picnic spot at the water intake. A similar walk follows the Turangi stream a little north of Ngatangiia. Matavera stream makes another good walk. Be prepared for mosquitoes.

Two other beautiful valleys are Takuvaine, behind Avarua, and Avatiu, inland from Avatiu Harbour. See details on these under Inland Drives. They also have walking tracks extending up into the valleys beyond where the roads end. The road heading inland from Avatiu Harbour ends at the start of the Cross-Island Track.

Any beach on Rarotonga is pleasant for strolling.

Places to Stay

Rarotonga has a wide variety of places to stay in every budget range. It also has an official policy that every arriving visitor should be booked into a place to stay before arriving on the island. See the Accommodation section in the Facts for the Visitor chapter for details on this requirement.

In large part this advance booking policy is designed to discourage people from camping on the beach, which is highly illegal – don't even think about camping on the beach because this will get you deported immediately. It's also designed to make sure everyone has a place to stay. There are only about 700 hotel rooms on Rarotonga and some of the hotels are routinely booked up months in advance.

Most of the places to stay on Rarotonga have some sort of kitchen or cooking facilities where guests can do their own cooking – a great convenience, not only for all the obvious reasons (being able to eat what you want, when you want to, much more cheaply than if you eat at restaurants) but also because the places to stay and the restaurants all tend to be scattered around the island, meaning a lot of travelling to restaurants if you must eat out, unless you want to constantly eat out at the same place. The large resort hotels and a few other hotels don't have kitchens in the rooms and so eating out will be an extra expense if you stay at one of these.

If you're looking for the most beautiful beaches on the island, choose one of the places to stay on Muri beach, or along the south side of the island. The beaches along the south and west sides of the island are all good for swimming – but not those on the north and east sides, where the reef is too close to shore, making the beaches rocky and the lagoon too narrow for swimming. If you want to see the sunset from your hotel then of course you must stay on the west side of the island.

A 12.5% tax (VAT) is charged on virtually every economic transaction in the Cook Islands, including the price of accommodation. Room rates are normally given with the VAT included; all prices given here include VAT. When asking prices be sure to clarify if the VAT is included; if it's not, you'll pay 12.5% more. Most places provide free airport pick-up, and have laundry facilities available for guests.

Places to Stay – bottom end

Rarotonga is experiencing a surge in budget accommodation, with a number of good old standbys and an equal number of newer establishments. All of the following places have kitchen facilities for guests to use, and are listed in an anticlockwise order around the island starting from Avarua.

Tiare Village Dive Hostel (☎ 23-466, ☎/fax 21-874, PO Box 719, tiarevil@ gatepoly.co.ck), a comfortable backpackers' haven, is on Kaikaveka Drive about 3km from the centre of Avarua, off the Ara Metua back road, out behind the airport. The hostel consists of one large house with three triple rooms and one double room, all sharing a common sitting area, kitchen and two bathrooms, plus three separate self-contained

A-frame chalets, each with one double bedroom and two single rooms. There's also a TV lounge, board games and a library for entertainment on rainy days. Snorkelling gear is available for NZ$5 per day. Fresh fruits and vegetables are in abundance here, which you are welcome to eat, and the place is famous for its hospitality. Nightly cost is NZ$16 per person, with discounts for weekly stays. The staff will take you into town and help you get oriented, hire a bike and the like the first day you arrive. Make sure you bring a mosquito coils.

The *Matareka Hostel* (☎ 23-670, fax 23-672, PO Box 587, hubaker@gatepoly.co.ck) is on Kaikaveka Drive, up the hill from the Tiare Village Dive Hostel – take the same turn-off from the Ara Metua back road and continue past the Tiare Village up to the very top of the hill. The hostel occupies the two houses at the top of the steep hill overlooking the airport. It's not bad if you have your own transport, but quite inconvenient otherwise, though they will rent you a mountain bike (NZ$5 per day) or scooter (NZ$12 per day), making it easier to get around and to get up that hill. It's pleasantly quiet up here, with spacious well-maintained grounds and a sweeping view over the sea. The top house is a big three-bedroom house, each bedroom having its own bathroom and sleeping three to four people, with a large communal kitchen and lounge area. The lower house has three twin or double rooms, again with a shared kitchen and sitting area. Nightly cost is NZ$25/35 a single/double room, or NZ$15 per person to share. Bring mosquito coils.

Further along the back road behind the airport, *May's Apartments* (☎ 21-877, fax 23-088, PO Box 856) in Nikao has six clean, modern two-bedroom apartments. There's a share rate of NZ$15 per person, or you can get a whole apartment to yourself for NZ$30/40/50 single/double/triple. Children under seven stay free. May Kavana, the friendly owner, works with flowers and arranges weddings by request.

The *Airport Lodge* (☎ 20-050, fax 29-223, PO Box 223) is on the main coastal road, near the end of the airport runway and opposite the radar station and the beach, about 5km west of Avarua. It consists o three duplexes, each with two self-contained one-bedroom units. Each unit sleeps two people except the one with two triple rooms which can sleep six. Nightly cost i NZ$25/40/45 a single/double/triple.

Aunty Noo's Beach Lodge (☎ 21-253, fax 22-212, PO Box 196) is in Arorangi, off the main road and close to the beach. This is the cheapest place to stay on Rarotonga – bed are NZ$10 per person, including a simple breakfast. Accommodation is quite basic with shared kitchen facilities and bedroom having only sheets for doors, but severa budget-minded young backpackers told u they love it. It's near the beach, the sunset it's in walking distance to everything, an there's an umukai on Sunday for just NZ$5 Aunty Noo (pronounced NO-oh) also rent a bungalow on the back road for NZ$40 a night.

The *Are-Renga Motel* (☎ 20-050, fax 29-223, PO Box 223) is on the main road in Arorangi, about 8km from Avarua. Mos accommodation is in comfortable little self contained one-bedroom apartments; there are also a few rooms with shared kitchen and sitting areas. The apartments are rather basic but if you're looking for a low-priced mote you may well find them ideal. Be sure to check out the 4 hectares (10 acres) of tropica gardens in the rear, with a variety of seasona fruit trees you are welcome to pick Singles/doubles are NZ$25/40, or there's a share rate of NZ$15 per person.

Maria's Housekeeping Apartments & Backpackers (☎ 21-180, PO Box 777) is a pleasant little duplex out behind the family home of Exham & Maria Wichman, in Arorangi – turn inland at the sign on the main road opposite Bunny's Diner and go abou 200m. The two self-contained units have a everything you need, including a large shared verandah; cost is NZ$15 per person in these, or NZ$10 per person in dorm rooms, with weekly discounts. Exham & Maria are a much-loved pair who operated historical tours of the island for many years

ow Exham has a home workshop where he
arves Tangaroa figures and wooden drums,
nd makes ukeleles and other island crafts.

Backpackers International Hostel (☎/fax
!1-847, PO Box 878, b.packer@gatepoly.
o.ck) in Kavera, not far from the Raro-
ongan Beach Resort, is an old favourite
▸ackpackers' hostel. It has recently been
▸xpanded and now has 27 rooms, with
ingles (NZ$28), doubles/twins (NZ$18 per
▸erson), triples and an eight-person dorm
NZ$16.50 per person); discounts are given
▸or stays of four days or more. There's a large
ommunal kitchen, comfortable indoor and
▸utdoor lounge areas, a rooftop sundeck and
▸ famous Saturday night island buffet. Bicy-
les, scooters and snorkelling gear are
▸vailable for hire. Look for the sign pointing
▸nland at the Kavera bus stop; the hostel is
▸he first two-storey house on your right.

Piri's Beachfront Hostel & Cottage (☎/fax
!0-309, PO Box 624), operated by Piri
▸uruto III (see Entertainment), is right on a
▸eautiful stretch of beach at Vaimaanga, on
▸he south side of the island. Rates per person
▸re NZ$12.50 in the dorm, NZ$14
win/double with shared facilities, NZ$15
win/double with private bath, or NZ$20 for
▸ single room. Guests receive discounts to
▸iri's shows and the Sunday umukai feast.

The *Beach Lodge* (☎ 20-270, fax 27-270,
▸O Box 611, raroinfo@citours.co.ck) is next
▸oor to the official residence of the Queen's
▸epresentative (QR) in Titikaveka, in a
▸eautiful spot opposite a white sandy beach
▸ood for swimming and snorkelling. Three
▸elf-contained two-bedroom apartments are
▸IZ$50 a night each, or NZ$13 per person on
▸ share rate, including an island breakfast.

The *Aremango Guesthouse* (☎ 25-210,
▸ax 25-211, PO Box 714) on the coast road
▸t Muri beach is friendly, clean, comfortable
▸nd well kept, with ample shared kitchen
▸acilities and outdoor sitting areas. Its 10
▸pacious bedrooms, each sleeping two or
▸ree people, are NZ$16.50 per person.

Vara's Beach House (☎ 23-156, fax 22-
▸9, PO Box 434, backpack@varasbeach.
▸o.ck) has one house right on Muri beach,
▸ith a volleyball court, barbecue area, picnic

tables and a luxurious villa up the hill with a
great view overlooking Muri lagoon, the
motu and the ocean beyond. Rates are
NZ$18 per person in dorms sleeping three to
five people, or NZ$21 per person in
double/twin rooms. Also up the hill are a
couple of cottages that can be booked as
self-contained houses for NZ$60 or NZ$75
per night. Vara's has many extras including
outrigger canoes, snorkelling gear and
mountain bikes.

The *Sunrise Beach Motel* is a straightforward motel but in addition to its regular
motel units it also has two budget units for
NZ$25 per person. See Places to Stay –
middle for details.

The *Ariana Bungalows & Hostel* (☎/fax
20-521, PO Box 925, bob@gatepoly.co.ck)
is about 200m inland from the coast road,
3km east of Avarua. The buildings are spaced
around a lush, green garden with fruit trees
ripe for the picking and a peaceful, quiet
atmosphere. There's a swimming pool, barbecue area, recreation room with pool table,
TV and video, a small shop and a self-service
laundry. Pushbikes and motorcycles are
available for hire. The Ariana has nine self-
contained bungalows, each with a fully
equipped kitchen, separate bedroom and
private balcony; these are NZ$60 for one to
three people. Two other buildings operate as
hostels, with shared kitchen and bathroom
facilities. The smaller, two-bedroom house
has singles/doubles for NZ$30/40. The
larger house has four bedrooms, but the pan-
elled walls come only part way up to the
ceiling; cost in this 'dorm house' is NZ$18
per person. There's a 10% discount for week-
long stays.

Places to Stay – middle

Club Raro (☎ 22-415, fax 24-415, PO Box
483, holiday@clubraro.co.ck) is about
2.5km east of Avarua. It's right on the waterfront but the beach here is not good for
swimming, so there's a waterfront swimming pool. Singles/doubles/triples are
NZ$75/88/120 in garden rooms, NZ$100/
110/140 in poolside rooms, or NZ$150 in

superior rooms, including a continental breakfast (the rooms have no kitchens). Corporate, group and all-inclusive rates are available on request. This 39-room hotel, with three bars and dining areas, is best known for its 'island night' entertainment at least two nights per week.

The *Kii Kii Motel* (☎ 21-937, fax 22-937, PO Box 68) is about 3km east of Avarua. This 24-room motel is on the beachfront, with a beachfront swimming pool since the beach here is not good for swimming. There's a choice of studio and one-bedroom units, all with kitchen; singles/doubles are NZ$54/67 in the budget rooms, NZ$68/87 in the standard rooms, NZ$86/108 in the deluxe rooms, or NZ$92/114 in the rooms overlooking the sea.

Wild Palms (☎ 27-610, fax 27-611, PO Box 489, drink@ronnies.co.ck) is on Kaikaveka Drive, off the Ara Metua back road out behind the airport, in a quiet garden setting about 3km west of Avarua. Six self-contained rooms, each with kitchenette, open onto a small swimming-pool area. Rooms are NZ$95 per night, with weekly discounts.

Ati's Beach Bungalows (☎ 21-546, fax 25-546, PO Box 693) is on the beachfront in Arorangi, on the west side of the island, on the main road near the CICC church. It's on a good stretch of beach, with a view of the sunset. Five small self-contained studio units in the house by the main road are NZ$80; these have no view. Four beachside studio bungalows are NZ$120, and a larger deluxe, two-bedroom, beachfront, family unit (sleeping up to seven people) costs NZ$250. Ati's is famous for its Sunday island buffet.

Etu Bungalows (☎/fax 25-588, PO Box 2136) has two free-standing, self-contained bungalows in a quiet, peaceful garden behind a family home on the main road in the south part of Arorangi. It's right opposite a good beach and you can help yourself to all the fruit you like. The bungalows are NZ$70 a night, or NZ$175 a week for long-term stays.

Daydreamer Accommodation (☎ 25-965, fax 25-964, PO Box 1048, byoung@

gatepoly.co.ck), at Vaimaanga on the south side of the island, has five clean, modern and pleasant units opposite a fine stretch of beach. All are spacious, airy and well equipped with kitchen, TV and phone. Bruce Young, the friendly owner, offers free island tours and snorkelling gear for guests. Four one-bedroom units are NZ$100; a two-bedroom unit is NZ$150. Children under 1 stay free.

Raina Beach Apartments (☎ 22-32 daytime, 20-197 evening, fax 23-602, PO Box 72, raina@gatepoly.co.ck), a curious looking three-storey concrete structure, is on the south-east side of the island, opposite beach excellent for snorkelling. Two one bedroom family units downstairs can sleep up to six people each. The upstairs units are smaller, without the separate bedroom, but they have the same lounge area, kitchen facilities and so on. Each unit costs NZ$10 for one or two people, NZ$20 for each extra person, no children under six accepted. The rooftop garden has a sundeck and a 360 view overlooking the lagoon and the mountains.

Aroko Bungalows (☎ 23-625, 21-625, fax 24-625, PO Box 850) has one of the most tranquil and beautiful settings on Rarotonga on the shore of Muri lagoon with a view across to Oneroa and Motutapu motu. It's a very simple place with just five small but cosy and attractive self-contained bungalows, each sleeping two; cost is NZ$80 in the garden bungalows, NZ$90 in the beachfront bungalows with verandahs overlooking the lagoon.

Sunrise Beach Motel (☎ 20-417, fax 24-417, Postal Depot 8, Ngatangiia), on the east side of the island just north of Avana Harbour, has eight small self-contained bungalows, some right on the beach with an ocean view. The lagoon here is very narrow so swimming is not so good, but it's not too far to walk to Muri lagoon. Rates are NZ$6 for one or two people, additional people NZ$15, and NZ$5 for children under five. A couple of budget units are NZ$25 per person

Sea View Lodge (☎ 26-240, fax 26-241 PO Box 176, seaview@gatepoly.co.ck) is luxurious two-bedroom home on the Ara Metua about 1km east of Avarua. It has many amenities including a jacuzzi on the verandah with a great view of the sea, well-equipped kitchen and sitting room, and a private office area. The cost is NZ$100 a night.

Oasis Village (☎/fax 28-214, PO Box 1093, oasis@gatepoly.co.ck), on the west side of the island near the beach and just south of the golf course, has four small free-standing one-room studio cabins, all with air-con and private bath, tea and coffee-making equipment but no kitchens. The cabins don't face the beach but they're not far from it, and there's beach access. The rate of NZ$120 per night includes a tropical breakfast at the Oasis Restaurant, which is also here.

The *Rarotongan Sunset Motel* (☎ 28-028, fax 28-026, PO Box 377, welcome@rarosunset.co.ck), on the beachfront on the west side of the island, about 6km west of Avarua, has 20 self-contained studio units with well-equipped kitchens, private verandahs and swimming pool. Twelve of the rooms can be interconnected. The cost is NZ$155 in the 11 garden rooms, and NZ$190 in the nine beachfront rooms. Breakfast is served in the bar, and there's a Sunday barbecue. Book ahead here; it's often booked up months in advance.

The *Puaikura Reef Lodge* (☎ 23-537, fax 21-537, PO Box 397, paul@puaikura.co.ck) on the south-west side of the island has 12 modern well-equipped units, each with kitchen and dining area. The family units are great if you're with children as the main sleeping area has a concertina door which you can slide across to shut off the living area. The cost is NZ$135 in these one-bedroom units, and there are also some studio units for NZ$110. The beach, narrow but pleasant and with good swimming, is only a few steps away across the road. There's also a tiny swimming pool, with a barbecue off to one side.

Lagoon Lodges (☎ 22-020, fax 22-021, PO Box 45, des@lagoon.co.ck) is on the coast road, opposite the beach, 400m from the Rarotongan Beach Resort. It stretches back from, rather than along, the road, so there's little traffic noise, and it's safe for children. There are 19 spacious bungalows set around a large 1.6-hectare (4-acre) garden, with a grass tennis court, trampoline, barbecue and swimming pool. In addition to six studio units, several of the bungalows are larger one or two-bedroom units – very spacious with a kitchen and living room area, a large verandah and virtually your own private garden. If you have children these larger units are among the best on the island. Prices are NZ$135 in the studio units, NZ$165 in the one-bedroom units, NZ$190 in the two-bedroom units, and NZ$425 in a large three-bedroom lodge. These prices include two adults and two children; extra adults/children are NZ$25/15.

The *Palm Grove Lodge* (☎ 20-002, fax 21-998, PO Box 23, palm@gatepoly.co.ck) on the south side of the island is a pleasant place with a variety of free-standing self-contained bungalows, a small swimming pool and large grassy grounds, beside a fine stretch of beach good for swimming and snorkelling. Six garden studio units, each sleeping three, are NZ$160; two one-bedroom garden villas, each sleeping up to four people, cost NZ$200; and seven beachfront studio units, each sleeping two, are NZ$240 per night. A bar/bistro is scheduled to open here soon, and these prices will then include breakfast.

The *Moana Sands Hotel* (☎ 26-189, fax 22-189, PO Box 1007, beach@moanasands.co.ck) in Titikaveka on the south-east side of the island has a two-storey block of rooms, 12 in all, each with a verandah facing directly onto the beach. It's a fine beach here, with kayaks, canoes, snorkelling and a barbecue area. Other activities can also be arranged, with the help of the very friendly and helpful staff. The rooms have no kitchens but they do have fridges, tea and coffee making facilities, toaster, microwave and electric frypan; there is also a restaurant and bar open three nights a week. Four of the rooms can be interconnected. The cost is NZ$179 per night.

The *Little Polynesian* (☎ 24-280, fax 21-585, PO Box 366), is right on the beach at Titikaveka lagoon. It's private and secluded, with eight beachfront studio units (NZ$175) and a lagoonside cottage (NZ$215), each with full kitchen. There's a swimming pool, a barbecue hut, picnic tables, and hammocks stretched under the palms. Snorkelling is excellent in the lagoon here; kayaks and snorkelling gear are free. Bicycles and motorcycles are available for hire. Children under 12 years are not accepted.

The *Muri Beachcomber* (☎ 21-022, fax 21-323, PO Box 379, muri@beachcomber.co.ck) is right on the shore of beautiful Muri beach. It has 16 self-contained, one-bedroom, seaview units, plus a couple of larger, poolside, one-bedroom garden units, for NZ$150/175 a single/double, plus three luxury free-standing one-bedroom watergarden villas for NZ$200/225. Children under 12 can stay in the garden units, but not in the seaview units or villas. The spacious grounds have a swimming pool, barbecue areas and a relaxing lily pond. The whole place is modern, well kept and well run. English and German are spoken there, and booking in advance is generally a must.

Places to Stay – top end

Rarotonga has some excellent places to stay in the top end range. Three of them – the Pacific Resort, Sokala Villas and Avana Marina Condos – are on Muri lagoon, two of them right on Muri beach.

The *Pacific Resort* (☎ 20-427, fax 21-427, PO Box 790, thomas@pacificresort.co.ck), right on Muri beach, is probably Rarotonga's most attractive medium-sized resort. The 49 self-contained units all have kitchens, one or two bedrooms, sitting rooms, private verandahs and good views of the beach, garden, and pond or swimming pool. Nightly cost is NZ$245 for one or two people in the 28 one-bedroom garden units, NZ$265 in the eight two-bedroom garden units, NZ$285 in the six beachside units, NZ$365 in the four beachfront units, NZ$485 in the four Pacific villa garden units, and NZ$520 in the three luxury Pacific villa lagoon units. Interconnecting suites are available. Children under 12 are free, sharing a room with their parents. All guests have free use of the watersports equipment (kayaks, windsurfers, snorkelling gear etc). The resort's intimate Barefoot Bar, right on the beach, has a lovely view; there's also the open-air Sandals Restaurant, and a weekly 'island night' performance.

Sokala Villas (☎ 29-200, fax 21-222, PO Box 82, villas@sokala.co.ck) is an assortment of seven timber, self-contained one-bedroom villas right on Muri beach. Each villa is different; five have their own private swimming pool, four are right on the beachfront, three are one storey and four are two storey with loft bedrooms. All are elegant and excellently appointed. This place is especially popular for couples and honeymooners. Children under 12 years are not accepted. Prices range from NZ$295 to NZ$440 per villa; ask about their 'early bird' discounts.

The *Avana Marina Condos* (☎ 20-836, fax 22-991, PO Box 869) are on Muri lagoon, overlooking Avana Harbour with a view across to Motutapu. The condos have their own jetty and each of the six units comes with its own boat; there's good swimming here, and a private beach. Five of the six units have two bedrooms and sleep up to five people; there's also one three-bedroom unit. Children are welcome. The cost is NZ$350 per night.

The *Manuia Beach Hotel* (☎ 22-461, fax 22-464, PO Box 700), in Arorangi on the west side of the island, was closed at the time of writing, but it's expected to re-open.

Large Resorts Rarotonga has only two large resorts – the *Rarotongan Beach Resort* and the *Edgewater Resort*. Their 'rack rates' – the prices you'll pay if you walk in off the street – are high, but most of their business comes from airline and travel agents' package holidays, which make the room rates cheaper.

The *Rarotongan Beach Resort* (☎ 25-800, fax 25-799, PO Box 103, sales@rarotongan.co.ck), on the south-west corner of the sland, has 151 guest rooms and it's the only international standard' hotel on Rarotonga. It has everything including its own beach with a beachfront swimming pool and spa pool, plenty of beach activities, tennis courts, a beachfront bar, two restaurants, various souvenir shops and huts, a travel desk, and car, motorcycle and bicycle rental. There's also a business centre with secretarial, photocopying, fax and email services, and even a conference centre.

The Rarotongan Beach Resort underwent major renovations and upgrading in 1997. It has four standards of rooms; the differences are principally whether you face the garden or the beach and some variation in equipment levels, though none of the rooms have kitchens. Singles/doubles are NZ$220 in garden rooms, NZ$270 in beachfront rooms, NZ$375 in paradise rooms and NZ$550 in suites. There is no extra charge for children under 16 years occupying the same room as their parents.

Even if you're not staying here, you can still come to partake of the many activities – anytime you come for a meal, a drink at the bar or whatever, you are considered a guest and you're welcome to use all the facilities including the swimming and spa pools, sun deck and those for beach activities. The resort beach has kayaks, outrigger canoes, snorkelling gear, volleyball, badminton and so on. An activities list at the front desk describes the various events being held each day.

All the resort's rooms and public areas are wheelchair accessible, and some rooms have specially equipped facilities for the disabled; this may be the only place in the Cooks built with special provisions for the disabled.

The *Edgewater Resort* (☎ 25-435, fax 25-475, PO Box 121, stay@edgewater.co.ck), on the beachfront at Arorangi on the west side of the island, has 180 rooms, making it the biggest resort in the Cook Islands. The resort has a beachfront swimming pool, tennis courts, cars, motorcycles and bicycles for hire, and a travel desk where you can book a variety of activities around the island. The rooms are quite straightforward with the three different categories differing mainly in their views (garden, partial beach view or beachfront) and furnishings. All have air-con, TV and in-house movies, but no kitchens. Prices are NZ$195 for garden rooms, NZ$220 for superior rooms, NZ$245 for beachfront rooms, NZ$325 for executive suites and NZ$390 for the VIP/honeymoon suite. Children under 12 are free. If you come on a package tour, as most guests do, prices are cheaper.

Places to Stay – renting a house

One of the best deals, especially if you're staying on the island for a while, is to rent a house by the week. A fully equipped two-bedroom house sleeping four or five people usually costs around NZ$100 to NZ$300 per week.

The challenge is to find one. The only real estate agent on Rarotonga that rents houses is the Cook Islands Commercial Realty Brokers Ltd (☎ 25-264, fax 25-265, PO Box 47, property@realty.co.ck), which rents houses for a minimum of three nights. Early bookings improve your chances of finding something. Cook Islands Tours & Travel (☎ 28-270, 20-270, fax 27-270, raroinfo@citours.co.ck, PO Box 611) also rents houses. Vara's Beach House, Aunty Noo's Beach Lodge and the Kii Kii Motel, all mentioned earlier, also have houses to rent.

Also check the classified section of the *Cook Islands News* and *Cook Islands Press*, where one or two rental houses are usually listed. The Tourist Authority may also be able to help you turn up something. Or you may have the best luck simply by asking around; there are plenty of houses available that are not advertised.

Places to Eat

The widest choice of eating places is found in Avarua, but there's also a scattering of places right around the island.

Restaurants Restaurants tend to be scattered at distances around the island, with more on the west than on the east side. Since you'll probably have to travel at least some distance to get to any of them, and most of them are quite small, reservations are a good idea. They're mentioned in an anticlockwise direction, starting from Avarua.

The *Oasis Restaurant & Hopsing's Chinese Wok* (☎ 28-213) in Arorangi is one of Rarotonga's best new restaurants. The open-air decor is simple but pleasant; the food is delicious and brings raves from practically everyone who eats here. Most Chinese dishes are around NZ$17; steak and seafood mains are NZ$23 to NZ$26, including salad. It's open for dinner Monday to Saturday from 6 pm; takeaways are available.

Alberto's Steakhouse & Bar (☎ 23-596) in Arorangi is another good place for a steak, open Monday to Saturday from 6 pm.

PJ's Sports Cafe (☎ 20-367) in Arorangi serves both Chinese and European food. Lunch is served Monday to Saturday, dinner every night, accompanied by live dinner music. The bar is open most days from noon to midnight; it's very popular, especially on Friday night, when it's open till 2 am.

The *Spaghetti House* (☎ 25-441), in Arorangi at the turn-off to the Edgewater Resort, has good pastas (meat or vegetarian) plus pizza, meat dishes and seafood. It's open for dinner every night from 5 to 9.30 pm, and also does takeaways.

The *Reef Restaurant & Bar* at the Edgewater Resort (☎ 25-435), one of the biggest restaurants on the island, has a weekly schedule of 'island night' buffets and theme dinners – all around NZ$25 to NZ$35 – and a couple of à la carte nights. There's a continental breakfast buffet every morning, and a menu of light meals and snacks (nachos, burgers, salads etc) served every day from 11 am to 9 pm. There's entertainment every night except Friday, when there's a theme dinner followed by a nightlife tour.

The *Tumunu Bar & Restaurant* (☎ 20-501), next to the Edgewater Resort, has a pleasant outdoor barbecue area and an indoor restaurant/bar with lots of attractive Polynesian touches. Seafood and steaks are the speciality here; try the big seafood platter. They also have vegetarian dishes,

children's meals and nightly specials. You'l feel right at home whether you dress up o go casual. There's a friendly weekly dart competition, and a roast pork dinner on Sunday. It's open every night from 6 pm on

The *Kaena Restaurant* (☎ 25-432, 25 433), 50m north of the Rarotongan Beach Resort, specialises in steaks and seafoods Put together a meal for two including all the house specialties – seafood chowder, fish o the day and a delicious banana crêpe fo dessert – and your bill will come to abou NZ$55. There's also an extensive wine, bee and bar list. The Kaena looks rather plain from the outside but it's attractive inside. It' open every night from 6 pm; reservations are recommended.

The Rarotongan Beach Resort (☎ 25-800 has casual dining around the pool and the beachfront terrace and bar. The more forma *Whitesands Restaurant* is a top-quality res taurant that serves three meals every day with a changing à la carte menu and a weekly 'island night' buffet (see the Entertainmen section). The resort's Sunday brunch (11 am to 3 pm) is a favourite on the island, with relaxed but festive atmosphere including string band, fashion parade, swimming and volleyball. On Sunday evenings there's a outdoor barbecue buffet (adults NZ$28, chil dren NZ$14) with a great view of the sunse

Vaima Cafe & Cocktails (☎ 26-123), i Vaimaanga about 2km beyond the Rarotongan Beach Resort, is a popular plac with beautiful island decor. The food is goo but not expensive – there's nothing on the menu over NZ$20. It's open every day from 11 am until late; in the evening there' romantic candlelight, and live music mos nights. Hotel transfers can be arranged.

Muri beach has three fine restaurants *Sails* (☎ 27-349), upstairs at the Rarotong Sailing Club, has an excellent view ove Muri lagoon, especially lovely when there' a full moon that seems to rise up out of th lagoon. Dinner main dishes include seafoo and steak; specialities of the house are th seafood chowder (NZ$10.50) and seafoo pasta (NZ$18). It's open for candleligh dinner every evening from 6 pm on. Dowr stairs, the *Boardwalk Cafe* serves simple fare in the daytime.

Nearby at the Pacific Resort, *Sandals Restaurant* (☎ 20-427) serves a continental buffet breakfast every morning and dinners from 6.30 pm nightly. Most nights there's an à la carte menu with steaks and seafoods, but they also have theme nights including an 'island night' buffet, a carvery night and a weekly barbecue, each NZ$33. Lunch is served in the beachfront *Barefoot Bar*, with both outdoor and indoor tables.

Down near the end of Muri beach, the *Flame Tree* (☎ 25-123 after 3 pm) is widely known as one of the best restaurants on Rarotonga, with delicious food, an elegant atmosphere and artistic decor. The international menu features dishes from India, Thailand, China, Japan, Singapore and elsewhere, with spicy and non-spicy selections. There are plenty of vegetarian dishes, plus seafood, steak, lamb and other meats. Appetisers are NZ$9 to NZ$14, soups NZ$6.50 and main courses NZ$18 to NZ$29. It's open for dinner every evening from 6.30 pm; reservations are recommended.

Island Buffets You'll get a good island-style buffet at any of the 'island nights' at the big resorts, where they present dancing and entertainment in addition to the food. If you just want to eat, a couple of the more modest places to stay have excellent island buffets, cheaper than the 'island nights'.

Ati's Beach Bungalows (☎ 21-546) in Arorangi has an excellent all-you-can-eat buffet with a great selection of delicious island foods every Sunday at 6.30 pm, for NZ$17.50 per person. Book by Saturday, as space is limited and this is one of the most popular Sunday dinners on the island. Transport can be arranged.

Backpackers International Hostel (☎ 21-349) has its island buffet on Saturday at 7 pm. It's NZ$12 for hostel guests, NZ$17 for others. It too is enormously popular; book by 4 pm Friday.

Piri Puruto III, of Piri's Beachfront Hostel & Cottage, does a traditional Cook Islands-style umukai every Sunday in which you can participate in the preparation and learn how it's done (see the Entertainment section, below).

Snacks & Takeaways There are just a few places around the island where you can get basic cheap takeaway food, but they all have tables so you can dine there or take the food away. They are listed here in an anticlockwise sequence, starting from Avarua.

In Arorangi, *The Flamboyant Place* in the little shopping centre opposite Dive Rarotonga has simple, inexpensive takeaways and hot food. It's open every day from 8 am until 1 or 2 am. Also in Arorangi, *Southern Fried Chicken* has fried and roast chicken, corn and coleslaw; it's open the same long hours as the SFC at Avatiu Harbour.

Bunny's Diner in Arorangi has basic breakfasts, burgers, sandwiches and the like, besides being a small grocery shop. It too is open long hours: Monday to Thursday 6.30 am to 9 pm, Friday and Saturday 6.30 am to 2 am, Sunday 6 to 10.30 pm.

Fruits of Rarotonga in Tikioki, on the south side of the island, is a popular little place selling reasonably priced home-made island fruit products like jams, chutneys and relishes. It also serves morning and afternoon teas and sandwiches. The owners boast that it's opposite the best snorkelling spot on the island.

Emil's Cafe (☎ 24-853), on the main road at Muri, is a favourite with locals and visitors alike for its good food, pleasant atmosphere and Emil himself, the cheerful owner, chef and host. Emil's has a basic takeaway menu with many welcome innovations, nightly specials, and good coffee.

On Muri beach, the Rarotonga Sailing Club has the pleasant *Boardwalk Cafe* on the downstairs deck overlooking the beach and lagoon – you can't beat the gorgeous view. It serves inexpensive light meals, snacks and desserts, plus drinks from the bar.

Just Burgers on the main road in Pue, just east of Avarua, makes inexpensive American-style hamburgers, french fries, milk shakes and the like.

Markets & Supermarkets In Vaimaanga on the south side of the island, Wigmore's Supermarket has a good selection of foods, good prices, and a wide variety of produce fresh from Wigmore's farm. Many locals on the south side of the island who used to go into town to shop now do their shopping here.

Many small shops are dotted around the island. They are convenient and are open longer hours than the supermarkets, but like 'convenience stores' in other countries, their prices are often higher.

Entertainment
Island Nights Cook Islands dancing is reputed to be the best in Polynesia, superior even to the better known dancing of Tahiti. There are plenty of chances to see it at the 'island nights' performances that seem to be on virtually every night of the week. The prices hotels quote for their 'island nights' – around NZ$35 – include buffet 'island meals'. If you turn up after the buffet and only want to watch the show you'll normally pay only a NZ$5 to NZ$10 cover charge. The show starts about 9 pm, and afterwards there's usually a live band.

The *Rarotongan Beach Resort, Edgewater Resort, Pacific Resort* and *Club Raro* all hold 'island nights' at least once or twice a week. They also hold barbecues and buffets which may include live entertainment. Sunday, when most other restaurants are closed, is the big day for hotel barbecues and brunches.

The tourist office hands out a free printed leaflet with up-to-date information on all the 'island nights' around the island.

Bars Friday night is Rarotonga's big party night. Most of the bars and nightclubs are in Avarua, but there are also a few possibilities around the island.

At the Edgewater Resort in Arorangi, the *Reef Restaurant & Bar* has entertainment of one kind or another every night except Friday. Nearby, the *Tumunu* restaurant/bar is cosy and there's a weekly darts competition. *PJs Sports Cafe*, also nearby, is a popular

bar/restaurant with a pool table, juke box and live dinner music every night.

The poolside/beachside bar at the *Rarotongan Beach Resort*, a lovely tropical style place with a great view of the sunset, is probably the most elegant bar in Rarotonga

The *Local Homestead Bar* on the back road in Kavera is a local watering hole with open-air tables and relaxed ambience.

Vaima Cafe & Cocktails in Vaimaanga has live music most nights.

On Muri beach, the Rarotonga Sailing Club has a pleasant upstairs bar at the *Sail* restaurant, with a great view overlooking the lagoon and the islands offshore. Downstairs the open-air *Boardwalk Cafe* has bar service in the daytime. Nearby, the *Pacific Resort* has the attractive beachfront *Barefoot Bar* with a lovely view of the lagoon and tables both indoors and out on the terrace.

The *Reef Runner Bar* on the south end of Muri beach is a pleasant, simple beachside bar in an open-air, thatch-roofed building tables are also on the beach and around the grounds. It's in a remarkably beautiful setting, near the Paringaru stream.

The *RSA & Citizens Club* opposite the airport is a casual bar and social club with pool tables, darts, and a live band on weekends. Locals come here to play pool and darts, and visitors are always welcome. They boast that their beer prices are some of the cheapest on the island. It's open every day from around noon to midnight.

Video There are innumerable video-hire shops around Rarotonga. Some hire video players, and even the TV to go with it. D&L Video Rentals (☎ 20-004), beside the Vaima Cafe in Vaimaanga, rents TVs for NZ$10 video decks for NZ$15.

Piri Puruto III Let's not forget Piri Puruto II (☎ 20-309) who zips up coconut trees demonstrates traditional firemaking and gives a generally entertaining and informative show at various locations around the island. His one-hour performance costs NZ$12 (NZ$6 for children), and it's worth it. He also takes tourists fishing on the reef

NANCY KELLER

NANCY KELLER

ft: Carving at Michael Tavioni's woodcarving stall, Punanga Nui market, Rarotonga
p Right: Stone statue by Michael Tavioni at the Sir Geoffrey Henry National Culture
 Centre, Avarua, Rarotonga
ttom Right: Sir Albert Henry's grave, CICC churchyard, Avarua, Rarotonga

NANCY KELLER

NANCY KELLER

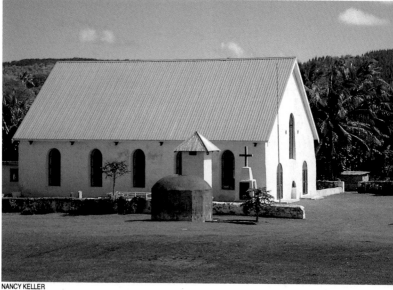
NANCY KELLER

Top Left: Graves decorated for Turama (All Souls Day), Catholic cemetery, Panama,
    Rarotonga
Top Right: Kea's grave, Mauke
Bottom: Ivirua CICC church, Tava'enga, Oneroa, Mangaia

or in the lagoon (NZ$30), does a fish barbecue dinner (NZ$10) and an 'early bird' coconut breakfast show (NZ$18) on various days of the week. Ring for a schedule, or pick up his pamphlet.

On Sunday Piri puts on a delicious umukai feast, cooked in an underground oven in the traditional Cook Islands Maori way. You can participate in the preparation to learn how it's done, then have a light lunch, see Piri's show and go for a swim while you wait for the feast to emerge. The cost is NZ$35; transport can be arranged. Children are half price for all Piri's activities.

Aitutaki, Manuae & Palmerston

Aitutaki

Population: 2332
Area: 18.3 sq km

Aitutaki is another Cook Islands' entrant in the 'most beautiful island in the Pacific' competition. It's the Cooks' second most populated island although in area it only ranks sixth. It's also the second most popular island in terms of tourist visits. The hook-shaped island nestles in a huge triangular lagoon, 12km across its base and 15km from top to bottom. The outer reef of the lagoon is dotted with beautiful *motu* (small islands) and they are one of Aitutaki's major attractions.

Aitutaki is also historically interesting, with a number of impressive *marae* (pre-European religious meeting grounds) which can still be visited today. Aitutaki is also historically significant because it was the first foothold in the Cooks for the London Missionary Society (LMS). Only after converting Aitutaki's population did they move on to Rarotonga.

Aitutaki has one of the best 'island nights' performances in the Cook Islands; try to arrange to be on the island on a Friday night to catch this authentic local occasion.

History

Various legends tell of early Polynesian settlers arriving at Aitutaki by canoe. The first settler was Ru, who according to various traditions came from either the legendary Polynesian ancestral homeland of Avaiki, or from Tubuaki, which may be the present-day island of Tubuai in the Austral Islands, now part of French Polynesia.

Wherever Ru's homeland was, it had become overcrowded so Ru, his four wives, his four brothers and their wives, and a crew of 20 royal maidens sailed off in search of new land. Eventually they landed on Aitutaki

HIGHLIGHTS

* Taking a cruise on Aitutaki's huge turqoise lagoon

* Climbing to the top of Mt Maungapu for supurb views of the entire Aitutaki island

* Big-game fishing beyond the islands' reefs

* Enjoying the magnificent snorkelling, sand bars and coral ridges within Aitutaki's lagoon

* Taking a circle tour of Aitutiki, visiting villages on the way

* Getting out to remote Palmerston on one of the Cooks' interisland ships

at the Akitua motu, and decided to make this their new home. Ru went to the highest point on the island, the top of Maungapu, and surveyed the island. He divided the land into 20 sections, one for each of the 20 royal maidens, but completely forgot about his brothers! One brother had been killed as the huge canoe was hauled onto land, rolling it over logs. The three remaining brothers left the island in anger – they had come all that way to settle new land, and yet Ru allotted them none. They continued over the ocean and eventually wound up in New Zealand.

The original name of Aitutaki was Ararau Enua O Ru Ki Te Moana, meaning 'Ru in search of land over the sea'. Later this shortened to a more manageable mouthful. Still later the name was changed again to its present one of Aitutaki – *a'i tutaki* means 'to keep the fire going' – but the old names are still used in legends and chants. Akitua, the motu now occupied by the Aitutaki Lagoon Resort, was Ru's landing place and was originally named Uri Tua O Ru Ki Te Moana, or 'Ru turning his back to the sea'.

Various canoes came after Ru's party, from Tonga, Samoa and islands in French Polynesia, landing on different parts of the island. Each new people had to be accepted by one of the 20 maidens or their descendants in order to have a space on the island to settle.

The island's European discoverer was Captain William Bligh, on board the *Bounty*, on 11 April 1789. The famous mutiny took place just 17 days later as the ship was en route to Tonga. Two years later in May 1791, Captain Edward Edwards came by in HMS *Pandora* searching for those mutineers, and in 1792 Bligh paid his second visit to the island.

In 1814 Captain Goodenough turned up with his ship *Cumberland* after his visit to Rarotonga came to its ill-starred conclusion. He left behind three Rarotongans whom he had taken with him on his sudden departure. In 1821 the missionary John Williams visited Aitutaki briefly and left behind Papeiha and Vahapata, converts from the island of Raiatea near Tahiti, to begin the work of bringing Christianity to the Cooks. Williams returned two years later to find Papeiha had made remarkable progress so he was moved on to greater challenges on Rarotonga.

Later European visitors included Charles

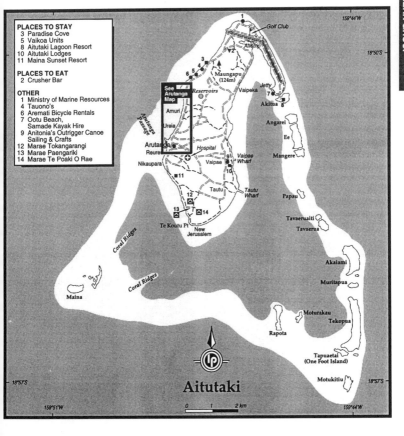

THE SOUTHERN GROUP

PLACES TO STAY
3 Paradise Cove
5 Vaikoa Units
8 Aitutaki Lagoon Resort
10 Aitutaki Lodges
11 Maina Sunset Resort

PLACES TO EAT
2 Crusher Bar

OTHER
1 Ministry of Marine Resources
4 Tauono's
6 Aremati Bicycle Rentals
7 Ootu Beach,
   Samade Kayak Hire
9 Anitonia's Outrigger Canoe
   Sailing & Crafts
12 Marae Tokangarangi
13 Marae Paengariki
14 Marae Te Poaki O Rae

Aitutaki

Darwin on the famous voyage of the *Beagle* in 1835. The first European missionary took up residence in 1839, and the 1850s saw Aitutaki become a favourite port of call for the whaling ships scouring the Pacific at that time. During WWII Aitutaki went through great upheaval when a large American contingent moved in to build the island's two long runways, which until 1974 were larger than Rarotonga's airport runway.

Orientation

You can make a tour of Aitutaki in just a few hours. The road runs near the coast most of the way, and passes through several pleasant villages. Arutanga, about halfway down the west coast, is the island's main settlement. Other villages include Amuri, Nikaupara, New Jerusalem, Tautu, Vaipae and Vaipeka. The numerous small motu around the edge of the lagoon are unpopulated.

Information

The New Zealand Department of Survey and Land Information's 1:25,000 topographical

Dogs & Pigs

There are no dogs at all on Aitutaki and nobody is allowed to bring them to the island. There haven't been any for quite a few years and there are numerous stories as to what happened to them. Probably the best is that the Aitutakians, like the Tahitians, savoured dogmeat and eventually ate them all. Another is that the dogs were thought to be carriers of leprosy, which at one time was rampant on the island. Still another story is that a dog mauled an *ariki's* (high chief's) child and he then banned all dogs. Whatever the reason, it's a relief not to be tripping over them all the time. And Aitutaki does have some healthy looking stray cats!

There are, however, plenty of pigs – that most popular of Pacific domestic animals. South Sea pigs have learnt to make coconuts a major part of their diet although well-kept pigs also have papaya and taro mash. They're tasty pigs. There are even some pigs, kept on one of the motu, which have learnt to dig up and break open the *pahua* clam shells which are an Aitutakian delicacy. ■

map of Aitutaki, widely available on both Rarotonga and Aitutaki, shows the island's roads and trails and the coral formations in the lagoon. *What's On in the Cook Islands* and *Jason's*, the two free tourist publications, contain maps of both Rarotonga and Aitutaki, with items of interest to visitors (hotels, restaurants, sights etc) clearly marked.

The post office is at the Cook Islands Administration Building at the intersection of the two main roads in Arutanga (the coast road and the road leading down to the wharf). Aitutaki issues its own special postage stamps which are not available on Rarotonga. The post office is open weekdays, 8 am to 4 pm.

The Telecom office, at the post office, is open the same hours. Here you can make long-distance phone calls, send and receive faxes, or buy a phonecard to use in the card phone outside the building which is accessible anytime.

Also at the Administration Building is the Treasury, where foreign currency and travellers cheques can be exchanged weekdays, 8 am to 3 pm.

Westpac has a branch opposite the Administration Building, but it's only open on Wednesday from 9.30 am to 3 pm. It gives cash advances on Visa, MasterCard and Bankcard, changes foreign currencies (cash and travellers cheques) and makes telegraphic transfers. The ANZ Bank agent, next door to Ralphie's Bar & Grill in Arutanga, is open on weekdays but changes only New Zealand travellers cheques.

The Aitutaki Lagoon Resort, the Rapae Hotel and Tom's Beach Cottage all give cash advances on credit cards, but only to their guests.

The Air Rarotonga office (☎ 31-888) on the main road in Arutanga is also the agent for Air New Zealand. It's open weekdays 8 am to 4 pm, Saturday 8 am to noon.

Ask at your hotel if you should boil your water before drinking it. At some places, the water comes from underground and should be boiled first; at others it may come from a special rainwater tank.

Activities

Beaches & Snorkelling Beaches on most parts of the main island are beautiful but not that good for swimming because the water is so shallow. From beside the Rapae Hotel you can walk all the way out to the outer reef on a natural coral causeway which starts 50m from the shore – at low tide it's not more than knee-deep all the way. There are interesting coral rockpools just inside the outer reef and there are places you can snorkel there. A little to the north of where this causeway meets the outer reef you can fish in the Tonga Ruta passage. The branches of the passage are very narrow – some as narrow as 30cm – but they are over 15m deep and full of fish. This is one of the main passages through which the lagoon drains, so the outgoing current is very strong as the tide ebbs – be extremely careful.

If you continue round the corner beyond the black rocks on the beach on the north side of the Rapae Hotel there's a slightly better beach, with water about 1.5m deep and some interesting snorkelling. Beware of stonefish in this area, however.

The snorkelling is pretty good along this same stretch of coast all the way up to the airport, even though the water is not deep. The reef here is close in and the coral formations support an abundance of life. Snorkelling is also good in the channel separating Akitua motu (where the Aitutaki Lagoon Resort is) from the main island, especially on the outer side of the channel, towards the reef, and on the lagoon side, around the far tip of the motu. Lots of local children come to this channel to swim.

Anywhere there's a jetty – beside the wharf in Arutanga, or around the east side of the island – there's water deep enough to swim in, and you're likely to find lots of friendly local children doing just that.

The best swimming, snorkelling and beaches are found out on the lagoon motu.

Lagoon Cruises Several operators offer trips on the lagoon and to the motu around it. Ask around, and at your hotel, about who is doing the cruises at the time you arrive.

Coconut Crabs

The flesh of the large blue-grey coconut crab is considered delicious on some Pacific islands, and it's been eaten to near extinction on some of them. However, the crabs are still common among the Cook Islands.

Coconut crabs are slow growers: they can take 20 years to reach their mature weight of 2kg or more, and live to a ripe old age. They live close to the water and come out at night to feed on the flesh of coconuts. How they crack open the coconuts is something of a mystery. Some people believe that they simply use their enormous claws to crack the coconuts open, but others claim they scale the palm trees and snip off a few coconuts which split open when they hit the ground. Whatever the truth, the mighty crabs will spend days devouring the coconut flesh. ■

THE SOUTHERN GROUP

Also ask exactly what is included in a cruise. Some go to only one island, some go to many; most are full-day cruises and include transport to and from your accommodation, snorkelling gear and a barbecue fish lunch on the motu. Prices are about NZ$40 to NZ$50 for a full day with lunch. All of them operate every day except Sunday, when the whole island takes a day off.

Bishop's Lagoon Cruises (☎ 31-009, fax 31-493; NZ$50) is a popular cruise operator, as is Tu's Cruise (☎ 31-264; NZ$40).

Aitutaki Lodges, the Maina Sunset Resort and the Aitutaki Lagoon Resort also offer lagoon cruises. Paradise Islands Cruises (☎ 31-248, fax 31-369), based at the Aitutaki Lagoon Resort, offers cruises for NZ$55 on a big 10.2m (34-foot) catamaran, the *Titi Ai Tonga*.

All of these operators use motorised boats of one kind or another. If you're in the mood for something quieter, outrigger canoes are an option. Anitonia's Outrigger Canoe Sailing & Crafts (☎ 31-207), based in Vaipae, offers lagoon cruises on a 7m (21-foot) outrigger sailing canoe, which holds just two passengers plus the captain. The cost is NZ$15/30 per person for a half/full-day trip, including snorkelling gear, fruit snacks and coconut drinks, but you can also do shorter trips, like a two-hour sunset sail for around NZ$10 per person.

Outrigger reef canoes are available at Tauono's (see the following section). A poled and guided tour, including snorkelling, swimming, fishing and a reef walk, costs NZ$25. For the same price you can hire a canoe for a whole day, or go on a guided reef-fishing trip.

Samade (☎ 31-526) at Ootu beach, near the Aitutaki Lagoon Resort, offers lagoon cruises, kayak rental, and a snack shack on a fine little beach.

Diving Another attraction is to dive outside the lagoon. Diving on Aitutaki is relaxed, visibility is good, and it's suitable for everyone from novices to experts. Features include drop-offs, multilevels, wall dives, deep dives, cave dives and more. The drop-off at the edge of the reef is as much as 200m in places and divers have seen everything up to, and including, whale sharks, humpback whales and an operating submarine!

Neil Mitchell at Aitutaki Scuba (☎ 31-103, fax 31-310, scuba@gatepoly.co.ck) is the professional diving operator on the island, affiliated with PADI and NAUI. Diving trips cost NZ$70 with their gear, NZ$60 if you bring your own, with discounts for multiple dives. You must be a certified diver to go on these dives, but you can also pay NZ$20 and go along to snorkel. They also offer diving certification courses (NZ$450 for a minimum four-day course) and other NAUI and PADI-sanctioned dive courses including a PADI 'Experience Scuba' dive inside the lagoon, with no previous diving experience required, for NZ$75. All prices include transfers to and from your accommodation.

Fishing You can go big-game fishing outside the reef with Aitutaki Sea Charters (☎ 31-281) or Clive Baxter (☎ 31-025). Both offer four to five-hour game fishing trips for around NZ$110 per person, including all gear. Marlin, tuna, wahoo and mahi mahi are all found outside the reef.

Barry Anderson (☎ 31-492) offers fishing trips inside the lagoon – there's spinning, live bait fishing, bone fishing, and if you bring your own gear you can go fly-fishing. Full-day fishing trips are NZ$150/180 for one/two people.

Tauono's offers reef fishing trips; see the separate section.

Golf A round of golf at the nine-hole golf course by the airport costs NZ$5.

Car, Motorcycle & Bicycle Motorcycles and bicycles can be hired from a number of places on the island. Ask at your hotel to see if they rent them; several hotels do.

In Arutanga, Swiss Rentals (☎ 31-600, fax 31-329) rents mountain bikes (NZ$7 per day), motorbikes (NZ$20 per day) and cars (NZ$50 per day), with discounts if you hire for four or five days; if you keep it for a week you get seven days for the price of five. German and English are spoken.

Rino's Rentals (☎ 31-197, fax 31-559) in Ureia rents bicycles (NZ$8 per day), motorbikes (NZ$20 per day) and Jeeps (NZ$70 per day), with discounts for rentals of over three days.

Aremati Bicycle Rentals (☎ 31-271), north of the Rapae Hotel, rents mountain bikes (NZ$7 per day).

Arutanga

Arutanga is a pleasant, sleepy little place redolent of the South Seas. There are a number of typical island trade stores and a weathered old CICC church picturesquely situated by the playing fields next to the harbour. Built in 1828 the church is the oldest in the Cooks, and also one of the most beautiful, with carved wood painted red, yellow, green and white all around the ceiling, more dark woodcarving over the doorways, simple stained-glass windows, and an anchor placed on the ceiling with the inscription Ebera 6:19 (Hebrews 6:19). A colourful mural over the altar shows angels announcing 'Tapu, Tapu, Tapu' ('Holy, Holy, Holy'). This church also has some of the best acoustics in the Cooks, wonderful for enjoying the spirited hymn singing. In the church yard there's a double-sided monument to the LMS's pioneering Reverend John Williams and to Papeiha, the Polynesian convert, who Williams left here in 1821.

The harbour is quiet although there are often a few visiting yachts moored offshore. Larger ships have to be unloaded by lighters, outside the lagoon. You can get an excellent view of the island's whole western coastline from the end of the jetty.

The Orongo Centre, beside the harbour, was built as a banana packing plant to handle the island's major export crop. It now contains the Seabreeze Cafe, the Aitutaki Women's Development Craft Centre and other small crafts shops, and the Aitutaki Growers Market, where local farmers and fishermen come to sell their products. The building occupies the site of the Orongo Marae, one of the island's most powerful marae; the large stones on the south side of the building are part of this marae.

New Jerusalem

On the south coast, New Jerusalem is a religious village built in the early 1990s. Its residents are all members of the Free Church. The village is constructed entirely of native materials, in the style of a traditional old Cook Islands village.

Marae

The Aitutaki marae are notable for the large size of the stones. The main road goes right through a big marae at the turn-off to the Aitutaki Lodges; the stones are along both sides of the road. The huge banyan tree arching over the road here is a memorable sight.

On the inland road between Nikaupara and Tautu, the signs saying 'Marae' and 'Marae/Jerusalem' will direct you to some of

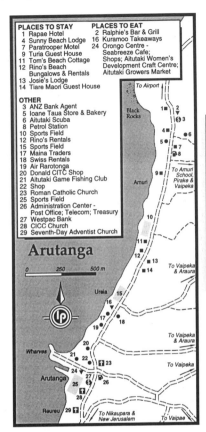

PLACES TO STAY
1 Rapae Hotel
4 Sunny Beach Lodge
7 Paratrooper Motel
9 Turia Guest House
11 Tom's Beach Cottage
12 Rino's Beach Bungalows & Rentals
13 Josie's Lodge
14 Tiare Maori Guest House

PLACES TO EAT
2 Ralphie's Bar & Grill
16 Kuramoo Takeaways
24 Orongo Centre - Seabreeze Cafe; Aitutaki Women's Development Craft Centre; Aitutaki Growers Market

OTHER
3 ANZ Bank Agent
5 Ioane Taua Store & Bakery
6 Aitutaki Scuba
8 Petrol Station
10 Sports Field
12 Rino's Rentals
15 Sports Field
17 Maina Traders
18 Swiss Rentals
19 Air Rarotonga
20 Donald CITC Shop
21 Aitutaki Game Fishing Club
22 Shop
23 Roman Catholic Church
25 Sports Field
26 Administration Center - Post Office; Telecom; Treasury
27 Westpac Bank
28 CICC Church
29 Seventh-Day Adventist Church

Arutanga

0   250   500 m

the most magnificent marae on the island. **Tokangarangi**, just off this road to your right, is a marae built by Temuna Korero, who came from Avaiki on the canoe Ua-Tuau-Au.

Farther south along this same road is Taravao – a sign nailed up on a tree announces the spot. From this crossroads there are two very large marae, one on either side of the road. The one on your left (east), **Te Poaki O Rae** ('The Stone of Rae'), covers about 1.6 hectares (4 acres). It has several groupings of stones but the tallest one, at 2.8m, is attributed to Rae, who brought it

Tairi Terangi Meets his End at Tokongarangi

In pre-European times a huge and powerful warrior, Tairi Terangi, came from Rarotonga to try to overpower Aitutaki. He started at the north of the island and worked his way south, defeating or killing everyone and everything in his path. As he forged southwards the people became increasingly terrified, and the *taunga* (high priests) tried to divine, with a fortune-telling power they had using coconut shells, what the outcome would be. In place after place, the shells prophesied the victory of Tairi Terangi – all the way to the south of the island, to the marae Tokongarangi. When the taunga cast the shells on this marae, they predicted that Tairi Terangi would be defeated.

Since Tokongarangi is practically at the southern tip of Aitutaki, if Tairi Terangi had prevailed here, it would have meant the defeat of the entire island. But when he arrived on the marae, a much smaller man, Pukenga, inspired with the divine power and assistance of Are Mango, god of sharks and god of this marae, killed him, releasing the whole island from the reign of terror. ■

from a more ancient marae elsewhere on the island. The line of stones on your right as you enter the marae area was where watchmen used to stand to guard the marae.

On the west side of the Taravao crossroads sign, another large marae, **Paengariki**, arrests your attention as you come over the hill, with its large expanse and big black volcanic stones. Only part of the marae is visible today; more stones, covering an area as large or larger than the visible marae area, are hidden in the dense bush on the south side. Each of the large black volcanic basalt stones has its own name. This marae is attributed to Kakeroa, who is said to have sailed to Aitutaki from Avaiki and married Ruano'o, a woman from Ru's canoe, though one genealogy places him only around 11 generations ago. Kakeroa is also credited with one of the stone groupings at the Te Poaki O Rae marae nearby.

All of these marae had recently become overgrown and it was not possible to visit them, but plans were in the works to clean all the marae on the island. You might want to ask if the marae have been cleared, before you go out to look for them.

Maungapu

Maungapu, at just 124m, is the highest point on the island. It's an easy 30-minute hike to the top, from where there's a superb view of the island and the entire lagoon. The route to the top takes off from opposite the Paradise Cove motel and is marked by a sign on the road. It starts off gently and gets steeper as you near the top.

Aitutaki Lagoon

The lagoon of Aitutaki is one of the wonders of the Cook Islands. It is large, colourful and full of life, although fortunately not sharks. The snorkelling is magnificent. The lagoon is dotted with sandbars, coral ridges and 21 motu, many of them with their own stories.

Maina Maina, at the south-west corner of the lagoon, offers some of the lagoon's best snorkelling on the coral formations near its shore and around the large powder-white sandbars just to the north and east. It is also the nesting place of the red-tailed tropicbird, which inspired Cook Islanders from as far away as Atiu to come seeking its red tail feathers to use in their spectacular headdresses. If you're here at the right time of year you may get to see them nesting on the island; their nesting season ends around December when they fly off to other lands.

Rapota Rapota, a volcanic islet farther east, was once a leper colony.

Akaiami Akaiami is the motu where the old flying boats used to land to refuel. You can still see their wharf on the lagoon side of the motu. There are some thatch houses near the wharf, used for short camping trips to the island.

Eastern Motu From Akaiami southwards, the eastern motu are interesting to explore, but the snorkelling is not so good because there is little coral. If you visit them during the wet season (December to April) be sure to bring mosquito repellent.

Tapuaetai Perhaps the most famous motu, and certainly the most visited by tourists, is Tapuaetai, or One Foot Island, with its lovely white stretch of beach. The brilliant, pale-turquoise colour of the water off this beach is truly amazing. The channel between One Foot Island and its neighbour, Tekopua, is very shallow and the pure white sand of the lagoon causes the water to gleam. There's no coral in the lagoon so the snorkelling is not so good, but the clear water compensates for this.

Tauono's

Tauono's (☎ 31-562) is operated by a couple renowned for their friendliness: Tauono, a local, and Sonja, his Austrian-Canadian wife. A wide variety of organic fruits, vegetables and herbs can be picked to order from their lush garden; they also sell deep-sea and reef fish, European-style cakes, coffee and herbal teas. Tauono and Sonja give free garden tours, and will do a traditional Maori *umukai* (underground oven feast) on request for 10 or more persons – you can help with the preparation and learn how it's done. German, French, English and Maori are spoken.

Tauono's also has outrigger reef canoes – see Lagoon Cruises.

Ministry of Marine Resources

Near the airport, the Ministry of Marine Resources (☎ 31-406, fax 31-529) is an interesting place. Five species of giant clams – the huge ones with wavy lips – are being raised in tanks here, and in a farm in the lagoon, for introduction into the lagoon. The parent clams were brought here from Australia and Palau because the populations of the local species was decreasing. Baby sea turtles are also raised here.

The research station is open weekdays, 8 am to 4 pm. A tour and educational video costs NZ$2, and is well worth it. Large groups should reserve in advance, but individuals can just stop by.

Organised Tours

Chloe & Nane's (☎ 31-248) offers circle island tours for NZ$30 per person, Monday to Saturday, and bus service to church on Sunday.

Places to Stay – bottom end

Paradise Cove (☎ 31-218, fax 31-456), on the north-west side of the island, is on a beautiful stretch of beach with fine white sand and good snorkelling. Singles/doubles are NZ$20/30 in a large house with shared kitchen, bathroom and lounge, or NZ$25/40 in six rustic free-standing bungalows right on the beach. Each bungalow has its own fridge, but shares bathroom and kitchen facilities. Though rustic, the bungalows are charming, built with all natural materials and

---

Aitutaki Gets a Mountain

According to legend, Aitutaki was once just a low atoll. The inhabitants decided they needed a mountain for their island, so they went off across the sea in search of one. Coming to Rarotonga, they spotted Raemaru, the mountain behind the village of Arorangi, and thought that it would be perfect. However, it was rather large for Aitutaki, so they decided they'd take just the top off and bring that home.

Late at night, they sneaked up the sides of Raemaru and encircled it, thrust their spears in until they had severed the top from the bottom, and took off with it. They held it aloft with their spears as they set off for Aitutaki in their canoes, spread out in the sea all around the mountain top.

When morning came, the Arorangi villagers looked up and noticed something was wrong. They set off in hot pursuit of the Aitutakians to reclaim their mountain. But the fierce Aitutakian warriors beat the Rarotongans back, using only their single free hands while still holding the mountain aloft between them with their spears in their other hands. After bringing the mountain top to Aitutaki they placed it in the north part of the island.

Raemaru today has a distinctly cut-off, flat-topped appearance. ∎

Tapuaetai (One Foot Island)

Tapuaetai (One Foot Island), out of all the 21 motu, wasn't always the major tourist attraction that it is today.

In 1978, a photographer working for Air New Zealand came to Aitutaki to take publicity photos and a photo of this islet's beautiful beach was used for a big promotional poster. Travel writers who came to the island sought out this idyllic stretch of beach and its fame soon spread.

Technically, the name Tapuaetai means not 'one foot' but 'one footprint'. There are several versions of how the motu got its name. One legend tells of how a father and son, fleeing warriors from the main island, sought refuge on Tapuaetai. Upon reaching the motu's shore, the father picked his son up and hid him in a tree. When the warriors arrived they killed the father but having seen only one set of footprints leading away from his canoe did not realise his son was there. The son returned to Aitutaki and told the story of how the single set of footprints had saved his life.

In another legend, a seafarer from Tonga was crossing the seas with his sister. She died but he wanted to bury her on land, not throw her to the sharks, so he kept her body in the canoe until he sighted land. He came into Aitutaki's lagoon near Tapuaetai and landed there, hoping to bury his sister on the motu. As he alighted from the canoe, however, some fierce Aitutakians emerged from the bush and he jumped back into the canoe and sailed away, still bearing his sister and leaving only a single footprint in the sand. ∎

thatched roofs. It's the only place we saw in the Cook Islands where you can sleep in a traditional *kikau* hut (thatched-roofed hut).

Further south, *Vaikoa Units* (☎ 31-145) has six self-contained studio-apartment units, each with kitchen and bath, for NZ$25/40/65 a single/double/triple. It's on a lovely stretch of white beach good for swimming and snorkelling, and you're welcome to use the outrigger canoes.

Several guesthouses are in Amuri on the main road between the Rapae Hotel and the centre of Arutanga. All offer similar facilities and standards, with several simple bedrooms sharing kitchen, bathroom and lounge.

The *Turia Guest House* (☎ 31-049), in a four-bedroom family home on the beach side of the road, charges NZ$15 per adult, and less for children.

Right on a beautiful stretch of beach and closer to town, *Tom's Beach Cottage* (☎ 31-051, 31-121, fax 31-409) is a friendly and relaxed place. You can have barbecues, lounge around or even sleep on the beach if you like. Singles/doubles/triples are NZ$25/38/48.

A little closer to town, *Josie's Lodge* (☎ 31-111, fax 31-518) and the *Tiare Maori Guest House* (☎ 31-119) are practically next door to one another and they're very similar to each other. Josie's Lodge has six regular

bedrooms, plus one larger family room sleeping four people. All the beds have canopy mosquito nets; singles/doubles/triples/quads are NZ$20/38/48/52. You can do your own cooking, or have meals prepared. The Tiare Maori Guest House has seven bedrooms for NZ$15/25/40, with use of the stove an extra NZ$2 per day.

Arekoe/Bamboo Bungalows (☎ 31-327, 31-228) has two self-contained studio bungalows about 100m inland from the post office. Singles/doubles/triples are NZ$35/45/50.

Places to Stay – middle

The *Paratrooper Motel* (☎ 31-563, 31-523), on the main road in Amuri, consists of several self-contained houses, all new and spotless. A one-bedroom house is NZ$67; two-bedroom houses are NZ$56 per bedroom if you share the house, or NZ$114 for the whole house. There are substantial discounts for stays of over three nights; also ask about backpackers' rates. This is a pleasant place to stay, with a friendly owner who's proud of his service to New Zealand.

Nearby, the *Sunny Beach Lodge* (☎/fax 31-446) has four self-contained studio units, all in a long row, costing NZ$72/80/95/110 for singles/doubles/triples/quads. It's on the beach side of the road, opposite Aitutaki

Scuba. *Tom's Beach Cottage* (see the Places to Stay – bottom end section) has a private self-contained one-bedroom 'honeymoon unit' by the beach for NZ$76/86 a single/double.

Also on the beach, but closer in to Arutanga, *Rino's Beach Bungalows & Rentals* (☎ 31-197, fax 31-559) has four self-contained studio units for NZ$65/85/115 a single/double/triple, two beachfront rooms for NZ$105/135/165, and two deluxe beachfront rooms with great views. Across the road is a three-bedroom house, complete with everything you need, for NZ$250 per week.

The pleasantly situated *Rapae Hotel* (☎ 31-324, fax 31-321) is set in lush gardens right beside the beach, about 2km north of the centre of Arutanga. It has 13 rooms, 12 of them studio doubles in duplex units – they're simple but comfortable with bathroom, tea and coffee making equipment and a big shady verandah. These standard rooms are NZ$80; a larger family unit, at NZ$100 per night, sleeps six and occupies the same space as a regular duplex, with separate bedroom and sitting room. The Rapae has a pleasant open-air, lagoon-view restaurant, Aitutaki's best 'island night' performance every Friday, bicycle hire for NZ$10 per day, motorbike hire for NZ$25 per day and car hire for NZ$75 per day.

Places to Stay – top end

The *Maina Sunset Resort* (☎ 31-511, fax 31-611) is an attractive new seaside resort in Nikaupara, about 1km south of Arutanga. Eight studio units without kitchen (NZ$140) and four one-bedroom units with kitchen (NZ$170) face a courtyard with a small swimming pool right on the beach. There's a restaurant, boat hire, snorkel gear hire, motorbike hire and other amenities.

Aitutaki Lodges (☎ 31-334, fax 31-333, aitlodge@gatepoly.co.ck) on the east coast of the island has six A-frame chalets, each with a kitchenette, one queen-size bed and one single bed, and a large verandah with a splendid view of the lagoon and the motu stretching away in the distance. The view is unsurpassed on the island; the only drawbacks are that the beach here is volcanic rather than white sand (but it does have a swimming pool), and you're about 3.5km from town (a half-hour's walk). Motorcycle hire is NZ$30 per day. You can cook for yourself or arrange for cooked meals; there's an open-air bar and dining room under a thatched roof. Singles/doubles/triples are NZ$186/192/237, including tropical breakfast and airport transfers.

At the far end of the airstrip, the *Aitutaki Lagoon Resort* (☎ 31-201, fax 31-202, akitua@gatepoly.co.ck) is on Akitua motu, which is joined to the main island by a footbridge. It has nine beachfront bungalows (NZ$286), 16 garden bungalows (NZ$427) and five deluxe beachfront bungalows (NZ$550), plus all the mod cons including two restaurant/bars, a swimming pool, and many activities on offer. Nearly everybody staying here will be on some sort of all-inclusive package deal booked through travel agencies, which may make it cheaper. The major drawback is the resort's considerable isolation from the rest of the island. The locals often call it the Akitua Resort, after the motu.

Places to Eat

Self-Catering The shops have the usual Cook Islands selection of tins and the usual limited selection of fresh fruits and vegetables. The choice is more restricted than on Rarotonga and the prices are higher. It's worth bringing some supplies with you, particularly if you plan to cook for yourself.

The Aitutaki Growers Market at the Orongo Centre by the wharf in Arutanga has locally grown produce, and if you come early (around 7 or 8 am) you may also find freshly caught fish. The Growers Market is open weekdays from 8 am to 3 pm but most of the buying and selling is done in the morning.

Tauono's (☎ 31-562) offers a wide variety of organic fruits, vegetables and herbs from the garden, all fresh-picked when you come. They also sell deep-sea and reef fish, European-style cakes, coffee and herbal teas.

The *Ioane Taua Store & Bakery* opposite

Aitutaki Scuba, near the Rapae Hotel, has fresh-baked bread and other baked goods.

Cafes, Bars & Restaurants In the Orongo Centre by the wharf in Arutanga, the *Seabreeze Cafe* is a pleasant open-air cafe/bar with a view of the lagoon and the wharf, selling basic foods such as curries, burgers, sandwiches and chips. *Kuramoo Takeaways* on the main road in Arutanga, with tables outdoors or under a thatched roof, offers similar fare. Both are simple and inexpensive places for a bite.

The restaurant at the *Rapae Hotel* is a relaxed open-air restaurant overlooking the lagoon and white beach. It has good food – their home-cured ham sandwiches are delicious and they have hot lunch and dinner main dishes for around NZ$12 to NZ$15, sandwiches, soups, starters and desserts for around NZ$6. On Friday night their excellent 'island night' buffet (NZ$30) begins at around 7.30 pm. A floor show and dance follows and being there for the buffet gets you a ringside seat. Book in advance.

Opposite the Rapae, *Ralphie's Bar & Grill* (☎ 31-418) serves lunch and dinner Monday to Saturday, and only dinner on Sunday. The menu has everything from fine dining to takeaways – there are seafood, steaks and pastas with prices about the same as the Rapae as well as inexpensive fare such as burgers and chips. Phone for free transport.

On the north side of the island, the *Crusher Bar* (☎ 31-283) is a true island-style place, with a thatched-roof, open-air dining room, lots of island decor, and live music and dancing every night except Friday. Their 'island night' buffet and floor show (NZ$25.50) is held on Thursday night. Sunday is roast and seafood night (NZ$16.50), and on Saturday there's a special backpackers' menu (NZ$10.50). Reservations are essential and free transport is provided. It's open from 6 pm, every night except Friday.

The bar/restaurant at the *Aitutaki Lagoon Resort* serves all meals and has a changing dinner menu served from 6.30 to 9 pm. Soups, starters and desserts are NZ$10.50 to

NZ$16.50, main courses around NZ$20 to NZ$25. Lavish buffets and island-style floor shows are put on twice a week, with a Wednesday night fishermen's catch (NZ$39) and Saturday barbecue night (NZ$30). The buffets are from 7 to 9 pm, with a floor show at 8.30 pm and a live band for dancing afterwards.

Tauono's (☎ 31-562) will do a traditional Cook Islands umukai when there are 10 or more people interested. You can help with the preparation and learn how it's done, go for a swim or canoe trip and then chow down. It's a great experience.

Kuru (Breadfruit) *Artocarpus altilis* (JK)

Entertainment
The 'island night' performance at the *Rapae Hotel* on Friday night is a social event only outdone by the Sunday church service. There's a buffet that is served from around 7.30 pm which costs NZ$25 and eating here, or simply being a Rapae Hotel guest, also gets you a ringside seat for the performance, but if you don't want to eat there's no cover charge or entry cost.

The band starts playing around 8 pm and the dancing gets under way around 9 pm. It's an hour of raucous fun. Large matrons return from the bar between the dancers, and show very clearly that they can still swing a hip as well as any upstart teenager! The finale involves pulling *papa'a* (foreigners) out of

The Coral Route

Aitutaki had a pioneering role in Pacific aviation as a stopping point in Tasman Empire Air Line's 'Coral Route'. Back in the 1950s TEAL, the predecessor to Air New Zealand, flew across the Pacific on an Auckland-Suva (Fiji)-Apia (Western Samoa)-Aitutaki-Papeete (Tahiti) route. The first leg to Suva was flown by DC-6s but the rest of the way was by four-engined Solent flying boats.

The stop at Aitutaki was purely to refuel, and this was carried out on the uninhabited motu of Akaiami. It took over two hours so passengers had a chance to take a swim in the lagoon. Flying in those days was hardly a one-stop operation: one day took you from Suva to Apia and the next day required a pre-dawn departure from Apia in order to make Papeete before nightfall. The flying boats were unpressurised so they did not fly above 3000m and they sometimes had to descend to less than 500m.

The old Solents carried their 60-odd passengers in seven separate cabins and in some degree of luxury. Food was actually cooked on the aircraft, in contrast to today's reheated airline meals. At that time the fortnightly flight into Papeete was the only direct air link between Tahiti and the rest of the world, and the aircraft's arrival was a major event.

Usually the trips were uneventful but on one occasion a malfunction at Aitutaki required off-loading the passengers while the aircraft limped on to Tahiti on three engines. It was a week before it arrived back to collect the passengers – who by that time had begun to really enjoy their enforced stay on hotel-less Aitutaki. On another occasion, the aircraft was forced to return to Aitutaki when the Tahiti lagoon turned out to be full of logs. The trip to Tahiti was attempted twice more before the lagoon was clear enough for a landing. One of the TEAL flying boats is now on display in the MOTAT transport museum in Auckland, New Zealand.

Solents were also used by British Airways (BOAC in those days) on routes from England through to India and Australia. A couple were still in use by Ansett Airlines in Australia for Sydney-Lord Howe Island flights right into the early 1970s, but flying-boat travel was really ended by WWII. Prior to the war, most long-range commercial flights were made by flying boats because suitable airports for long-range land planes did not exist. After the war not only had large, long-range aircraft been greatly improved but there were airport runways capable of handling them all over the world. The flying-boat days were over. ■

the audience and getting them to show what they've learnt. By this time most people have had enough to drink for the embarrassment to be minimal. The band continues on until around 1 am with an increasingly unsteady but highly entertaining crowd.

Ralphie's Bar & Grill opposite the Rapae also has Friday night entertainment, with a floor show immediately following the one at the Rapae and then a dance following that. Those who want to see both floor shows rush from the Rapae to Ralphie's, and then the crowd drifts back and forth between the two dances.

The *Aitutaki Lagoon Resort* has its entertainment on Wednesday and Saturday nights, with a buffet starting at 7 pm and a floor show and dancing afterwards (see the Places to Eat section). If you wish to come for the entertainment only, it's NZ$10.

The *Crusher Bar* on the north part of the island features dinner, live music and dancing every night except Friday, with an 'island night' performance on Thursday nights. Transport can be arranged.

The *Aitutaki Game Fishing Club* at the foot of the wharf in Arutanga is a simple place to enjoy a cheap beer, friendly and relaxed atmosphere, and a beautiful view of the sunset. Its schedule is informal but it usually opens around 4 pm.

Things to Buy

Island crafts are available at the Aitutaki Women's Development Craft Centre and at several other little shops in the Orongo Centre building by the wharf in Arutanga. Aitutakian crafts include pandanus purses, bags, mats and hats, white rito church hats, shell-and-rito fans, shell jewellery, wooden drums, ukeleles, kikau brooms, and colourful pareu and T-shirts. In Vaipae, Anitonia's (see the Lagoon Cruises section) carves wooden drums, makes ukeleles (small and large, four and eight string) and other handicrafts.

Getting There & Away

Air Aitutaki's large airstrip was built by US forces during WWII. It's the only airport in the Cooks with a two-way runway and it could handle much larger aircraft than those currently used. You could fly Boeing 737s into Aitutaki.

Aitutaki was the first outer island in the Cooks to have regular air links with Rarotonga. Air Rarotonga (☎ 31-888 in Aitutaki) operates three flights a day to Aitutaki, plus a day tour, except on Sunday when there are no flights at all. Regular fares are NZ$142 each way on most flights. The last flight of the day from Rarotonga to Aitutaki and the first flight of the day from Aitutaki to Rarotonga are cheaper on a 'Super Saver' fare (NZ$118 one way, NZ$190 return), but only if you book and purchase your ticket locally, in cash, within 14 days of travel.

All the Rarotonga travel agents offer package deals for transport and accommodation on Aitutaki. Day tours are another option; see Day Tours in this section.

Sea See the Getting Around chapter earlier in this book for information on passenger freighter ship services between Rarotonga and Aitutaki. Often a stop on Aitutaki is included in trips between Rarotonga and the northern group islands.

Aitutaki is a popular yachting destination, but the narrow reef passage is too hazardous for large ships to enter so cargo is taken by lighters outside the reef.

Organised Tours Air Rarotonga offers day trips from Rarotonga to Aitutaki, departing from Rarotonga airport at 8 am and returning there by 6.30 pm. Trips include a tour of the island, a lagoon cruise with snorkelling gear provided, lunch on one of the motu beaches, and plenty of time for swimming, snorkelling and soaking up the sun. Cost is NZ$289 (children aged two to 15 years are NZ$145, and children under two are free). Bookings can be made directly with Air Rarotonga (☎ 22-888, fax 20-979) or through Rarotonga travel agents.

Getting Around

The Airport A bus (☎ 31-379) connects with all arriving and departing flights; cost is NZ$5 between town and the airport. Some hotels provide airport transport for their guests.

Car, Motorcycle & Bicycle Hire For information see Car, Motorcycle & Bicycle in the Activities section earlier in this chapter.

Manuae

Population: unpopulated
Area: 6.2 sq km

The two tiny unpopulated islets of Manuae and Te Au O Tu belong to the people of Aitutaki, 101km away. Occasionally copracutting parties visit from Aitutaki, as they have done for a century or more.

The two islets are the only parts of a huge volcanic cone to break the ocean's surface. The cone is 56km from east to west, 24km north to south. The other high point on the rim of this vast cone is the Astronomer Bank,

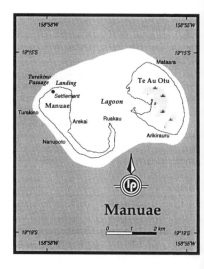

13km west of Manuae, which comes to within 300m of the ocean's surface.

History

Captain James Cook was the European discoverer of the atoll. He sighted it in 1773 during his second voyage, and in 1777 on his third voyage he paused to investigate but did not land. The islands were named the Hervey Islands by Captain Cook, a name which for a time was applied to the whole southern group, but now that name is rarely used.

In 1823 the missionary John Williams visited the island and found about 60 inhabitants. There were only a dozen or so in the late 1820s and the missionaries took them to Aitutaki. Later a series of Europeans made temporary homes. The best known was the prolific William Marsters (read on) who in 1863 was moved to Palmerston with his three wives.

Palmerston

Population: 49
Area: 2.1 sq km

Palmerston is something of a Cook Islands oddity: it's only a little north of Aitutaki, otherwise the northernmost of the southern group islands, but it's also far to the west of the other southern islands. Furthermore, unlike the other southern islands it's an atoll, more like the northern group islands. As a result it sometimes gets treated as part of the northern group.

The lagoon is 11km wide at its widest point and 35 small islands dot the reef. At low tide the lagoon is completely closed off and visiting ships have to anchor outside the reef.

History

Captain Cook sighted the island in 1774 when it was unpopulated. He did not stop on that occasion but in 1777 when he passed by on his third voyage his ships did pause and

boats were sent ashore to seek provisions. A passing missionary ship en route to Tahiti stopped at Palmerston in 1797; in 1811 another ship stopped to collect bêches-de-mer and shark fins, valued as delicacies by the Chinese.

In 1850 the crew of the *Merchant of Tahiti* discovered four starving Europeans on the island. When they took them to Rarotonga the ship's captain laid claim to the island, then passed the claim to a Scottish trader in Tahiti named John Branden. This gentleman placed a representative on the island and some time later discovered William Marsters, a European, living on Manuae island and persuaded him to move to Palmerston in 1863.

William Marsters became a living legend. The present inhabitants of the island are all Marsters, descended from William and his three Polynesian wives. They not only populated Palmerston: to this day you'll find people with the surname Marsters all over the Cooks and it's a common name on cemetery headstones. Old William Marsters died on 22 May 1899 at the age of 78 and is buried near his original homestead.

At one time the population of the island was as high as 150 but it's a quiet and little-visited place today. If you did come to Palmerston you'd have to stay a long time, as transport is very infrequent.

The green turtle is so-named because of the colour of its fat. It feeds mainly on sea grasses and sometimes comes ashore to bask in the sun.

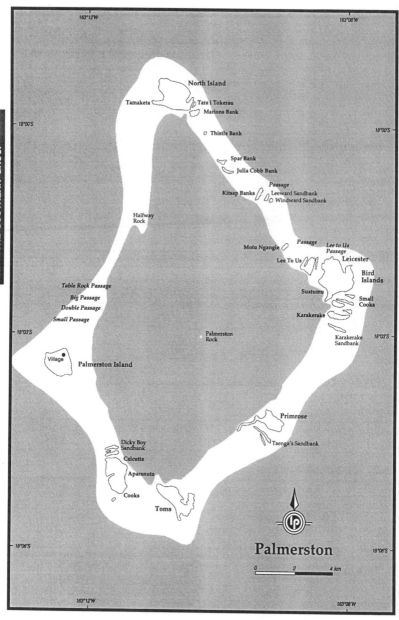

Palmerston

Places to Stay

Palmerston has no organised accommodation for visitors. If you do come, Reverend Bill Marsters can arrange accommodation with local families.

Getting There & Away

There are no flights to Palmerston, and inter-island passenger freighter ships stop very infrequently. See the Getting Around chapter for details on shipping services in the Cooks.

Nga Pu Toru – Atiu, Takutea, Mauke & Mitiaro

Atiu, Mauke and Mitiaro are often referred to by the collective name Nga Pu Toru, 'The Three Roots'. The three islands are in close proximity – it takes only 10 minutes to fly from one to another, and they can easily be visited as a group. They are also similar geographically, characterised by a narrow lagoon, a raised coral reef (*makatea*) around the outside edge, and a higher interior. Over the centuries there has been a lot of travel between the three islands. Takutea, an unpopulated sand cay near Atiu, is a wildlife sanctuary.

Atiu

Population: 960
Area: 26.9 sq km

The third largest of the Cook Islands, Atiu is noted for its raised coral reef, or makatea. Unlike all the other Cook Islands, including Mangaia with its similar geography, the villages on Atiu are not on the coast. The five villages – Areora, Ngatiarua, Teenui, Mapumai and Tengatangi – are all close together in the centre of a hill region. Prior to the introduction of Christianity, the people lived spread out around the lowlands, where the taro is grown. When the missionaries persuaded the people to come upland and move the original settlements together, they effectively created a single village – the island's administration centre and CICC church form the centre, and the villages radiate out from this centre on five roads, like the five arms of a starfish.

Atiu is surprisingly interesting for the visitor – there are some fine beaches, magnificent scenery, excellent walks, ancient *marae* (pre-European religious meeting grounds) and the makatea is riddled with

HIGHLIGHTS
• Seeing the kopeka birds in Anatakitaki ('Cave of the Kopeka'), and exploring the ancient burial caves on Atiu
• Taking a tour of the Atiu Island Coffee plantation
• Walking the Vai Momoiri Track to the inland villages of Atiu
• Seeing the intricate textile arts at the Atiu Fibre Arts Studio
• Attending a service at Mauke's Divided Church, where a line down the centre separates the denominations
• Swimming in the fresh-water pools of Mauke and Mitiaro's makatea caves
• Visiting the lakes, and surrounding swamp land and peat on Mitiaro

limestone caves, some of them used as ancient burial sites. You can also see coffee production, visit the fibre arts studio and there's couple of a fine place to stay. Most visitors stay for only a couple of days, but that really isn't long enough. Atiu is not, however, a place for easy lazing around – you have to get out and do things; burn some energy. This was one of our favourite places in the Cooks and the island really deserves more visitors!

History
Atiu's traditional name is Enua Manu, which can be translated as 'land of birds' or 'land of insects'. Numerous legends tell of early settlers arriving by canoe and of visits by legendary Polynesian navigators. What is more certain is that some time before the first European arrival three *ariki* (paramount high

THE SOUTHERN GROUP

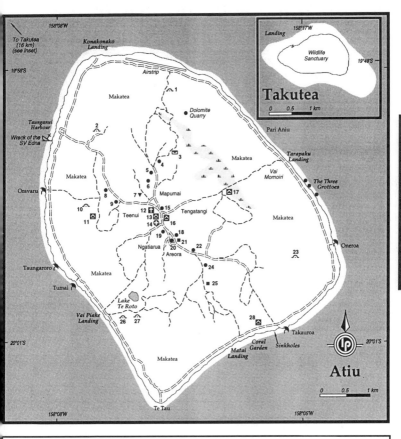

PLACES TO STAY
21 Are Manuiri
25 Atiu Motel; Kura's Kitchen

PLACES TO EAT
7 Atiu Fibre Arts Studio; Workshop & Gallery; Tivaivai Cafe

OTHER
1 Te Ana O Raka Burial Cave
2 Vaiori Burial Cave
3 Post Office & Telecom
4 School
5 Bakery
6 School
8 Akari Tumunu
9 Power House
10 Burial Cave
11 Orongo Marae
12 CICC Church
13 Government Administration Building; Te Au Tapu Marae
14 Hospital
15 Atiu Nui Maruarua Hall; Women's Craft Centre
16 Te Apiripiri Marae
17 Vairakai Marae
18 The Hut
19 ADC Shop
20 Bakery
22 Atiu Island Coffee Factory
23 Anatakitaki Cave ('Cave of the Kopeka')
24 Matavai Tumunu
26 Pou-Atea Cave
27 Rima Rau Burial Cave
28 Marae

chiefs) controlled the island and began to extend their power over the neighbouring islands of Mauke and Mitiaro. Atiu has had a colourful and bloody history – the Atiuans were the warriors of the Cooks and specialised in creating havoc on all their neighbouring islands.

The European discovery of Atiu is credited to Captain Cook on 3 April 1777. The previous day the Atiuans had made friendly visits to his ships, the *Resolution* and *Discovery*. The Atiuans were uninterested in any items they were offered for trade, but they wanted a dog. Fortunately the Tahitian, Omai, who Cook had taken back to England on his previous voyage, offered one of his dogs.

The next day the captain sent three of his boats ashore to try to procure supplies. His men spent a long day being feted (and pickpocketed) by the Atiuans, but came back effectively empty handed. At one point, when a large oven was being prepared, Omai was so frightened it was intended for himself and his companions that he came straight out and asked the Atiuans if they were preparing to eat them. The Atiuans expressed shock at the mere thought of such an idea but subsequent tales of the Atiuans' eating habits amongst the people of Mauke and Mitiaro makes you wonder about their ingenuousness.

With his men safely back on board, Cook sailed away and managed to find the necessary provisions, principally for the cattle he had on board, on the neighbouring island of Takutea, where he left 'a hatchet and some nails to the full value of what we took from the island'.

Forty years were to pass before the next European contact. In late 1822 or early 1823 two Polynesian 'teachers' were sent from Bora Bora near Tahiti. They were singularly unsuccessful, although when the Reverend John Williams turned up a few months later on 19 July 1823 searching for Rarotonga, he quickly persuaded the Atiuans to take the first steps of burning their 'idols', destroying their marae and starting work on a church.

About eight or nine months prior to Williams' arrival, an Atiuan named Uia had made a prophecy that soon some people would arrive on Atiu in a huge canoe with no outrigger, their bodies, heads and feet covered, with a mighty god in heaven called Jehovah, and that the Atiuan gods would be burnt with fire. The chiefs were indignant and ordered that Uia be caught and punished, but he escaped the chiefs' wrath and was never heard of again. On board the mission ship was an ariki from Aitutaki, who told Rongomatane, the leading Atiuan chief, that Aitutaki had already converted to Christianity and that many of the gods there had already been burnt; this also influenced him greatly.

The day after Williams' arrival, Rongomatane took the mission party to his own marae and challenged them to eat the sugar cane from a sacred grove. When Williams, Papeiha and the rest of the group ate the cane and did not drop dead on the spot Rongomatane became an instant convert, ordered all the idols on the island burnt and told his people to come and listen to the missionaries' teachings.

Rongomatane told Williams that he had two other islands close by – Akatokamanava (Mauke) and Nukuroa (Mitiaro) – and that he would like the people on those islands to receive the gospel as well. He accompanied Williams' ship to these two islands, converting the inhabitants with amazing speed. This conversion of Mauke and Mitiaro had a rather macabre sidelight. Some time before Williams' visit a dispute had evolved between Atiu and Mauke. Rongomatane had rushed off to Mauke bent on revenge and virtually wiped out the islands' inhabitants. Having killed, cooked and eaten their fill, the Atiuans took back canoe-loads of cooked Maukeans for the rest of the Atiuans to sample.

This was not the first time Rongomatane had descended upon Mauke and the Atiuans had also worked off their appetites on the unfortunate inhabitants of Mitiaro. It's hardly surprising that shortly after, when Williams and his new Christian convert, only recently a bloodthirsty cannibal chief, turned up on Mauke the inhabitants of the island embraced Christianity with such alacrity and fervour!

After Williams' profitable visit to Atiu, Mauke and Mitiaro, he still had not found Rarotonga, the island he was looking for in the first place. Rongomatane had never been to Rarotonga, but he knew where it was and easily directed Williams towards it. Taking the ship to Oravaru beach on Atiu's western shore, they lined up the stern of the ship with the big rock in the lagoon, Williams took a compass reading and sailed off in a bee-line to find Rarotonga, arriving on 26 October 1823.

The missionaries subsequently made occasional visits to Atiu from Tahiti but in 1836 the Tahitian convert Papeiha was sent back from Rarotonga and started the serious work of bringing Christianity to the island.

Gospel Day is still celebrated on Atiu on 19 July every year, often with *nuku* plays acting out the drama of how the gospel came to Atiu.

Geology

Atiu's geology is fascinating. It's thought that Atiu rose out of the sea as a volcano cone around 11 million years ago. The cone was worn down to a shoal, then upheaval raised the shoal to form a flat-topped island. Further eons produced a wide coral reef around the island but then, about 100,000 years ago, the island rose another 20m out of the sea. The coral reef then became a coastal plain, stretching back about 1km from the new coastline to the older central hills. In the past 100,000 years a new coral reef has grown up around most of the island, but this is only 100m wide.

The island today is rather like a very low-brimmed hat with a flat outer rim. This outer rim, or makatea, is principally rough and rugged, fossilised coral densely covered in tropical greenery including shade trees, coconut trees, vines, ferns and mosses. The makatea starts off around 5m in height at the coast and gradually slopes up to around 20m at its inner edge. Then instead of sloping up

THE SOUTHERN GROUP

Bush Beer Schools

Don't miss the opportunity to visit a *tumunu* while you're on Atiu. It's a direct descendant of the old kava ceremony of premissionary times. Kava was a drink prepared from the root of the pepper plant *piper methysticum*. It was not alcoholic but it certainly had an effect on its drinkers – ranging from a mildly fuzzy head to total unconsciousness. Drinking kava was always a communal activity with some ceremony involved; you could not be a solitary kava drinker. In several Polynesian countries, including Fiji, Tonga and Samoa, kava is still popular today, but in the Cook Islands the missionaries managed to all but totally stamp it out. During that missionary period, however, when drinking was banned, the tumunu came into existence and men would retreat to the bush to drink home-brewed 'orange beer'. The tumunu is the hollowed out coconut palm stump which was traditionally used as a container for brewing the beer.

Tumunu are still held regularly at various places on the island, although the container is likely to be plastic these days and the beer will be made from imported hops, much like any western home brew. Technically, however, the bush beer schools are still illegal. The staff at the place where you're staying can arrange an invitation for a visit to the local tumunu. Traditionally the tumunu is for men only, and women rarely participate, but for tourists the rules relax somewhat and any visitor, male or female, is welcome.

There's still quite a tradition to the tumunu gathering. The barman sits behind the tumunu and ladles the beer into a coconut-shell cup. Each drinker swallows his drink in a single gulp and returns the empty cup to the barman who fills it for the next in line. You can pass if you want to but by the end of the evening everybody is decidedly unsteady on their feet – including, sometimes, the barman who is supposed to stay sober and keep everyone in line! At some point in the evening the barman calls the school to order by tapping on the side of the tumunu with the empty cup and then says a short prayer. Guitars and ukeleles are usually around to provide music and accompaniment to song. As a visitor to the tumunu you should bring 1kg of sugar or the equivalent in cash as a donation towards the next brew. ∎

immediately into the central hills – the old volcanic core – there's a circular band of swamp. It seems that water running off the hills permeates the edge of the makatea and has eroded it away to form this damp swamp area. It's extensively used for taro cultivation but it's also a breeding ground for mosquitoes! Inland from the swamp is the inner plateau, the most fertile area of the island, where coffee and other crops are grown.

Economy

A number of crops are grown for local consumption but the island's only major export crop is its coffee. Taro is also an important crop on the island.

Information

The administration centre and the CICC church form the centre of the island. Foreign currency can be exchanged at the administration centre. Cash advances on credit cards (Visa, MasterCard or Bankcard) are available from the ADC Shop in Areora village. There are banks on the island but they are only for local savings accounts.

The post and Telecom offices are in the same building, in Mapumai village. It's open weekdays, 8 am to 4 pm.

Electricity on Atiu operates every day from 5 am to midnight.

What to Bring Two important items to bring with you to Atiu are a torch (flashlight) and mosquito repellent. The places to stay will lend you a torch for cave exploring but you'll want a backup in case of emergencies when underground. The mosquitoes in the swamp region are voracious and exceedingly numerous, especially during the rainy season from around mid-December to mid-April.

Leave your fancy restaurant clothes behind on Rarotonga. If you'll be poking around in caves or on the makatea you'll need things like old T-shirts, torn shorts and worn-out running shoes. The big exception is if you plan to go to a dance or to church. Fancy dress is not needed, but women must wear a dress or skirt and sleeves (and a hat, if you have one) to church, and men must wear long pants.

Standards of modesty on Atiu, as on all the outer islands, are more conservative than on Rarotonga and locals become upset about anyone going without a shirt or wearing very short shorts or swimming gear in town. The first time that guests of the Atiu Motel went to town wearing their swimming gear, motel owner Roger Malcolm received a visit from the Island Council complaining that his guests had been walking around the island in their underwear!

Books If you want more information on Atiu there are some interesting books available. *Atiu through European Eyes*, subtitled 'A Selection of Historical Documents 1777-1967', is a collection of references to Atiu from books and reports. *Atiu, an Island Community* is a study of Atiu's current conditions and customs, written by Atiuans. *Atiu Nu Maruarua* is a bilingual collection of legends about Atiu told in Atiuan Maori and English. All of these books are published by the University of the South Pacific (USP) and are available at USP's Rarotonga Centre in Avarua. The information about Atiu and Atiuans in chapter four of Ronald Syme's book *The Lagoon is Lonely Now* is insightful and amusing.

Caves

The makatea is riddled with limestone caves complete with stalactites and stalagmites. You'll stumble across many small ones in any ramble through the makatea so take a torch (flashlight). Take your bearings too as it's very easy to get totally confused underground and when you finally find your way out it may be by a different exit. A walking stick is a great help when walking in the sharp makatea, so either bring one along, cut yourself one or ask your guide to cut you one.

Tours of the various caves on Atiu typically take about two to three hours and cost around NZ$10 per person. You must go with a guide, partly because the caves can be difficult to find but also because the cave

re on owned land and permission must be
obtained before you enter. Many of the caves
were used for burials, although when and
why nobody knows. If you visit one of these
aves do not move or take any of the bones.
At the very least there will be a curse on you
f you do! The place where you're staying
an help you to arrange a guide.

The Te Ana O Raka burial cave, south of
he airstrip, is just off the road and very easy
o find. The family landowners require visi-
ors to go with a guide, however, partly to
nsure the safety of both the cave and the
isitors – the cave is extensive, with numer-
us entrances and exits, and it is very easy to
et confused. Aue Raka (☎ 33-086) offers
ours of the cave and other local sights.

In the south-east of the island is
Anatakitaki or 'Cave of the Kopeka'. The
ave is reached by a longish walk across the
nakatea from the plateau road. Kopekas are
iny birds, very much like swifts, which nest
n huge numbers inside the cave. When they
ome out to hunt insects they are never seen
o land; only in the cave do they rest. Inside
ne pitch dark cave they make a continuous
hattering, clicking noise which they use to
ind their way around, like bats.

Some of the chambers in this extensive
avern are very large. Although this is the
nain kopeka cave they do nest in smaller
umbers in at least one other cave. One
egend relates how a Polynesian hero, Rangi,
vas led to this cave which concealed his
nissing wife, by a kingfisher bird – ask your
uide to tell you.

In the south-west the Rima Rau burial
ave is a smaller cave reached by a vertical
othole. There are many bones to be seen in
nis cave and nearby there's a very deep
nkhole with a deep, cold pool at the bottom.

Lake Te Roto is noted for its eels, a
opular island delicacy. On the western side
f the lake, a cave leads right through the
nakatea to the sea. You can wade through it
or a considerable distance if the water in the
ake is low enough. Vaine Moeroa (known as
VM') goes eeling in the cave every three
eeks or so, and will take visitors along; ask
: the place where you're staying to be put in

touch with him. Be prepared to get very
muddy.

Warning Take great care when you are
walking across the makatea – the coral is
extremely sharp. It's often like walking
across razor blades and if you slipped and fell
you'd be sliced to pieces. Wear good shoes
too; if you stubbed your toe while wearing
thongs you'd probably cut it right off.

Beaches & Coast

Atiu is not a great place for swimming – the
surrounding lagoon is rarely more than 50m
wide and the water is generally too shallow
for more than wading and gentle splashing
around. You can swim at Taunganui
Harbour, as many of the locals do, where the
water is clear and deep enough for good
swimming and snorkelling.

There are, however, countless beautiful,
sandy strips all along the coast. You can
easily find one to yourself and when you tire
of sunbathing just slip into the water for a
cooling dip. Some of them are easily reached
but to get to others a little pushing through
the bush is required, although the coastal
road is rarely more than 100m from the coast.
Thatch-roofed shelters have been erected
near several beaches including Taungaroro,
Matai and Takauroa.

Oravaru beach, on the west coast, is
thought to be where Cook's party made its
historic landing. There's a large rock in the
water just off the beach, which the chief
Rongomatane used in directing John Williams to Rarotonga. Farther south is the
longer sweep of Taungaroro beach, backed
by high cliffs and sloping fairly steeply into
the water. South again is Tumai beach and
there are plenty of others.

On the north-east coast there's a 1km-long
stretch where there is very little fringing reef
and the sea beats directly on the cliffs. At the
end of the road there's a rarely used emergency boat landing, Tarapaku, and there's
also a pleasant stretch of beach. More
beaches, and three lovely seaside grottoes,
are south between Tarapaku Landing and
Oneroa beach. The grottoes can only be

visited when the sea is calm on the east side of the island.

The south-east coast takes the brunt of the prevailing northerly winds and the sea, washing fiercely over the reef, is often unsafe for swimming. There are, however, a series of picturesque little beaches including Matai Landing and Oneroa. Oneroa is the best beach for finding beautiful shells; a surprising number of old shoes are also washed up!

South of Oneroa is the turn-off to Takauroa beach. If you walk about 100m back along the rugged cliff face there are some sinkholes deep enough for good snorkelling. They are only safe at low tide or when the sea is calm.

At low tide, the lagoon from Takauroa beach to Matai Landing drains out through the sinkholes and tropical fish become trapped in a spot known as the Coral Garden, which becomes a fascinating natural aquarium. The Coral Garden can be reached by walking along the reef from Takauroa beach, but only at low tide, when there are no waves washing over the reef; at other times it is dangerous and not worth visiting.

The most popular beaches on the island are Matai Landing and Taungaroro, because of their beauty and ease of access.

Vai Momoiri & Vairakai Marae
The steep road between Tengatangi village and Tarapaku Landing is worth taking, as it passes through all different kinds of vegeta-tion including plantations, taro patches, makatea and littoral forest. The road passes the impressive 37m-long wall of the Vairaka Marae, built of 47 large limestone slabs, six cut with curious projections on their top edges. It also passes Vai Momoiri, a deep canyon filled with brown water and con-nected by a short tunnel to a second, simila sinkhole. Wild pawpaw trees line the road (you're welcome to pick the fruit), and at the beach end of the road is a thatched shelter where you can rest and relax.

Other Marae
Atiu has a number of interesting marae remains. One of the best known is the Orongo Marae near Oravaru beach. An inter national Earthwatch party came in 1985 to clean up the marae, which was practically an excavation project since it had become so overgrown that it was almost lost in the jungle. Unfortunately, however, the site ha now become overgrown once again. You must have a guide to visit this marae because it's difficult to find and it's on private land Signs of an ancient village can still be seen around the marae.

Te Apiripiri Marae where Papeiha is said to have first preached the gospel in 1823 i behind the tennis courts and house opposite the administration centre. There's little left of the marae apart from some stalactites o stalagmites lying on the ground but there's a memorial stone to mark the spot. Te Au Tapu a marae still used for investiture ceremonies is between the administration centre and the palace of Ngamaru Ariki.

Coffee Plantations
Coffee has been grown on Atiu for over a century now, but its development has been somewhat erratic.

Coffee was introduced to Atiu by early 19th century traders and missionaries. By the beginning of the 20th century it played an important economic role, with almost 5 tonnes of coffee exported in 1906. Produc tion and export declined after that, however for the next 40 years. By the 1940s it was produced only for local consumption.

THE SOUTHERN GROUP

Atiu's coffee production was revitalised in the 1950s when a few growers once again began working the old coffee plantations and brought in some new Kenyan coffee varieties. The government also became interested, establishing nurseries and two small farms. About 16 hectares (40 acres) of coffee were brought into cultivation, and green coffee beans were exported. Once again, however, production went into decline and by 1980 the industry had dwindled to the point where coffee was again picked only for local consumption.

This was the state of the industry when German-born Juergen Manske-Eimke moved from Nigeria to Atiu in 1983 and changed his occupation from economist to coffee grower. In 1984 he imported modern machinery and equipment from Germany and the USA, set up a coffee factory, and the Atiu Coffee Growers Association was formed.

The Atiu coffee business is now rebounding and Juergen hopes that the 7.5 tonnes of coffee the island currently produces will expand to twice that level. At present about 22 hectares (54 acres) of coffee is planted on the island, but that could potentially be expanded to around 50 hectares (125 acres), which could yield up to 37 tonnes of green coffee or 33 tonnes of roasted coffee annually. Now that coffee grown on Aitutaki is being processed on Atiu, Juergen estimates that the combined yield should come to approximately 15 tonnes per year. The supermarkets and fancier restaurants of Rarotonga alone use about half of the factory's production and Atiuan coffee is now being exported to New Zealand, Tahiti and the USA.

The coffee has a ripening cycle of approximately 290 days, which means it is not always harvested at the same time of year. Because of the small scale of production and relatively low labour costs Atiuan coffee is 100% sun-dried and hand selected. Coffee growing on Atiu has its problems – wild pigs, too much sunshine and the perennial Cook Islands land-ownership questions all cause hassles. It's good coffee though, and you can buy a 250g package from the Tivaivai Cafe

on Atiu for NZ$10.50 (cheaper than in Rarotongan shops) or by mail order.

Juergen gives tours of the coffee plantations, pulping factory and the factory where it's hulled, roasted and packed. Tours cost NZ$10 per person and require a minimum of two participants. The tour ends with a cup (or two) of Atiuan coffee at the Atiu Fibre Art Studio's Tivaivai Cafe in Teenui, operated by his wife Andrea. Bookings are made through the Atiu Motel or directly (☎ 33-031, fax 33-032, adc@adc.co.ck; PO Box 13, Teenui, Atiu, Cook Islands).

Atiu Fibre Arts Studio

The Atiu Fibre Arts Studio specialises in *tivaevae* (appliqué works), the colourful patterned bedspreads which are among the most famous handicrafts of the Cook Islands. Tivaevae are normally made only for home use. Cost for a machine-sewn double to queen-size tivaevae is about NZ$500 to NZ$1100; a hand-sewn one, requiring countless hours to make, costs NZ$1300 and up. You can buy one on the spot or custom order it in the pattern and colours you want. Tivaevae are available in traditional or contemporary patterns, and are made using traditional or contemporary methods.

The studio also produces a variety of other textile arts using appliqué techniques similar to those used in making tivaevae, plus fabric painting and hand-dyed fabrics. All products of the studio are exhibited in its gallery, workshop and cafe building in Teenui, open weekdays from 8 am to 4 pm, Saturday 8 am to 1 pm.

Andrea Eimke, operator of the studio and originally from Germany, can tell you everything you want to know about the local arts and crafts. Andrea is interested in promoting cultural exchange, inviting artists and craftspeople to come and share their skills with the studio and learn Atiuan crafts. For visiting artists she can arrange accommodation, craftmaking facilities and anything else that might be needed. Contact Andrea Eimke, PO Box 13, Teenui, Atiu, Cook Islands (☎ 33-031, fax 33-032, adc@adc. co.ck).

Tutaka & Tivaevae

Twice a year, a committee goes around to inspect all the houses on Atiu for their condition and cleanliness. This *tutaka* is done in many of the Cook Islands, but on Atiu it's made into a big occasion, with the local ladies bringing out all their best handicrafts to proudly put on display in their homes. The major tutaka of the year is just before Christmas, with another in the last week of June. It's easy to spot the inspection committee going around, since they're all in uniform, and if you ask permission you can join them. The tutaka inspection is held on a Wednesday and Thursday, and that same Friday there's a big ball with prizes handed out for the village that wins the competition.

An exhibition of *tivaevae*, the colourful patterned bedspreads and cushions which are one of the most distinctive local handicrafts, takes place the last week of November in the CICC Sunday school hall. Or you can see them on display anytime at the Atiu Fibre Arts Studio. ■

Other Attractions

The CICC church in the centre of the village has walls over 1m thick and is in the traditional island style. A couple of dusty display cases with some Atiuan artefacts are in the library of Atiu College.

Atiu has a surprising number of tennis courts – a few years ago the five villages got into a tennis court building competition, each attempting to build a better one than the next! There are now nine tennis courts on the island.

Organised Tours

You can arrange for a two to three-hour Cultural Tour visiting the marae, historical spots and other points of interest on the island. The cost is flexible, depending on the number of people going and the mode of transport. Ask at the place where you are staying to arrange a guide. See the Caves section earlier in this chapter for details on cave tours.

Place to Stay

The *Atiu Motel* (☎ 33-777, fax 33-775), is about the only organised accommodation on the island, is about 1km out of Areora on the road leading down to the beach. Roger & Kura Malcolm have four units from NZ$90/100/110 a single/double/triple. They are delightful, individual A-frame chalets making maximum use of local materials.

Each chalet has a single and double bed and a mezzanine area where another person or two could sleep. There's also one large family unit sleeping up to six people. All have a verandah in front, and a kitchen area where you can do your own cooking – each unit comes with a fridge and cupboard full of food and at the end of your stay you're simply billed for what you've used. Island meals can also be arranged, and there's an outdoor barbecue where guests often get together.

The motel has a lawn tennis court with lawn bowls every Saturday afternoon. Beside this is a large open-air thatch pavilion and bar where dances are held every Saturday night.

Bookings for the motel can be made at the Air Rarotonga office on Rarotonga (☎ 22-888, fax 20-979) and at Rarotonga travel agents.

For something cheaper and simpler there's the *Are Manuiri* (☎ 33-031, fax 33-032, adc@adc.co.ck), right in the centre of Areora village. It's a pleasant three-bedroom house with shared kitchen, living room, dining room and thatched verandah. Two of the bedrooms have two beds, and the third has three. Prices are NZ$25 per person for shared room, and NZ$40 for a room to yourself. Return airport transfers are NZ$10 per person. Mountain bikes are available for NZ$10 per day. Andrea and Juergen, the German couple who operate the coffee factory and the Atiu Fibre Arts Studio, are part-owners and they'll see you're well looked after.

Places to Eat

The *Tivaevae Cafe* at the Atiu Fibre Arts Studio serves Atiu Island Coffee, homemade cakes, breads and jams, good breakfasts and fresh fruit juice. It's open weekdays from am to 4 pm, Saturday 8 am to 1 pm.

Kura's Kitchen at the Atiu Motel provides evening meals for motel guests and casual diners. Book before 3 pm.

Atiu has several trade stores, two bread bakers and three doughnut makers. Maroro (flying fish), an Atiuan delicacy, are caught in butterfly nets on the 10th, 11th and 12th nights after the new moon during the spawning season, from June to December.

Entertainment

Dances are held in the thatched open-air pavilion bar at the *Atiu Motel* every Saturday night, beginning around 9 pm. They feature a rousing local band and occasional floor shows. Being the only regularly scheduled entertainment on the island, the dances attract visitors and locals alike.

Dances are also held on occasional Friday nights at the *Atiu Nui Maruarua Hall* opposite the CICC church. People of all ages appear and it's always good fun.

For more sedate entertainment, lawn bowls are held on the tennis court at the Atiu Motel on Saturday afternoon.

Things to Buy

The Hut, in the centre of Areora village, sells tivaevae and other handicrafts. Patikura Jim, the owner, also sells handicrafts from her home (behind the hut) and at the Atiu Motel. A Women's Craft Centre may be opening, which will be another place to buy handicrafts.

Woodcarving is popular on the island, and many carvers sell from their homes. You can easily see their workshops along the road as you pass through the villages.

Atiu Island Coffee and goods from the Atiu Fibre Arts Studio are other popular souvenirs of Atiu.

Getting There & Away

Air Air Rarotonga (☎ 33-888 on Atiu) flies between Rarotonga and Atiu every day except Sunday. The 40-minute flight costs NZ$127 (double for return). The same flights also operate from Atiu to Mitiaro and from Mitiaro on to Mauke; there are no direct flights between Atiu and Mauke. Since these

No Dancing in Hurricane Season
Up until 1990, dances on Atiu had an interesting twist between 1 January and 31 March, a holdover from the 'blue laws' days. The original LMS missionaries who founded the CICC church managed to convince the people of Atiu that if they held dances during the hurricane season, it could cause a hurricane to strike the island! Until 1990, the CICC was still opposed to dances being held at that time. The Roman Catholics, however, had no such compunctions so dances usually managed to go on regardless. ■

flights take only 10 minutes each, it's easy to visit all three islands. Air fares are cheaper – NZ$96 per sector – for a multi-island pass.

Rarotonga travel agents organise package tours either to Atiu alone or as part of an Island Combination tour. See the Getting Around chapter for details.

Atiu's airport is on the north-east corner of the island. Both of the places to stay provide airport transfers for guests.

Sea Interisland passenger freighter ships sail to Atiu; see the Getting Around chapter for details.

The all-weather harbour at Taunganui, built in 1974, is too small to take ships so the passengers and freight are unloaded onto aluminium boats while the ship stands offshore. 'Boat day' is an island event and worth witnessing if you happen to be here at that time.

Prior to 1974, getting ashore on Atiu could be a pretty fraught business. In fact some say the Atiuans, once the terror of Mauke and Mitiaro, could have been the terror of many more places were it not for their lack of harbour facilities. As it was the Atiuans could never build really big ocean-going canoes. Instead they used smaller canoes and once offshore lashed two together to make a larger and more stable vessel.

Getting Around

Atiu is great for walking but you need transport to get around. The Atiu Motel rents motorcycles for NZ$25 per day. Clara George (☎ 33-115) provides a taxi service.

Mountain bikes (18-speed) can be rented from Are Manuiri (see the Places to Stay section) for NZ$10 per day.

The Wreck of the *Edna*

There isn't much left of it but you can still see the wreck of the *Edna* just south of Taunganui Harbour. Originally stranded out on the reef, the bow of the wreck was washed up onto land during a hurricane and it's now wedged into a crevasse near the harbour. The stern, 3m under water just off the reef, can be seen by snorkelling or diving.

A 45m (135-foot) sailing cargo ship, the *Edna* was a Dutch ship built in 1916 as a riveted-iron fishing lugger. Her American captain, Nancy Griffith, brought her from Hawaii to the Cook Islands in 1987, and for some years the ship transported passengers and freight around the Cook Islands.

The proud ship met her end on Atiu on 28 November 1990, at about 1.30 am, when a small 'cell' – a spin-off from a hurricane that was passing near Palmerston – slammed into Atiu as the *Edna* was anchored offshore. Although Griffith and the crew were all on board and immediately leaped into action to save the ship, the *Edna* had been flung onto a shoal of coral, and all efforts to save her proved futile. ■

Both places to stay give preference to their own guests, but will also rent vehicles to non-guests.

Takutea

Population: unpopulated
Area: 1.2 sq km

Clearly visible from Atiu, this small sand cay is only 6m above sea level at its highest point. The island has also been called Enua iti which simply means 'small land'. Cook visited Takutea in 1777, shortly after he left Atiu, and paused to search for food for the livestock on his ship.

Takutea is 16km north-west of Atiu and copra-collecting parties used to come from Atiu. Today Takutea is unpopulated and rarely visited, except by the occasional fisherman who seldom steps ashore. Many seabirds including frigates and tropicbirds nest on the island. Takutea is maintained as a wildlife sanctuary by the Atiuan chiefs on behalf of the people of Atiu, who own the island.

Mauke

Population: 646
Area: 18.4 sq km

Mauke is the easternmost of the Cook Islands. It's one of the more easily visited islands since there are regular flights and it can easily be combined with a visit to nearby Atiu and Mitiaro.

History

Mauke takes its name from its legendary founder Uke but there are several versions of what the name means. The most obvious is simply 'land of Uke' but another claims that it means 'clean Uke'. This legend tells of Tangiia, one of the two famous mariners who settled Rarotonga (the Ngatangiia district of

Mauke

157°21'W · 157°19'W

Anareia
Angataura
Anaue
Airstrip
Uriaata
Oneunga
Kimiangatau
Makatea
Raungauni Landing Harbour
Oiretumu
Anaputa
Ngatiarua
Arapaea
Areora
Makatea
Makatea
Aanga
Anaiti
Tukume
Makatea
Anaraura
Teoneroa
Utu
Rererua
Anaokae

0   0.5   1 km

20°08'S · 20°11'S

THE SOUTHERN GROUP

arotonga still bears his name today), oming to ask Uke's aid in going to war gainst the Samoans. Uke replied, 'my hands e clean' – he did not want war. It is said that ke came to Mauke in search of a peaceful lace to live, and he wanted to continue to ve in peace.

Prior to this, Mauke was known as katokamanava, which means 'my heart is rest, at peace'. These were the first words tered by Uke when he arrived from the gendary homeland Avaiki, landing at rapaea on the eastern coast in the huge anoe *Paipaimoana*, carrying a large group f settlers. Mauke is still referred to as katokamanava in song, dance, legend and formal address.

Uke arrived on Mauke with a wife he had ought from the Vanuatuan island of rromango – the same island where the mis- onary John Williams would later be killed d eaten. They had six children, four boys d two girls. The two girls were renowned

for their exceptional beauty, and when the two famous Rarotongan settlers, Tangiia and Karika, came seeking these girls for marriage, they went to live on Rarotonga. Uke's sons also went to other islands, and thus Uke became a common ancestor for all the islands of the southern group.

Prior to the arrival of Christianity, Mauke was totally dominated by the island of Atiu. The Atiuans would descend on murderous, cannibal raids. Akaina, an Atiuan chieftain, settled on Mauke and spirited away the wife of an island chief. Swearing revenge the jilted chief killed Akaina and most of his compatriots but one escaped and, in a small canoe, made the perilous crossing to Atiu. Incensed by this affront to Atiuan power Rongomatane, the great chief of Atiu, set out for Mauke at the head of a fleet of 80 war canoes. The terrified Maukeans took refuge in caves but many of them were hauled out, beaten to death with clubs, cooked and eaten. Satisfied that justice had been done Rongomatane installed an Atiuan named Tararo as chief and sailed back to Atiu.

The surviving islanders regrouped, however, and under Maiti attacked the Atiuans. Unfortunately for the Maukeans Tararo survived and once again an emissary sailed off to alert Rongomatane. And once again the Atiuan war canoes sallied forth to Mauke. This time the Atiuans showed at least some restraint and spared a number of the women and children, taking them back to Atiu as slaves, the cooked flesh of their husbands and fathers accompanying them in the canoes.

The first European to arrive on Mauke was the pioneering missionary John Williams on 23 June 1823. And who accompanied Mr Williams? Why none other than that unpleasant previous visitor, Rongomatane! It's hardly surprising that the Maukeans were converted to Christianity with an ease and speed that astonished the missionaries. Despite Christian influence Mauke still remained subject to Atiu with ariki appointed from Atiu.

Author and island personality Julian Dashwood (known as 'Rakau', the Maori word for 'wood', on the island) lived for years on Mauke where he ran the island store. See the Books section in the Facts for

---

The People of Mauke

On one of their murderous forays to Mauke, the Atiuans tempted the unfortunate inhabitants out of their cave hideaways by claiming they were on a friendly visit and inviting them (the Maukeans) to a feast that they (the Atiuans) were setting up. This was not totally untrue, as the unfortunate people of Mauke found, but they did not anticipate their role at the feast. They were henceforth labelled 'Mauke kaa-kaa' ('Mauke the easily fooled').

Some say that when deciding which women to eat, the Atiuans always ate the ugliest and spared the most beautiful, which accounts for the extraordinary beauty of Maukean women today! ■

---

the Visitor chapter for more information. His second book, *Today is Forever*, is largely about Mauke.

Geology

Like Atiu, Mangaia and Mitiaro, Mauke is a raised atoll with a surrounding makatea. Inland from this fossil coral reef a band of swampland surrounds the fertile central land. The central area of the island is flat, rising virtually no higher than the makatea. In contrast to Atiu and Mangaia where the central area is hilly, Mauke rises barely 30m above sea level at its highest point. Like Atiu, Mitiaro and Mangaia, Mauke has numerous limestone caves in the makatea, which is densely forested with lush jungle-like growth.

Economy

Mauke's economy is primarily agricultural with a variety of fruits and vegetables grown mostly for local consumption. One important island export is *maire*, a type of leaf traditionally used for making *eis* (necklaces) in Hawaii, where they are called *leis*; a shipment of maire eis leaves Mauke bound for Hawaii each week. Mauke Miracle Oil, pure coconut oil made with a special medicinal plant, is another important export. A handful of cattle are raised on the island.

Mauke is noted for its pandanus mats, purses and hats and for *kete* baskets. Bowls shaped like the leaves of the breadfruit tree and carved from *miro* wood are another traditional Maukean craft. Tivaevae are also made on Mauke, but only for home use.

Information

Electricity operates on Mauke from 5 am to midnight. The Telecom and post office is in Ngatiarua village, in the centre of the island. It's open weekdays from 8 am to 2 pm, with a card phone outside that you can use anytime.

Caves

Like Atiu and Mangaia, Mauke has makatea riddled with limestone caves, many filled with cool water and wonderful for a swim on

The Divided Church

Mauke has two villages in the centre, Areora and Ngatiarua, and one on the coast, Kimiangatau. The coastal village was built in 1904 because some of the Maukeans had decided to become Roman Catholics and could no longer tolerate living with those who still followed the London Missionary Society.

Religious disputes were nothing new to the Maukeans as the 1882 CICC church illustrates. At that time there were still just two villages and they got together to build the church. When the outside was complete, however, the two sides could not agree on how the inside should be fitted out. Eventually the argument became so acrimonious that the only solution was to build a wall down the middle and let each village have its own church within the church.

A new pastor eventually managed to convince his congregations that this was hardly in the spirit of neighbourly Christianity and the wall was removed, but the two sides of the church are still decorated in different styles and each village has its own entrance. Inside, the two villages each sit on their own side of the aisle and they take turns singing the hymns! The pulpit, with old Chilean dollars set into the railing, is centrally placed but there's a dividing line down the middle and the minister is expected to straddle the line at all times. The interior of the church is painted in soft pastel colours.

Today, Mauke's population is nearly half CICC, and nearly half Roman Catholic, with the rest made up of a few families of Mormons, Seventh-Day Adventists and Baha'is. ∎

NANCY KELLER

Ziona, the divided church, Mauke

hot day. Walking through the makatea to the caves is like walking through a lush jungle, with coconut palms and shade trees, pandanus, mosses, ferns and tropical greenery in wild profusion. The shade is welcome on a hot day.

The easiest cave to reach, and also one of the larger ones on the island for swimming, is Vai Tango, just a short walk from Ngatiarua village. You'll probably need someone to show you how to get there the first time, but that's no problem as everybody knows where it is. It's often full of children on Saturday and after school, but at other times you may get it all to yourself.

Other interesting caves in the north part of the island, just a short walk off the main road, are Vai Ou, Vai Tunamea and Vai Moraro. Vai Ou is in a beautiful, lushly tropical grotto, with an ancient coral pathway leading to it. Vai Moraro is also known as the 'Crawling Cave' – you have to crawl down through a slit in the rockface to get in. It opens up into a big cave inside, but the pools are small,

although deep, and they taste like salt water. Be especially careful walking around in this one, as the rocks are wet and very slippery. Just a little farther on is Vai Tunamea.

Motuanga Cave or the 'Cave of 100 Rooms', each with its own pool, is Mauke's best known cave. The cave is entered on land and extends out toward the sea and under the reef. In some of the last rooms you can reach, the waves can be heard crashing above you.

There is nobody around today who has reached all of Motuanga's 100 rooms; they say that nowadays you can only get into 12 of them. But there is a legend of one man, Timeni Oariki, who did swim through all of them, finally emerging out into the sea where he was eaten by sharks. So he never got to tell anybody about it!

Marae

Like all the other Cook Islands, Mauke has many marae, or ancient religious meeting grounds.

The best preserved, and still used for ceremonial functions, is the Puarakura Marae. There's a triangular area enclosed within a rectangle within another larger rectangle, with seats for the ariki, the *mataiapo* (heads of sub-tribes) and the *rangatira* (landed gentry).

Out past the old airstrip is Marae Rangimanuka, the marae of Uke, Mauke's famous ancestor and namesake. It's hidden in an overgrown area but it's not difficult to get to with a guide who knows the way.

Near the harbour, the Marae O Rongo was once a huge marae but all you see today are a few large stones and a coral platform under what was a very big tree until it was destroyed by fire. According to tradition, this is the only marae on Mauke where anyone was killed and eaten. The marae is behind the government administration building; the little road going along the left (inland) side of the building leads right to it.

Paepae'a, a new marae built in 1997 for Tamuera Ariki, is an impressive marae on the road between Ngatiarua and the airport.

Beaches

A road runs right around the coast of Mauke, a distance of 18km. The fringing reef platform is narrow but Teoneroa beach is fairly good as is the beach at Arapaea Landing o the eastern side of the island. The beaches o the southern side of the island like Anaoka are pleasantly secluded. Other beaches, lik Anaraura and Teoneroa, have picnic area with thatched shelters providing welcom shade on a hot day. Oneunga, on the east side is also a nice little beach for a picnic. A around the island, the waves have beaten th shoreline cliffs into overhanging formation

Heading south from the Tiare Holida Cottages, the very first turn-off towards th sea leads you to Kopupooki ('Stomac Rock') beach. The name comes from a cav situated to your left as you face out to sea go just past the last outcrop of rock that yo see from the beach and you come to thi lovely cave full of fish, and good for swim ming and snorkelling. You can only reach at low tide; at other times, the poundin waves make it too dangerous. Except for th harbour, this is about the only place dee enough for a good salty swim, since the ree all around the island is quite shallow. Man more little caves and beaches are dotte around the island.

Places to Stay & Eat

The *Tiare Holiday Cottages* (☎ 35-083, fa

Kovitoa Ariki & Marae O Rongo

Kovitoa Ariki had two sons, Koumu and Kaivaiva, and when his wife died he remarried to a woman who had five small children. Because he wanted to be sure that his own two sons, who were away on Atiu at the time, would inherit his title, he concocted a plan to get rid of the five small children of his wife.

He took the children out to his plantation on successive occasions, and each time sent them off on various errands, keeping one with him to help him. When the rest of the children returned, they found their step father had prepared meat in an *umu* (underground oven) and their little brother or sister was gone. Each time, Kovitoa told the children that he had killed a pig in the bush and that their brother or sister had gone home. When the child was not at home upon their return, he said it must have been spirited away by the Atiu people.

Finally, when there were only two children left, the older one was becoming very suspicious. When Kovitoa sent him away, he hid in the bush, and saw his brother killed. He ran back to the village and told the people what Kovitoa had done. Not long after that, when Kovitoa was sleeping, someone bashed his head with a coconut grater, and he was roasted and eaten on his own marae, Marae O Rongo.

As the people were washing Kovitoa's body down at the present-day harbour, with the roasting oven blazing away, one of Kovitoa's two sons arrived in a canoe from Atiu. He ended up avenging his father's death by killing his assassin in his sleep with the same coconut grater that had been used on his father, and he took over his father's ariki title. ■

Kea's Grave

One of Mauke's beaches, Anaiti, has a special history. Up on the cliff to the right of the beach as you face the sea is a mound of grey coral stones. This is the grave of Kea.

Kea's husband, Paikea, was out fishing one day in his canoe when Kea, up on the cliff, saw a huge storm coming across the sea. She shouted to her husband to come back to land, but he didn't hear her. The storm caught him at sea and blew him farther and farther away from the island. Kea believed her husband was dead, and she cried and cried on that cliff overlooking the sea until she died of grief, and the people buried her there.

In the early 1970s, after a severe storm, Kea's bones became exposed, the surrounding sand having been washed away. The people covered her bones again with big coral stones which are still there today.

Paikea had not died at sea, however. He was blown very far by the storm, but he finally did reach land – the island of Mangaia. The people there did not want him to stay and were at the point of killing him when a woman who was half-Maukean took him under her protection. With her help, he escaped from Mangaia and sailed to Rarotonga. On Rarotonga, Paikea stayed in Ngatangiia, but later departed for New Zealand and never returned to the Cooks again.

There are a couple of versions of the story of which canoe Paikea took when he went to New Zealand. One version says he went as a crew member on the *Takitumu* canoe, in the Great Migration around 1350 AD – one Paikea did go on the *Takitumu*. Another version says that he went slightly later on a different canoe, the Orouta, which was shaped like a whale and of which he was the captain.

The Orouta ended its voyage at Whangara, on the east coast of New Zealand's North Island, between where Gisborne and Wairoa are today. A marae in Whangara bears a carving of Paikea on the apex of the rooftop at the entrance; he is sitting atop a whale, which represents his canoe. Paikea is today the revered ancestor of a large clan of New Zealand Maori.

But Kea remains in her grave here on the shore in Mauke, where she died of grief for her lost love. ■

35-102) is right on the coast, near to the village and to Kopupooki, one of Mauke's better beaches. It has three simple cottages, each with cement walls, thatched roof and its own fridge; a kitchen/dining area, showers and toilets are nearby. Singles/doubles are NZ$30/35 in these units. There's also one self-contained family unit, sleeping up to four people, for NZ$50 a night. If all of the units are full, there is also overflow accommodation – the staff can always arrange a room somewhere. Discounts are offered for stays of over five days, or if you help out around the place. The friendly owners, Tautara & Kura Purea, will meet you with eis at the airport, show you around the island, take you to the Divided Church on Sunday if you want to go, and to any special occasions on the island.

The *Mauke Cove Lodge* (☎ 35-130, 35-388, fax 35-094, aguinea@gatepoly.co.ck), operated by Aunty Tini and Aunty Pi, is a large two-bedroom, two-bathroom house at the north edge of Kimiangatau village. Singles/doubles are NZ$32/50, plus NZ$20 for each additional adult; the house can sleep up to six people.

You can do your own cooking at either place, or arrange for meals to be prepared for you. Island or caves tours, fishing trips and other activities can be arranged.

Things to Buy

There's nothing commercially organised, but if you want to buy any of the island's products or handicrafts, it can be arranged. Ask at the place you're staying.

Getting There & Away

Air Air Rarotonga (☎ 35-888 on Mauke) flies three times a week between Rarotonga and Mauke. The cost is NZ$142 (double for return) for the 50-minute flight. A visit to Mauke can easily be combined with a visit to Atiu and Mitiaro; stopping at more than one island brings the fare down to just

NZ$96 per sector on a multi-island pass. Rarotonga travel agents organise package tours including air fare and accommodation. See the Getting Around chapter for details.

Mauke now has an airstrip on the island's north coast, replacing the older one in the centre of the island.

Sea See the Getting Around chapter for details on passenger freighter ship services among the Cook Islands. A visit to Mauke can often be combined with visits to some of the other southern islands.

Getting Around

Both hotels rent motorcycles (NZ$20 per day) and bicycles (NZ$8.50 per day) to guests and nonguests alike, and both provide airport transfers.

Mitiaro

Population: 319
Area: 22.3 sq km

Mitiaro is not one of the Cooks' most physically beautiful islands, but there are a few enjoyable things you can do there to pass a pleasant few days. The people on the island are usually happy to see a new face; when you stop to talk to them they are very friendly. They all live in one small village on the west side of the island. To see the sights of Mitiaro, especially the caves and the marae, you'll need a local person to guide you. This can easily be arranged at the place where you stay.

History

Like Mauke the island of Mitiaro was subject to repeated raids from Atiu, but unlike the Maukeans the Mitiaroans did not hide in caves. They stoutly defended their fortress, Te Pare, but were, nevertheless, eventually overcome by the Atiuans. The small and declining population that lives on Mitiaro today is thought to be almost entirely descended from raiding Atiuan warriors. The

Reverend John Williams arrived on Mitiaro on 29 July 1823 accompanied by Rongomatane as he had been on Mauke and the island was soon converted to Christianity, but Atiuan raids continued, even after the arrival of Christianity, into the 1840s.

Before Christianity came to Mitiaro, the people lived in inland villages – Taurangi Atai, Auta, Mangarei and Takaue. As on Rarotonga, when the missionaries came they moved the people out to live on the coast, where they built a village centred around the church. The old village sites are now the plantation areas where the food is grown.

Geology

Mitiaro is another southern island with a raised coral limestone outer plain, or makatea. Like Mauke, but to an even greater degree, the interior of the island is very flat – the makatea rises to a maximum of 9m above sea level, the interior foodlands to about 12m. Much of the interior of Mitiaro is swampland, just 1m above sea level. Two parts of this swamp are deep enough to be labelled as lakes: Te Rotonui ('big lake') and Te Rotoiti ('small lake').

People, Economy & Culture

All the inhabitants of Mitiaro are related to one another in some way. The local ladies sometimes bemoan the situation, saying 'We'll *never* find a husband on this island. All the men here are our cousins!' In fact the people of Mitiaro, Mauke and Atiu are all in much the same situation and a great deal of intermarriage has taken place down through the years. Everybody on Mitiaro seems to have family on Mauke, Atiu, Rarotonga and even farther afield, and there's much visiting back and forth.

With everyone on Mitiaro being a relative it makes for a high degree of cooperation. There's not much money around, but agriculture and fishing produce abundant yields, there's a lot of sharing and everyone gets what they need.

Until the early 1990s, the Mitiaro schools only catered for children up to about age 12; after that they had to go to Atiu, Rarotonga or New Zealand to continue their studies. This system routinely broke up the families on Mitiaro; it was certainly a cause of the small population figure because children rarely returned to the narrow social and economic horizons of the island.

In the early 1990s secondary school classes were added to the program at the small Mitiaro school, making it possible to continue one's education on Mitiaro up to Form 5 (about age 16), fulfilling the Cook Islands' education requirement. The students can now sit their final exams on Mitiaro, achieving both the Cook Islands and New Zealand school certificates if they pass the tests. If they still want further education they can then go to Rarotonga, New Zealand or farther afield.

Not being forced to leave the island to attend school has resulted in more young people staying. There are very few unemployed young people on the island. Plantation work or fishing is about all Mitiaro has to offer though, and the work is in family-related businesses. This is great for

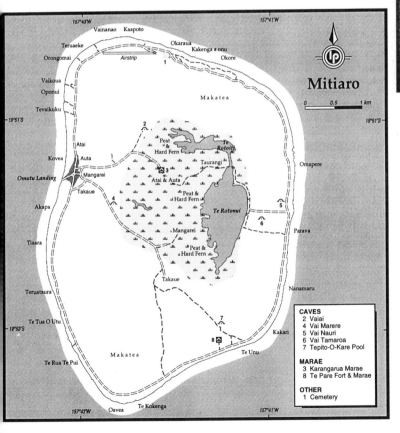

Mitiaro

CAVES
2 Vaiai
4 Vai Marere
5 Vai Nauri
6 Vai Tamaroa
7 Tepito-O-Kare Pool

MARAE
3 Karangarua Marae
8 Te Pare Fort & Marae

OTHER
1 Cemetery

THE SOUTHERN GROUP

▲▽▲▽▲▽▲▽▲▽▲▽▲▽▲

Terevai
The women of Mitiaro have a delightful custom known as *terevai*. A group of women get together and go to one of the island's pools, often to Vai Nauri or Vai Tamaroa. Along the way, they sing the old bawdy songs of their ancestors – many of them action songs, with graphic movements accompanying the lyrics. The mood gets exuberantly racy and by the time the women have trekked out to the pool, everyone is in high spirits. At the pool a prayer, a hymn and a chant precede a synchronised leap into the water. ■

▽▲▽▲▽▲▽▲▽▲▽▲▽▲▽

feeding the family but not for getting cash money, as all the fish and plantation produce is used here on the island and most of it gets traded back and forth among families. On the one hand, there's plenty of work for the young people to do and everyone on the island has plenty to eat; on the other hand, those who want to do anything other than plantation work, fishing or traditional handicrafts, or those who want to earn money somehow, must still leave the island eventually.

Although most people on Mitiaro now live in western-style houses, they usually have outbuildings made of traditional thatch which may serve as cookhouses, fishermen's shacks and the like. A few people do still live in traditional thatch huts; it's an interesting sight to see an electricity meter hooked up to a hut made of sticks and pandanus!

Many traditional handicrafts are still made on Mitiaro, and many traditional customs are still practised. Women weave long pandanus strips into floor mats, fans, handbags and other craftwork. Big bowls are carved of solid wood and canoes are still made in the traditional way. Fishing and planting are done according to the phases of the moon. Boys grow up learning the habits of each type of fish – at what phase of the moon it will be found, where, at what depth and doing what. The traditional arts are still taught to both boys and girls.

Information
Electricity is available daily from 5 am to midnight. The post and Telecom offices are in one building, open weekdays from 8 am to 4 pm. If you need to change money change it before you come to Mitiaro.

What to Bring Be well prepared to ward off mosquitoes when you come to Mitiaro; a significant portion of the island is covered by either lake or soggy swampland, providing an ideal breeding ground.

If you'll be doing any walking on the island, you'll need that repellent, and if you'll be doing any walking across the makatea, be sure to bring some sturdy shoes. Old ones are best because they'll definitely receive a beating in the razor-sharp makatea. Don't try to walk across the makatea in sandals or thongs as you could easily cut yourself very badly.

You may want to bring some food with you – food in the small village shops is considerably more expensive than on Rarotonga.

Since the power goes off at midnight, be sure to bring a torch (flashlight). Also bring sunglasses – the white surface of the roads on Mitiaro is extremely reflective and bright all around the island.

▲▽▲▽▲▽▲▽▲▽▲▽▲▽▲

Sweet Peat
There are many areas of natural peat on Mitiaro, principally around the lakes, adjacent to the foodlands and in the swamp. A particularly rich strip is located by the Parava boat landing on Te Rotonui, where the road meets the lake. A 1988 study concluded that the peat could not be efficiently used for energy, but farmers do use it to enrich the soil.

When you walk near the lake, or on the roads through the swamp towards the plantation lands, there is a pleasant peat smell in the air. Crossing the peat to the lake is quite an adventure as it can wobble like jelly beneath your feet. In places, logs have been placed to spread the weight. ■

▽▲▽▲▽▲▽▲▽▲▽▲▽▲▽

Plantations

In the old days people made their villages where they grew their food. Even after moving the houses to the seaside village in the 1800s, they have continued using the same traditional plantation areas. Nowadays there are roads across the makatea and you can drive there, although many people still make the long trip on foot. The new visitor may wonder why they don't simply grow their produce closer to the village but there's a good reason for it: the old agricultural areas with their surrounding peat deposits are the most fertile spots on the island, as well as being at the highest elevation.

The CICC Church

The inhabitants of Mitiaro are all concentrated in one village on the west coast. The village is an amalgamation of the villages moved to the coast when the missionaries arrived. The white-painted CICC church – the third church that the London Missionary Society (LMS) built in the Cooks – with its blue trim, parquet ceiling decorated with black and white stars, and stained-glass windows is a fine sight and the singing on Sunday is superb. There's also a small Catholic church and an Assembly of God church.

Marae & Fort

There are marae in the inland areas where the villages used to be although many are now overgrown. In 1988 an international team of archaeologists led by Dr Hiro Kurashina of Japan located and excavated the Takero marae, in the old Takaue village area. The huge stone seat of the ariki – he must have been a very big fellow – had been broken in two and they found the other half and put the seat back together. The side that was lost had turned white while the other side was brown, so today the seat is two different colours. There are several old graves near the marae.

The same team returned in 1989 and excavated another marae, Karangarua, in the old Atai village area. It's a huge marae, large enough for hundreds of people to gather, with seats for the ariki and other important

people. You're welcome to visit but you'll need a guide to find it.

In the south-east part of the island are the stone remains of the ancient Te Pare fort, built as a defence against Atiuan raids. An underground shelter was large enough for the people to congregate in during times of danger, while above was a lookout tower from which approaching canoes could be seen. Footsteps could be easily heard on the loose stone pathway to the fort. The important marae in the fort complex ensured there was spiritual as well as physical protection. Despite all this, the fierce Atiuan warriors eventually overpowered the islanders. The present three ariki of Mitiaro – Ma'eu O Te Rangi Ariki, Tiki Tetava Ariki and To'u Ariki – are descended from the foremost Mitiaro warriors, who were appointed by the Atiuan conquerors to represent the people.

To visit the Te Pare fort and marae, you must first ask permission of Tiki Tetava Ariki, the ariki to whom the marae belongs. His speaker will take you to the fort; there's an easy walking track across the makatea and a visit is well worthwhile.

Cemetery

Many old cemeteries are dotted around the island, indicating that in the past the population may have been much more widely spread than it is today. The cemetery on the north side of the island is the most interesting one. It has a few modern-style cement tombs, but also many older graves simply marked by an upright slab of coral. At almost every grave, both old and modern, some possessions of the deceased person are left at the headstone. Most of the graves have a plate, bowl, cup, glass, bottle and/or silverware sitting by the headstone – some carefully placed, just as if someone was going to sit down to a meal, others more haphazardly piled up. They are placed there so that if the spirit of the deceased comes, they can eat a meal on their own dinnerware!

Immediately after a death, the family brings food out to the grave and leaves it until it is gone. This may continue for a month or two, until it is felt that the spirit has departed, but the plates and cutlery are left permanently. There is a very strong belief that the spirit continues to live on after death, and every effort is made to ensure that the spirit will not become angry with the living. Tin or enamel bowls and cups adorn older graves, while newer ones have modern plates and cutlery. One grave has a whole box full of medicine bottles, some still containing the medicine; another has a baby bottle and a tiny pair of baby shoes.

Lakes

It's hard to tell where the surrounding swamp ends and the lakes begin. Except in one spot, where a road leads right up to the shore of Te Rotonui, the lakes are hard to approach and although the water is clear the lake bottoms are horribly muddy. If you approach the lakes by any other means than that one road, the ground becomes increasingly soggy and wallows more and more unsteadily under your feet the closer you get to the lake. Where the road arrives at Te Rotonui, though, the ground is firm, there's a boat landing and a pleasant picnic spot.

You can also approach the lakes from the Taurangi plantation area, which is quite easy since there is no makatea to cross – only a wide strip of very black mud. If you have a motorbike you can take it all the way to the end of the Taurangi area pathway. From there it's only a 15-minute walk to the lake but the mud you have to cross may deter you.

The local men often fish in the lakes for the prolific fish and the famous eels. The eels are caught at night by blinding them with a light and then hitting them with a bush knife. They can also be caught by baited hooks, or by hooking them around the body and hoisting them out of the water. There are plenty of eels in the lakes; 10 or more eels can easily be caught in a couple of hours. Milkfish, another renowned delicacy, are also plentiful in the lakes, due to a Japanese project stocking the lakes with fish brought from Aitutaki, Penrhyn and Hawaii.

Beaches, Caves & Pools

Mitiaro has some fine little beaches and the

reef at low tide is excellent for walking on all around the island. In common with the other islands with makatea it also has a number of beautiful caves, with pools of fresh water that make great swimming holes. The makatea looks parched and dry; you would never guess that out there somewhere are cool, clear pools, hidden under the ground. The water in the pools, as well as in the lakes and the swamp, rises and falls with the tide. There's no trace of saltwater in the pools but they must somehow be connected to the sea.

Just a 10-minute walk from the village on the Takaue road, Vai Marere is the only sulphur pool in the Cook Islands. All you see from the road is a big hole in the ground but it opens up into a large cave with stalactites. The water is darker than in other pools, possibly due to the sulphur content. It's refreshingly cool and makes your skin and hair feel wonderfully soft.

Vai Tamaroa and Vai Nauri are on the eastern side of the island. Vai Tamaroa is about a 15-minute walk across sharp makatea from the coast road; the start of the track is marked by a sign commemorating a Boys Brigade project in 1985. You'll need a local to take you there because the trail across the makatea is faint. A road to Vai Nauri has now been cut, so you can drive right up to it.

Vai Nauri is a large, brilliantly clear pool in a big cave. You can reach the water either by climbing down one side and wading in or by going around to the other side and leaping off the 3m cliff, like the locals do. It's beautiful to sit peacefully in the cool cavern and listen to the water dripping down from the stalactites on the ceiling, falling like rain.

Vai Tamaroa is another large pool, but open to the sky. All around it are cliffs about 10m high, and the locals love to jump down into the water, climbing back up the cliffs again for another leap. The women hold their terevai gatherings at both Vai Tamaroa and Vai Nauri.

Vaiai or the Sandalwood Cave, named for the sandalwood that grows there, is in the north of the island and also has a good fresh-water swimming hole. However, people rarely go there nowadays because the track is difficult to find since it was destroyed by a cyclone a few years ago. You'll need a good guide.

Tepito-O-Kare, in the south-east part of the island, is too small for swimming but it has fresh water good for drinking. Fishermen used to stop by here to quench their thirst as they walked back inland from Te Unu after fishing trips.

Places to Stay & Eat

Two guesthouses in family homes, both in Atai, provide accommodation for visitors. Mii O'Bryan (☎ 36-106, fax 36-683) has a three-bedroom house with a big verandah; the nightly cost of NZ$50 per person per day includes all three meals. Mii rents out motor-bikes (NZ$10 per day) and bicycles are available.

The *Mitiaro Guest House* (☎ 36-153, fax 36-683), operated by Mikara & Joe Herman, charges NZ$60 per person per day, including all three meals. They also rent out motor-bikes (NZ$25 per day) and bicycles (NZ$10 per day).

Limited food supplies are available at the small village food shops but prices are higher than on Rarotonga; you may want to bring some supplies with you. Mitiaro's dried bananas wrapped in banana leaves (*piere*) are a local delicacy, as are the eels and milk-fish, and there's a good variety of fish and fresh produce. Passionfruit and mangoes simply fall on the ground under the trees and coconuts are everywhere.

Things to Buy

Mitiaro women still make a variety of woven pandanus products for everyday use – floor mats, table mats, fans, handbags, baskets and the like. Pandanus no longer grows on Rarotonga and has been virtually eliminated on Atiu too, but it still grows profusely all over Mitiaro. Carved wooden bowls are another possibility.

There are no commercial outlets for these goods, but you should be able to arrange to purchase some – ask around.

Getting There & Away

Air Air Rarotonga (☎ 36-888 on Mitiaro) flies to Mitiaro three times a week. The cost is NZ$142 (double for return) for the 50-minute flight.

A visit to Mitiaro can easily be combined with visits to Mauke and/or Atiu – each is only a 10-minute flight from Mitiaro, and if you visit more than one island, the cost per sector is reduced to NZ$96. Rarotonga travel agents can include Mitiaro on a multi-island package tour with air fare, accommodation and hotel transfers all included. See the Getting Around chapter.

Sea See the Getting Around chapter for details on passenger freighter ship services among the Cook Islands. Stops at Mitiaro are often made in conjunction with visits to Atiu and Mauke.

Getting Around

Motorbikes and bicycles can be rented from both of Mitiaro's guesthouses.

THE SOUTHERN GROUP

Mangaia

Population: 1104
Area: 51.8 sq km

The second largest of the Cook Islands, Mangaia, is not much smaller than Rarotonga, although its population is much less and has declined sharply in recent years. The island is a geological oddity, very similar to Atiu. Like Atiu the central hills are surrounded by an outer rim of raised coral reef known as *makatea*. The lagoon inside the fringing coral reef is very narrow and shallow.

Although Mangaia's geography is basically similar to Atiu's it is much more dramatic. The makatea rises rapidly from the coast and in most places it drops as a sheer wall to the inner region. There are places where you can climb to the top of the cliff for impressive, uninterrupted views. The inner cliff of the makatea is such a major barrier that some of the cuttings through it are quite spectacular, one through to Ivirua in particular.

All the streams and rivers running down from the central hills run into a dead end at the inner cliff of the makatea, filtering through the makatea and emerging as small freshwater springs at or near the seashore. After heavy rains, streaks of Mangaia's red soil can be seen stretching from the makatea out into the sea from these water runoffs.

Scrub, ferns, vines, coconut palms and other trees grow on the makatea. Taro swamps are found around the inner edge of the makatea where water collects between the hills and the coral flatlands, and in the central valleys, which are the most fertile part of the island and are planted with various crops. Much of the island's hilly central area is planted with Caribbean pine trees, which prevent erosion and are expected to become an important timber crop.

Pineapples, which a few years ago were the island's principal export crop, are still grown but not on the grand scale that they

HIGHLIGHTS

- Wandering around the high, sheer inland cliffs & rich agricultural valleys
- Walking through the lush vegetation and cuttings in the makatea
- Climbing to the plateau of Rangimotia
- Exploring Teruarere burial cave and other caves
- Canoeing across Lake Tiriara to explore the cave at the far end

once were. After one year in the early 1990s when hundreds of boxes of pineapples rotted on the wharf waiting for shipment, most farmers now raise pineapple only on a small scale for local consumption. Mangaia pineapples are still justly famous – big, sweet and juicy. Mangaia taro is also said to be some of the finest in the Cook Islands.

The World Health Organisation built a dam and water reservoir in 1986, solving many of Mangaia's water problems. However, there was an 11-month drought in 1996 which again caused water problems for the island. You'll still see water tanks beside many houses, storing the rainwater from the roofs.

History

The Mangaians have an unusual legend of their early history. Most Polynesian islands have some sort of legend about a great ancestor arriving on a fantastic canoe, but not the Mangaians: nobody sailed from anywhere to become Mangaia's first settler. Rangi, Mokoaro and Akatauira, the three sons of the god Rongo, father of Mangaia, simply lifted the island up from the deep, becoming its first settlers and the ancestors of the Nga Ariki tribe.

The traditional name of the island was Auau ('terraced'), short for Auau Nui O Rongo Ki Te Au Marama ('big terraced land of Rongo in the world of daylight'). The spiritual name of the island was Akatautika ('well-poised'). The island's current name is comparatively recent – it is short for a name bestowed by Tamaeu, an Aitutakian who arrived on Mangaia in 1775, two years before Captain Cook made the first European discovery of the island. Mangaia means 'peace' or 'temporal power'. The name apparently relates to the interminable battles between the island's various groups and the

peace which was finally established when one leader eventually achieved *mangaia*, or power, over the whole island – after 42 separate battles which had various victors.

Captain Cook claimed the European discovery of Mangaia during his second Pacific voyage. He arrived on 29 March 1777 but the reception was not the friendliest and it was not possible to find a place to land, so the *Resolution* and *Discovery* sailed on to a more friendly greeting at Atiu.

The reception was even less inviting when John Williams turned up on Mangaia in 1823. The pioneering missionary had left

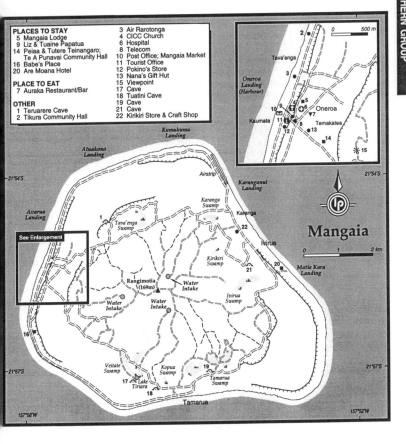

PLACES TO STAY
5 Mangaia Lodge
9 Liz & Tuaine Papatua
14 Peiaa & Tutere Teinangaro;
   Te A Punavai Community Hall
16 Babe's Place
20 Are Moana Hotel

PLACE TO EAT
7 Auraka Restaurant/Bar

OTHER
1 Teruarere Cave
2 Tikura Community Hall

3 Air Rarotonga
4 CICC Church
6 Hospital
8 Telecom
10 Post Office; Mangaia Market
11 Tourist Office
12 Pokino's Store
13 Nana's Gift Hut
15 Viewpoint
17 Cave
18 Tuatini Cave
19 Cave
21 Cave
22 Kirikiri Store & Craft Shop

Mangaia

Mangaian hut

Aitutaki to search for Rarotonga, which he eventually found by way of Atiu. Coming first upon Mangaia he attempted to set Polynesian missionary 'teachers' ashore but the Mangaians attacked them, so he quickly dropped the idea and sailed off again. On 15 June 1824, however, Tiere and David, two Polynesian missionaries from Tahaa, the island sharing the same lagoon with Raiatea in present-day French Polynesia, were landed on the island and, as elsewhere, the conversion to Christianity was soon underway.

Traditionally, the Mangaians had a reputation for being a dour, ethnocentric lot – an attribute which perhaps helped to keep the aggressive Atiuans at bay. The warriors of Atiu wreaked havoc on Mauke and Mitiaro but never had much success against Mangaia.

More recently Mangaia has suffered from a dramatic population decline. Since the mid-1970s the population of the island, stable for some time at around 2000, has fallen by almost half.

Orientation

Oneroa, Tamarua and Ivirua, the three main villages, are all on the coast, with Oneroa on the west side of the island, Ivirua on the east side and Tamarua on the south. Oneroa, the main village, has three parts: Tava'enga and Kaumata are on the northern and southern parts of the coast, respectively, with Temakatea up above, reached through a road cut through the makatea cliff. The airstrip is on the north side of the island.

Information

Mangaia's tourist office (☎ 34-289, fax 34-238, PO Box 10), in the Ministry of Outer Islands Development building at the bottom of the Temakatea road cutting, is open weekdays from 8 am to 4 pm. The director, Poko Otheniel, is exceptionally friendly and helpful.

The post office is in the government building opposite the tourist office; it's open on weekdays from 8 am to noon and 1 to 4 pm. The Telecom office, in the upper (Temakatea) part of Oneroa not far from the hospital, is open weekdays from 7.30 am to 4 pm. Here you can make long-distance telephone calls, send and receive faxes, and there's a cardphone outside the door that you can use anytime.

Electricity operates daily from 5 am to midnight.

Churches & Marae

There are typical, old CICC churches in Oneroa, Ivirua and Tamarua. The Tamarua church, surrounded by a shady grove of iron-wood trees, is especially beautiful – look for the woodcarving and the sennit-rope binding on the roof beams. In front of the Oneroa church an interesting monument details the ministers of the church, both *papa'a* (foreigners) and Maori, and also the Mangaian ministers who have worked as missionaries abroad.

Mangaia has numerous premissionary marae. There are 24 around the island, but you'd need a local expert to find them. Tuara George (see the Caves section) can take you. Many marae are remote, overgrown and disused – marae on Mangaia are no longer used in modern ceremonies, as they still are on most other Cook Islands.

An island-beautification project is scheduled to clear and clean some of Mangaia's marae. The tourist office will have information.

Rangimotia & Island Walks

Rangimotia (169m) is the highest point on the island. It's not really a peak, more of a high plateau. You know when you're at the top but you have to explore in several directions to see all the coast. From the Oneroa side of the island there's an old dirt road, suitable for 4WDs, motorcycles or mountain bikes, right to the top. At the top the track forks and you can follow either fork back down to the coast. The roads follow the ridges of Mangaia's rolling hills and even when the roads are indistinct it's easy to find your way.

If you've taken the fork heading towards Ivirua, you can turn south from Ivirua and head to Tamarua, the third village on the island. The dirt road runs just inland from the makatea for most of the distance. Along this stretch the makatea is not edged with much of a cliff but shortly after the trail climbs back onto the raised coral there is an impressive drop, and at a point shortly before Tamarua you can turn off the road for a view over an area of taro swamp. From Tamarua the road runs close to the coast with numerous paths down to the reef. Or you can take the shorter direct route back to Oneroa. This is a pleasant but quite long day's walk, probably over 25km in total.

There's no limit to the walks you could take in the interior of the island – in recent years the forestry service has cut an extensive network of firebreaks and rough dirt roads.

Several of the cuttings through the makatea cliffs are beautiful for short walks, with narrow roads winding between the high grey makatea cliffs, lush with vegetation. The cutting from Ivirua village heading inland to the taro swamp behind the village is probably the most beautiful on the island; the one heading south from the Temakatea part of Oneroa village to Tuaati beach is also very attractive.

Caves

The makatea is riddled with caves but the largest and most spectacular is Teruarere. Tuara George, who lives in Oneroa, is the guide for this cave. He charges around NZ$20 per person for a two to three-hour cave tour, passing by a number of ancient human skeletons inside the cave. If he's not on the island, ask at Babe's Place about organising a tour.

Teruarere, a burial cave, was rediscovered in the 1930s by Tuara's grandfather, Tuaratua, and Robert Dean Frisbie – see the Books section in the Facts for the Visitor chapter. Teruarere means 'jump' (possibly because people used to jump down into the cave opening).

You do have to climb down into the opening. The branches of a tree emerge at ground level and at the other end of this opening there's a fine view out from the makatea cliff. As you enter, the high, narrow cliffs seem to close overhead. At first there are several small openings high above you and a tree root winds down through one to floor level. Then you have to slither through a low, muddy opening and the cave becomes much more enclosed. Be sure to bring a torch (flashlight) and insect repellent as there are many mosquitoes near the cave entrance. The cave is not difficult to explore but wear old clothes because you'll get quite dirty and muddy.

This is a very dramatic cave and most of the time it is very high, though narrow. It holds many crystalline, glistening-white stalactites and stalagmites but the most interesting feature, apart from the human skeletons, is simply how far it continues. There are no major side chambers but the main cavern continues on and on: Tuara George's father, George Tuara, reckons that it continues for at least 2km. Although he has been going into the cave for nearly 50 years he has never reached the end, and it's said that no one else ever has either.

Mangaia also has many other caves, and many people who could take you to see them. Each cave is on private land, so arrangements must be made with the appropriate landowner in order to visit. Babe's Place and the Are Moana Hotel (see the Places to Stay section) have guides taking visitors to see different caves and they do an exchange, giving visitors an opportunity to see more than one cave. The tourist office also has information on cave trips.

Mangaia also has several legendary caves as yet undiscovered. One is said to contain the bones of ancient Mangaians of gigantic size. Another, Piriteumeume, is said to be filled with the skeletons of countless Mangaian warriors, each with his weapons laid beside him.

Beaches & Lake

Countless little beaches and bays dot the coastline although nowhere is there the kind of white, sandy beach with good swimming that you can find on some of the other Cook Islands. The reef is very shallow and generally close to the coast. About the only place you can go swimming with water deep enough to go over your head is at the wharf at Avarua Landing near Oneroa. Many locals swim at the wharf, afterwards going across the makatea about 100m to the left (south) to where a small freshwater spring gushes up from the makatea beside the seaside, with refreshing cool water and tiny fish. The spring is too small for swimming but you can sit in the water to wash off the sea salt.

On the south-west side of the island, Tuaati beach is a tiny unmarked beach too shallow for swimming, but you can splash around and it's very attractive. There's also a sandy beach at Karanganui Landing on the north-east side of the island, where again you can get wet but it's too shallow for swimming.

Lake Tiriara is the only lake on the island but it's difficult to distinguish it from the surrounding swamp, where high reeds grow. You may need to ask a local to point the lake out to you. From the road, you can follow a trail until you bump into the high makatea cliff near the lake. Turn to your left, and walk until you reach the lake – a very muddy walk as you get near. A canoe is usually moored at this point, which you can paddle across the lake and into a cave at the far end of the lake.

Organised Tours

Clarke's Tours offers tours to suit anyone's interest, including cave trips, special-interest trips, and beach and inland picnics. A full-day tour of the whole island costs NZ$30 per person. Contact Clarke through Babe's Place (see the Places to Stay section). Island tours and cave trips can also be arranged through the Are Moana Hotel.

Other

Other enjoyable activities on Mangaia include reef walking, reef fishing with a long bamboo pole, torch fishing at night and deep-sea fishing by canoe.

Places to Stay

All the places to stay on Mangaia make some provision for their guests to eat, either cooking meals for you or allowing you to prepare your own. Most accommodation is in Oneroa, the island's principal village.

The *Mangaia Lodge* (☎ 34-206, 34-260) near the hospital in Temakatea, the upper section of Oneroa, has three very large bedrooms in a sprawling old colonial-style home. The nightly cost is NZ$20 per person; you can do your own cooking, or meals can be arranged by request. Group rates are also available.

Babe's Place (☎ 34-092, fax 34-078) in the Kaumata section of Oneroa, beside the sea and near Tuaati beach, has a large and modern three-bedroom house sleeping up to six people, plus four new motel-style units. Singles/doubles/triples are NZ$75/120/150, which includes airport transfers and three meals a day. There's a bar open on Friday and Saturday nights for a dance; this is the only regularly held dance on the island.

In Ivirua, the *Are Moana Hotel* (☎ 34-278, fax 34-279) has several tiny, free-standing, one-room cabins around large grounds near the sea, with a good beach just a short walk away. The nightly cost of NZ$70 per person includes breakfast and dinner, or NZ$75 with all three meals. The owners, Jan & Tu Kristensson, offer many activities including island and cave tours, and reef fishing. They can give you advice about where to go snorkelling, but you'll have to have your own gear.

Back in Oneroa, another option is to stay in a family home with some of Mangaia's friendly locals. In the Temakatea section of Oneroa, near the hospital and overlooking the sea, *Liz & Tuaine Papatua* (☎ 34-164) rent a large bedroom for NZ$35 per person with meals included, or NZ$25 per person if you do your own cooking. Also in Temakatea, *Peiaa & Tutere Teinangaro* (☎ 34-168) rent a bedroom in the family home for NZ$25, and you do your own cooking.

For groups of four or more people, there's also the option of staying at one of Oneroa's community halls. Each has everything you need, including fully equipped kitchen, showers and foam mattresses. The cost is NZ$50 per night for the hall, whatever the size of the group. In Temakatea there's the pleasant *Te A Punavai Hall*; contact Peiaa & Tutere Teinangaro (see above), who live next door. Or there's the *Tikura Community Hall*, beside the sea in the Tava'enga section of Oneroa; contact Mrs Ngatamaine Ruatoi (☎ 34-042).

If all else fails and you are stuck for somewhere to stay, Mangaia's government representative, Atingakau Tangatakino (just call him 'the GR') says you should give him a ring (☎ 34-013, 34-082).

Places to Eat

Check out the *Auraka Restaurant/Bar* (☎ 34-281) in the Temakatea section of Oneroa – it's clean, friendly, and they'll make you anything you like to eat. It has a pleasant ambience, with both indoor and patio tables. A bakery also operates here, and fresh eggs are sold. It's on the back road behind the hospital, about 300m north of the road cutting.

Babe's Place and the *Are Moana Hotel* (see the Places to Stay section) both prepare meals for their guests. Casual diners are also welcome, just ring ahead to tell them you're coming.

Clarke's Tours offers a traditional *umukai* (underground oven feast) for groups of four people or more; the cost of NZ$20 per person includes the opportunity to see how the *umu* (food) is prepared and laid down. Contact Clarke through Babe's Place.

If you're staying long you might want to bring some of your own food with you. There are several trade stores around but their selections are rather limited. Pokino's Store in Oneroa is probably the best-stocked shop on the island but even its selection is limited.

Fresh vegetables are in particularly short supply at certain times of the year. There's a weekly Friday morning market beside the post office in Oneroa where you can get whatever fruits and vegetables might be around.

THE SOUTHERN GROUP

Pupu Eis

Almost everyone on Mangaia makes *pupu eis*, long necklaces of tiny white or yellow shells. The tiny pupu shells from which the eis are made come from tiny black land snails that can only be found after rainfall. Boiling the shells in caustic soda produces the typical yellow colour, but they can also be grilled to make them white, or dyed a variety of colours. They're then individually pierced with a needle and threaded to make the finished ei. It's a time consuming business.

On Rarotonga, pupu eis from Mangaia fetch as much as NZ$90 a dozen, and they are even more expensive elsewhere in the Pacific, but you can get them for around NZ$40 to NZ$50 a dozen on Mangaia. ∎

Entertainment

The only regularly scheduled entertainment on the island is the dance on Friday and Saturday nights at *Babe's Place* – a good chance to mix with the locals.

Things to Buy

Various arts and crafts are practised on Mangaia, and the island now has two small crafts shops. Nana's Gift Hut (☎ 34-254 after 4 pm), operated by Nga Teaio, is in a traditional pandanus hut by the side of the road in the Temakatea section of Oneroa. Handicrafts include hats, purses, bags, fans and mats all made from pandanus, as well as *pupu eis*, shell jewellery and more. Around the island in Ivirua village, Moe Lucre operates the Kirikiri Store & Craft Shop (☎ 34-133).

The people who make the arts and crafts welcome interested visitors stopping by to have a look. All of the following craftspeople live in Oneroa.

Mangaian ceremonial adzes are a well-known Pacific artefact in world museums. Mayor Tuaiva Mautairi (☎ 34-001) makes both the pedestal and hafted types in various sizes, all in the authentic style with intricate carving, basalt heads and sennit binding. He also makes *pate* (a Mangaian style of decoratively carved wooden drums), wooden fruit bowls and various other wood carvings, and calcite-stone taro pounders.

George Tuara makes ceremonial adzes, wooden drums and other carvings, plus model canoes, taro pounders, reef shoes, earrings and coconut bracelets. Glenn & Alex Tuara of Rapeuru Stone Carving (☎ 34-227) make stone taro pounders.

Tako Ruatoe (☎ 34-010) and Teremoana Tutu make household baskets, pandanus mats and long fishing baskets. Teremoana Ruatoe (☎ 34-010) makes *tivaevae*, cushions and pillow cases. Plenty of other women also make tivaevae but they are usually made only for home use.

Getting There & Away

Air Air Rarotonga (☎ 34-888 on Mangaia) flies between Rarotonga and Mangaia four times a week; the 203km flight takes 40 minutes and costs NZ$127 (double for return). If you visit any other southern group islands, a multi-island pass reduces the cost of each flight sector to NZ$96. See the Getting Around chapter for details.

Sea Passenger freighter ships operate from Rarotonga to the other Cook Islands, including Mangaia. See the Getting Around chapter.

Getting Around

Babe's Place (see the Places to Stay section) rents motorbikes for NZ$20 per day; the Are Moana Hotel rents them for NZ$25 or NZ$30 per day. Peiaa & Tutere Teinangaro rent motorbikes for NZ$20 per day, and a pick-up truck (see the Places to Stay section).

Walking is fine, especially the route across the island via Rangimotia, but the distances are quite long and you can't count on getting a ride from a passing vehicle as there is so little traffic. Tony Wheeler tried his luck one day while researching the first edition of this book and walked all the way from Ivirua via Tamarua to Oneroa, several hours' walk, and only saw one truck passing by – the wrong way. The situation still hasn't changed.

The Northern Group

The Northern Group

The northern islands of the Cooks are scattered coral atolls, specks of land in a vast expanse of sea. They are all low-lying and from a ship cannot even be seen from much more than 10km away. Severe hurricanes can send waves right across many of the islands.

Although atolls such as these conjure up the romantic image of a Pacific island – complete with sandy beaches, clear and shallow lagoons, swaying palm trees – in fact, life is hard on an atoll. Fish may be abundant in the lagoon but atoll soil is only marginally fertile and the range of foodstuffs which can be grown is very limited. Fresh water is always a problem. Shallow wells are often the only source of drinking water and the supply is generally limited and often not very pleasant to drink.

In the modern world atoll life has another drawback apart from these natural ones, and that is sheer isolation. Today, people want economic opportunity, education for their children and contact with the outside world.

On a tiny island where the only physical contact is a trading ship coming through a few times a year these things are clearly not available. Returning islanders and radios

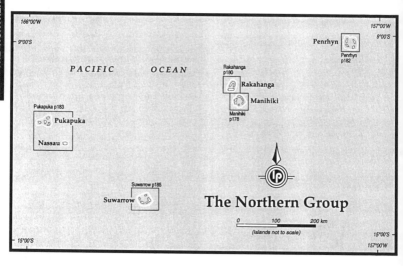

The Northern Group

have whetted appetites for the outside world and consequently many of the northern islands are suffering from a declining population.

Literature

Several of the northern islands have figured prominently in the literature of the Cook Islands, both past and present. See the Books section in the Facts for the Visitor chapter, where many are mentioned.

Getting There & Away

If you want to visit islands of the northern group you can fly to Manihiki, Penrhyn or Pukapuka, though the flights take a long time from Rarotonga (about 3½ to four hours) and are quite expensive. In fact it's only recently that the northern group islands have had regular air service at all – up until the early 1990s the distance to these islands made the cost of flying there prohibitively high. The cost is still high – it costs just as much to fly to the northern group islands from Rarotonga as it does to fly to New Zealand, and can take even longer – but if you do get up there, you'll find these remote islands quite unspoiled.

Rarotonga travel agents caution that flights to the northern group are scheduled for only once a week, but that adverse conditions, such as bad weather, limited fuel supplies and too few bookings, can sometimes cause the flights not to run. They recommend that you take out travel insurance to cover unavoidable delays when you fly to the northern group islands.

Otherwise the only regular way of getting to the northern group islands is on the interisland passenger freighter ships. The ships unload and load at the islands by day so if you're doing a circuit of the islands you can spend a day or two on a number of them. If you want to stay longer you may be stuck with waiting until the next ship comes by, which could be quite a long time. On the islands with airstrips you could always take the boat one way and fly one way. The Getting Around chapter has information on all the air and sea services travelling from Rarotonga to the northern islands.

Although only Manihiki and Penrhyn have guesthouses for visitors, on any of the islands the infrequent visitors are made welcome and some arrangement will always be made. Plan to pay your way, however, both in cash and with food or other supplies. Food supplies are limited on the islands and the arrival of a ship is always a major occasion.

Manihiki

Population: 662
Area: 5.4 sq km

Manihiki is reputed to be one of the most beautiful atolls in the South Pacific. Although Aitutaki is sometimes called 'the Bora Bora of the Cook Islands' and is justly renowned for its beauty, those who have visited Manihiki often come back saying that Aitutaki is only second best.

Nearly 40 islands, some of them little more than tiny *motu*, encircle the 4km-wide and totally enclosed lagoon of Manihiki. The main village is Tauhunu but there is a second village, Tukao. Manihiki has no safe anchorage for visiting ships which consequently stay offshore.

What it does have is pearls and pearl shells, especially the famous Manihiki black pearls which are the economic mainstay of the island and a significant export for the Cook Islands. The abilities of the island's pearl divers are legendary – they can dive effortlessly to great depths and stay submerged for minutes at a time.

Manihiki and Rakahanga were formerly lived on by the same group of people; they migrated between the two islands until the missionaries showed up and changed things.

History

Although some authorities believe the Spanish explorer Pedro Fernandez de Quiros was the first European to come upon

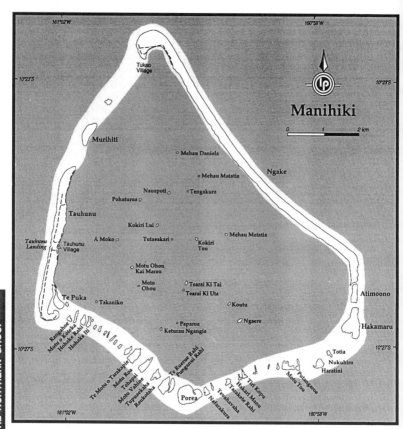

Manihiki, credit is normally given to Captain Patrickson of the US ship *Good Hope* in 1822. He and a successive stream of whalers and traders bestowed a series of names upon the island, none of which stuck.

Christian missionaries came to Manihiki in 1849 after a Manihiki canoe en route to Rakahanga was blown off course, rescued by a whaler and left at Manuae. The missionaries took the canoe passengers back to Manihiki and left two Polynesian missionary teachers at the same time. They also left disease. The ensuing epidemic quickly convinced the islanders that they had not been

behaving themselves and should embrace Christianity.

Manihiki at that time was something of a subsidiary of Rakahanga, 42km away, and the people of Rakahanga commuted to Manihiki as necessary. In 1852 the missionaries convinced the people to divide themselves between the two islands and settle permanently. See the Rakahanga section of this chapter for more about relations between the two islands.

The women of Manihiki were famous for their beauty, a reputation which continues to this day. In the late 19th century, however,

Hurricane Martin Strikes Manihiki
On 1 November 1997, during an especially bad year for El Niño, Manihiki was struck full-on by Hurricane Martin. Winds were severe, and high waves washed right over the island, completely submerging the land. Both of the island's villages were destroyed. Miraculously, considering the extent of the devastation, only 19 lives were lost. When plans were being made for rebuilding the villages, there was talk of rebuilding in safer locations.

As this book was going to press it was still uncertain what changes would be taking place in the rebuilding of Manihiki. You may find Manihiki different from its description in this chapter – even the villages may be in different places. Ask the tourist office and travel agents on Rarotonga for current information. ■

that idea led to raids by Peruvian slavers and a variety of other Pacific ne'er-do-wells. In 1869 'Bully Hates' spirited off a number of islanders, supposedly for a visit to Rakahanga; in reality they ended up as plantation labourers in Fiji.

In 1889, when relations between the British and French in the Pacific were tense, the islanders fell out with their missionaries and invited the French from Tahiti to take over the island. A French warship duly turned up but the missionaries speedily hoisted the Union Jack and the French opted for discretion rather than valour. Later that year the island was officially taken under the British wing.

Literature

Manihikian literary giants are few and far between but one Manihikian author, Kauraka Kauraka, published a number of books; see the Books section of the Facts for the Visitor chapter. Sadly, Kauraka passed away on Rarotonga in 1997; he is sorely missed. His grave is on Manihiki.

Places to Stay

The *Manihiki Guesthouse* (☎/fax 43-307) in Tauhunu village offers accommodation with shared facilities in a modern house with a good kitchen. The cost of NZ$56 per person per night includes all three meals, plus airport transfers. The friendly owners, Bernardino and Jane, offer tours and activities.

Getting There & Away

Air Air Rarotonga flies between Rarotonga and Manihiki once a week. The cost is NZ$475 (double for return) for the 3½-hour flight. Depending on demand, the flights may be routed through Pukapuka (1½ hours away) or Penrhyn (one hour).

Travel agents on Rarotonga offer packages to Manihiki which include air fare, accommodation, meals and airport transfers; these may work out cheaper than buying the flights and accommodation separately, especially when purchased at least seven days in advance of travel. It pays to phone around and compare offers.

Sea See the Getting Around chapter for details on sea travel to Manihiki.

Lost en Route
Although missionaries tried as early as 1852 to put an end to voyaging across the 42km between Rakahanga and Manihiki, people continue to shuttle back and forth, sometimes with harrowing results. In June 1953, for example, nine islanders set out at night to sail from Manihiki to Rakahanga. Come dawn they were lost – a squall had blown them off course and where they were, relative to the two islands, was a mystery. Where they were relative to Pukapuka, 500km downwind, can't have been such a mystery because they decided to sail there. Five days later, in an extraordinary navigational feat, they arrived in Pukapuka.

In 1965 another small boat from Manihiki suffered engine failure midway between the islands and was swept away to the west by the steady 3 to 4-knot current that runs between the islands. Sixty-five days and almost 3500km later the crew landed at Erromango in Vanuatu. The book *The Man who Refused to Die: Techu Makimare's 2000 Mile Drift in an Open Boat Across the South Seas* by Barry Wynne (Souvenir Press, London, 1966) recounts the tale of this extraordinary voyage and the persistence of Techu Makimare, the hero of the crew. ■

Rakahanga

Population: 249
Area: 4.1 sq km

Only 42km north of Manihiki, this rectangular atoll consists of two major islands and a host of smaller motu almost completely enclosing a central lagoon about 4km long and 2km wide at its widest points.

Without the pearl wealth of Manihiki, the island of Rakahanga is conspicuously quieter and less energetic. Copra is the only export product although the islanders grow breadfruit and a taro-like vegetable. The rito hats woven on Rakahanga are particularly fine. The population is concentrated in the village of Nivano on the south-west corner of the atoll.

History

Legends tell of Rakahanga being hauled up from under the sea by three brothers and the island of Manihiki breaking off from the island and drifting away. There are various similar legends including one which tells of the island subsequently being populated entirely by the offspring of one man and his wife, the man taking his four daughters as additional wives.

On 2 March 1606 the commander of the ships *Capitana* and *Almiranta*, Pedro Fernandez de Quiros, who as navigator to Mendana had already discovered Pukapuka 10 years earlier, sighted the island. He reported that the islanders were:

… the most beautiful white and elegant people that were met during the voyage.

Furthermore, he continued, the women were exceptionally beautiful and:

… if properly dressed, would have advantages over our Spanish women.

Such reports were no doubt the genesis for many romantic notions of the South Seas! De Quiros was not the only member of the expe-

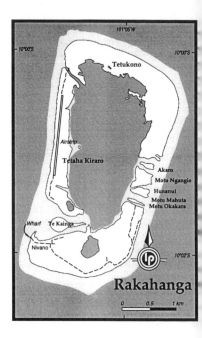

Rakahanga

dition to be impressed. A Franciscan friar accompanying the expedition named the discovery the island of Gente Hermosa, 'beautiful people'. At this time Rakahanga and Manihiki islands were both owned by the people of Rakahanga who used to commute between the two islands.

Over 200 years were to pass before the island was again visited by western ships, first a Russian expedition in 1820 then a series of whalers and trading ships. As usual a number of easily forgotten names were bestowed on the island. In 1849 Polynesian missionaries arrived on Manihiki, although at that time it was still only settled by temporary groups from Rakahanga. The journey between the two islands was often hazardous and often resulted in numerous deaths at sea. In 1852 the missionaries convinced the islanders to divide themselves between the two atolls. Travelling between Manihiki and Rakahanga can still be dangerous.

Getting There & Away

Rakahanga has an airstrip but no regular flights operate to the island. The only way to get to Rakahanga is by boat.

Penrhyn

Population: 600
Area: 9.8 sq km

Penrhyn, often still called by its traditional Maori name, Tongareva, is the northernmost of the Cook Islands and its lagoon is unlike most of the other Cook atolls in that it is very wide and easily accessible. From Omoka, one main village, Te Tautua, the other main village, isn't visible except for its church roof. Not only is the lagoon accessible to ships, it also has plenty of sharks, although most are harmless.

Penrhyn was famous throughout the Pacific at one time for its natural mother-of-pearl which is still found to this day. More recently, Penrhyn has joined Manihiki in the lucrative business of pearl farming. Some interesting shell jewellery is produced on the island, and Penrhyn is also noted for its fine rito hats.

History

Polynesian legends relate that the island was fished up from the depths of the ocean by Vatea, the eldest son of the great mother in Avaiki. He used a fish-hook baited with a star but when that did not work he tore a piece of flesh from his thigh, baited the hook with that and promptly pulled up the island from the deep. He then hung the hook in the sky.

The Maori name Tongareva could translate as something like 'to the south of the great emptiness' – there's a lot of nothing to the north of Penrhyn – or 'Tonga floating in space'. Another Maori name, Mangarongaro, is also sometimes used although some people say it was originally only the name of one of the islands in the atoll. There

is no direct translation but a *mangaro* is a kind of coconut.

Although the local name Tongareva is still widely used the atoll takes its most European name from the British ship *Lady Penrhyn* which dropped by in 1788 on the way back to England from Australia. The ship was one of the 11 which carried the original convict settlers out to Sydney in Australia. After the *Lady Penrhyn* it was 28 years before a visit by the Russian ship *Rurick* in 1816.

The earliest western accounts of Penrhyn all comment on the unusual fierceness and erratic behaviour of the island's inhabitants. The following extract is a typical description from a visit by the US ship *Porpoise* in 1841:

... each and all of them were talking in a language altogether unintelligible and in voices peculiarly harsh and discordant accompanying their words with every unimaginable contortion of the body and with the most diabolical expressions of countenance every muscle being brought into play and made to quiver apparently with rage and excitement, and their eyes fairly starting from their heads. It is utterly impossible for the mind to conceive and altogether out of my power to find words to express or convey any adequate idea of a scene so savage ...

None of these early visitors dared to go ashore and they all tried to keep the inhabitants distinctly at arm's length. Despite this impression, when the American ship *Chatham* ran onto the reef in 1853 they were treated well, to the surprise and relief of the crew and passengers. Some of them were to remain on the island for almost a year before being rescued. EH Lamont, the trader who had chartered the unfortunate vessel, wrote *Wild Life among the Pacific Islanders* about his time on the island. He obviously entered into atoll life wholeheartedly because he married three women while he was there! Dr R in his account was the Dr Longghost of Herman Melville's *Omoo*.

The first missionaries arrived in 1854 and those warlike and terrifying islanders quickly became obedient churchgoers. So obedient that the four Polynesian teachers landed by the missionaries 'sold' their flock to Peruvian slavers in 1862 to 1863. They

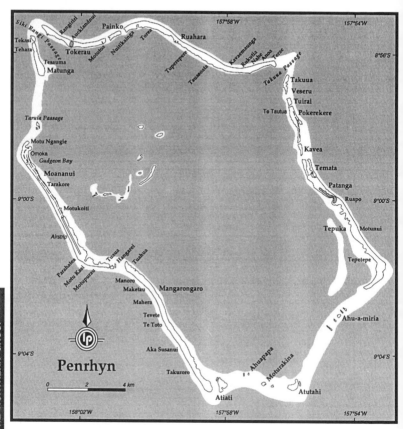

Penrhyn

0   2   4 km

netted $5 a head and went along to South America as overseers for a salary of $100 a month. The island's population was decimated by the activities of the slavers, who dubbed the island 'the island of the four evangelists'. That disastrous slaving foray left Penrhyn with a population of only 88 – down from an estimated 700 before the trade began, with around 470 persons taken to Peru, and another 130 to Tahiti. The population had rebounded to 445 by 1902 but the entire chiefly line disappeared during this period, so today Penrhyn is the only island in the Cooks with no *ariki* (paramount chiefs).

Literature

For an interesting account of the island's history during the 19th century look at *Impressions of Tongareva (Penrhyn Island), 1816-1901,* edited by Andrew Teariki Campbell, available at the USP Centre on Rarotonga.

Places to Stay

Soas Guesthouse (☎ 42-018, fax 42-105) in Omoka village offers basic, clean accommodation with shared facilities. The cost of NZ$61 per person per day includes three meals a day, plus airport transfers. The Tini family who operates the guesthouse will assist with activities.

Getting There & Away

Air Penrhyn has an airstrip near Omoka village as a result of its use as an American airbase during WWII. The remains of the *Go-Gettin' Gal*, a four-engined bomber, still remain there although it's gradually being used up as a source of scrap metal.

The airstrip was disused for many years, but Air Rarotonga now operates weekly flights between Rarotonga and Penrhyn; the cost is NZ$525 for the four-hour trip (double for return). The flights may be direct, or routed through Aitutaki or Manihiki.

Travel agents on Rarotonga offer packages to Manihiki which include air fare, accommodation, meals and airport transfers; these may work out cheaper than buying the flights and accommodation separately, espe-

cially when purchased at least seven days in advance of travel. It pays to phone around and compare offers.

Sea Penrhyn is also served by the interisland shipping services. See the Getting Around chapter for details.

Pukapuka

Population: 780
Area: 1.3 sq km

Shaped like a three-bladed fan, Pukapuka's atoll has an island at each 'blade end' and another in the middle. The northernmost island gives its name to the whole atoll although it is also known, usually in parentheses, as 'Wale'. The only landing place is reached by narrow and difficult passages

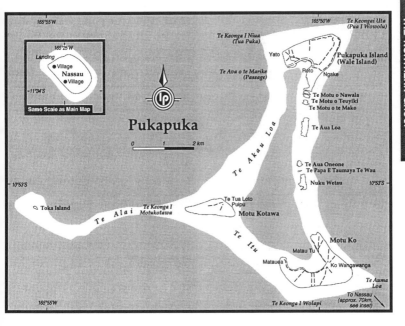

through the reef on the western side of Wale Island.

There are three villages – Ngake, Roto and Yato – all on Wale Island. Copra and smaller quantities of bananas and papayas are grown. The relative proximity to Samoa has resulted in the islanders' customs and language relating more closely to Samoa than to the rest of the Cooks. There is a notably decorated Catholic church on the island and excellent swimming and snorkelling, particularly off the central island of Kotawa. Pukapuka is noted for its finely woven mats.

History

Early legends relate tales of the island rising from the deep with men inside it and of great voyages. Another tale tells of a great tidal wave about 400 years ago which left only two women and 15 men alive on the island; with considerable effort (on the women's part!) they managed to repopulate it. There may be some truth to this tale as the islanders recall that it was during the rule of the fourth chief after the great disaster that the first western visitors arrived.

That first western visitor was the Spanish explorer Alvaro de Mendana who, with his navigator Pedro Fernandez de Quiros, sailed from Peru in 1595 and later that year discovered an island which he named San Bernardo. Although they did not attempt to land nor did they see signs of life, it is generally accepted that the island they sighted was Pukapuka. Over 150 years later in 1765 the British ships *Dolphin* and *Tamar* again sighted the island and again decided against attempting a landing due to the high surf. They named the atoll the Islands of Danger and Pukapuka is still sometimes referred to as Danger Island.

Further sightings and namings continued and finally in 1857 Polynesian missionaries were landed, followed in 1862 by a visit by the pioneer missionary William Wyatt Gill. A year later the population of the island was decimated by slave raids from Peru. In 1865 the London Missionary Society (LMS) ship *John Williams* which had spent so much time

in this region was wrecked on Pukapuka's reef.

During the 20th century, South Seas character Robert Dean Frisbie lived for some time on the island and wrote *The Book of Puka-Puka* and *The Island of Desire*. His daughter Johnny Frisbie also wrote of the island in *Miss Ulysses from Puka-Puka*. Modern maps of Pukapuka are still based on Robert Dean Frisbie's 1925 survey.

Getting There & Away

Air Air travel to Pukapuka has been initiated only very recently. The island's airstrip was officially opened in early 1994, and Air Rarotonga began operating flights to the island via Manihiki. The cost between Rarotonga and Pukapuka, about a five-hour flight including a stop at Manihiki, is NZ$525 (double for return); between Pukapuka and Manihiki it's a 1½ hour flight (NZ$159). Check with Air Rarotonga to see if flights to Pukapuka are still operating, before you make plans.

Sea Pukapuka is served by the passenger freighter ships coming from Rarotonga; see the Getting Around chapter for details. Since the island is closer to Samoa than to Rarotonga, some boat traffic also goes back and forth between Pukapuka and Samoa.

Nassau

Population: 99
Area: 1.3 sq km

The tiny island of Nassau was named after an American whaling ship. There's no atoll, just a fringing reef around a tiny, 500m-long sand cay. There is a coconut plantation and taro is grown in the centre of the island.

History

Lying 88km south-east of Pukapuka, the island was effectively the property of the Pukapukans. It was probably first discovered by Europeans in 1803 and each successive visitor gave it a new name, usually that of their ship. For some reason, however, it was the American whaler *Nassau's* visit, comparatively late in 1835, which gave the island its present name.

The island did not have a permanent population although occasional groups from other islands stopped for longer or shorter periods.

An American attempted to grow coconuts and other plants from 1876 and in later years a number of European-owned copra plantations were established. In 1945 these were sold to the colonial government for £2000. Six years later they were sold to the chiefs of Pukapuka for the same figure. Their temporary work groups have become a virtually permanent population.

Getting There & Away

The only way to get to Nassau is by the infrequent shipping services.

Suwarrow

Population: 4
Area: 0.4 sq km

The atoll of Suwarrow is one of the best known in the whole Cook Islands due to a prolonged visit by one man. Between 1952 and his death in 1977, New Zealander Tom Neale lived on the island for extended periods as a virtual hermit and his book *An Island to Oneself* became a South Seas classic. If you want to know all about how to live on an atoll, this book is a must.

Although Tom Neale is long gone – he is buried in the cemetery opposite Rarotonga's airport – his memory lives on and yachties often call in to the atoll. It's one of the few atolls in the northern Cooks with an accessible lagoon. Tom's room is still furnished just as it was when he lived there. Visiting yachts

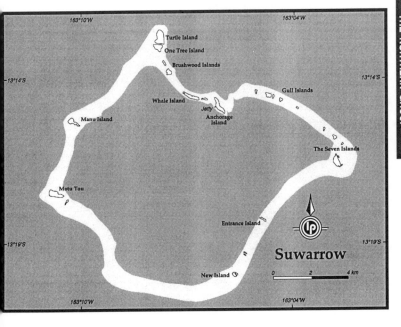

fill in a logbook left in the room. Pearl divers from Manihiki also visit occasionally.

Tom Neale wasn't the only writer to live on, and write about, Suwarrow. American-born Robert Dean Frisbie survived a terrible hurricane in 1942 and wrote of it in *Island of Desire*. His daughter Johnny Frisbie also wrote about the same hurricane in *The Frisbies of the South Seas*. Although the lagoon is large, the scattered islands of Suwarrow are all very small and low-lying. Hurricanes have brought waves which wash right across even the highest of the islands and in 1942 the Frisbie group only survived by tying themselves to a tree.

Today the island is populated only by a caretaker and his family. There has been talk of establishing pearl farming in Suwarrow's lagoon, as on Manihiki and Penrhyn. Suwarrow, Manihiki and Penrhyn are the only islands in the Cooks where the pearl oysters grow naturally.

History

Suwarrow's curious name is neither English nor Polynesian. It was named by the Russian explorer Mikhail Lazarev in 1814 after his ship *Suvarov*. Nor has it always been uninhabited. There was an unsuccessful attempt to produce pearl shell here in the early part of the 20th century, and in the 1920s and 1930s copra was produced until a devastating termite infestation halted production. Coastwatchers from New Zealand kept an eye on Japanese activity from Suwarrow during WWII and the remains of their buildings can still be seen on Anchorage Island.

There were earlier visitors. In the mid-19th century the American whaler *Gem* was wrecked on the reef. A ship came from Tahiti to salvage the whaler's oil cargo and one of the visiting ship's officers dug up a box containing $15,000. Where this cache came from has never been satisfactorily explained, although the coins were thought to date from the mid-1700s and may have been connected with the first British Pacific expedition under Commodore George Anson in 1742. In 1876 another visitor found Spanish coins dating from the 1600s.

In 1860 the atoll was the scene of a dramatic and tragic dispute. First, a group of eight people, one of them an Englishman, drifted to Suwarrow after an abortive Manihiki-Rakahanga voyage. Later, a group of Penrhyn pearl divers with a European boss turned up and later still another European visitor was left on the atoll. Shortly after the arrival of the third European an argument broke out between the pearl divers and their leader and all three Europeans were murdered.

In the mid-1870s more evidence of an early European visit was discovered when signs of habitation, various artefacts and skeletons were unearthed. Were they left by shipwrecked Spaniards? Or were they the remains of the English crew lost on a cutter from the ship *Pandora*, sent to the Pacific in 1791 to search for the mutineers of the *Bounty*?

Getting There & Away

Sea The only way to get to Suwarrow is on the extremely infrequent shipping services or by private yacht.

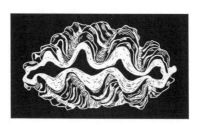

Glossary

adze – axe-like hand tool with ceremonial importance in the Cook Islands

Ara Metua – ancient Polynesian road around the circumference of Rarotonga, inland from the newer coast road

Ara Tapu – coast road around Rarotonga

ariki – paramount chief; traditional head of a tribe, the same as a king or queen

Atua – God; the Christian God

Avaiki – legendary Polynesian ancestral homeland. No-one today knows precisely where Avaiki was, but many Polynesian islanders and New Zealand Maori, say their ancestors originated from Avaiki (spelled variously throughout Polynesia). The spirits of the dead are believed to return home to Avaiki after death

bush beer – locally produced moonshine beer brewed from oranges, bananas, pawpaws or hops; also called 'home brew'

bush beer school – communal drinking session where bush beer is consumed; also called a *tumunu*

CICC – Cook Island Christian Church, the Protestant church which continues from the original London Missionary Society churches

copra – coconut 'meat' from which coconut oil is produced, an important product throughout the Pacific. The problem with copra is the price is very volatile – it has reached as high as US$450 a tonne but currently is much, much lower

ei – necklace

ei kaki – flower *ei* draped around the neck like a necklace; traditionally given to anyone arriving or departing on a journey

ei katu – flower tiara

ekalesia – church

eke – octopus

enua – land

House of Ariki – assembly of all the Cook Islands ariki; this is the 'upper house' of government, but it has only advisory, not legislative powers

ika – fish

kai – food

kaikai – feast

kakerori – the Rarotonga flycatcher, a rare bird endemic to Rarotonga

kikau – palm leaves, woven or thatched; a kikau hut is a traditional thatch-roofed hut

kopeka – a cave-dwelling swiftlet from Atiu

koutu – ancient Polynesian open-air royal courtyard, used for gatherings and political functions

Koutu Nui – assembly of all the *mataiapo* and *rangatira*

LDS – Church of Jesus Christ of the Latter-Day Saints (Mormons)

LMS – London Missionary Society, the original missionary force in the Cook Islands and in many other regions of the Pacific

maire – an aromatic leaf; maire *eis* are made on the island of Mauke for export to Hawaii

mataiapo – head of a sub-tribe, a rank down from an *ariki*

makatea – raised coral reef which forms a coastal plain around several islands of the southern group including Mangaia, Atiu, Mauke and Mitiaro

mana – spiritual power or influence

Maori – the Polynesian people of the Cook Islands and also of New Zealand, also the language of these people; literally means 'indigenous' or 'local'

marae – ancient open-air family or tribal religious meeting ground, marked by stones

maroro – flying fish

matu rori – sea cucumbers, bêches-de-mer

maunga – mountain

moana – sea; ocean

motu – lagoon islet

ngati – clan

pandanus – type of leaf used for thatching the roofs of traditional houses and for mats, baskets, bags and *rito* hats

papa'a – Europeans and other foreigners; also, the English language

pareu – wrap-around sarong-type garment

pate – carved wooden slit drum

pupu – tiny shells used to make necklaces

rangatira – landed gentry; lowest rank of Cook Islands royal hierarchy, below *mataiapo* which is below *ariki*

ra'ui – a traditional method of conservation used in the Cook Islands. A ra'ui is called by the traditional leaders for the purpose of conservation of a particular area or resource; during a period of ra'ui nothing can be taken from the designated ra'ui area.

rito – bleached pandanus or bleached, young palm leaves, used to make a variety of woven handicrafts including hats, fans and handbags

SDA – Seventh-Day Adventist church, another popular Protestant church in the Cooks

Tangaroa – in traditional Polynesian religion, Tangaroa was the god of the sea and fertility; his well-endowed figure appears on the Cook Islands' one dollar coin and is a symbol of the Cook Islands

tapere – district subdivision

tapu – holy; sacred

taunga – expert

tiare – flower

tiare Maori – gardenia

tiki – symbolic human figure

tivaevae – colourful, intricately sewn appliqué works traditionally made as burial shrouds but also used as bedspreads, with smaller versions used as furniture covers, cushion covers and pillowcases

tivaivai – alternate spelling for *tivaevae* used on the island of Atiu

tumunu – hollowed-out stump of a coconut tree used to brew bush beer; also refers to bush beer drinking sessions

umu – traditional Polynesian underground oven

umukai – traditional Polynesian food (*kai*) cooked in an underground oven (*umu*); also a feast of foods cooked in an umu

vaka – canoe

Index

Abbreviations

Maps

Text

LONELY PLANET PHRASEBOOKS

Building bridges,
Breaking barriers,
Beyond babble-on

Listen for the gems

Speak your own words

Ask your own
questions

Master of
your
own
image

- handy pocket-sized books
- easy to understand Pronunciation chapter
- clear and comprehensive Grammar chapter
- romanisation alongside script to allow ease of pronunciation
- script throughout so users can point to phrases
- extensive vocabulary sections, words and phrases for every situation
- full of cultural information and tips for the traveller

'...vital for a real DIY spirit and attitude in language learning' – Backpacker

'the phrasebooks have good cultural backgrounders and offer solid advice for challenging situations in remo locations' – San Francisco Examiner

'...they are unbeatable for their coverage of the world's more obscure languages' – The Geographical Magazine

Arabic (Egyptian)
Arabic (Moroccan)
Australia
  Australian English, Aboriginal and Torres Strait languages
Baltic States
  Estonian, Latvian, Lithuanian
Bengali
Brazilian
Burmese
Cantonese
Central Asia
Central Europe
  Czech, French, German, Hungarian, Italian and Slovak
Eastern Europe
  Bulgarian, Czech, Hungarian, Polish, Romanian and Slovak
Ethiopian (Amharic)
Fijian
French
German
Greek

Hindi/Urdu
Indonesian
Italian
Japanese
Korean
Lao
Latin American Spanish
Malay
Mandarin
Mediterranean Europe
  Albanian, Croatian, Greek, Italian, Macedonian, Maltese, Serbian and Slovene
Mongolian
Nepali
Papua New Guinea
Pilipino (Tagalog)
Quechua
Russian
Scandinavian Europe
  Danish, Finnish, Icelandic, Norwegian and Swedish

South-East Asia
  Burmese, Indonesian, Khmer, La Malay, Tagalog (Pilipino), Thai ar Vietnamese
Spanish (Castilian)
  Basque, Catalan and Galician
Sri Lanka
Swahili
Thai
Thai Hill Tribes
Tibetan
Turkish
Ukrainian
USA
  US English, Vernacular, Native American languages ar Hawaiian
Vietnamese
Western Europe
  Basque, Catalan, Dutch, French, Ge man, Irish, Italian, Portugues Scottish Gaelic, Spanish (Castilia and Welsh

LONELY PLANET JOURNEYS

JURNEYS is a unique collection of travel writing – published by the company that understands travel better than anyone else. It is a series for anyone who has ever experienced – or dreamed of – the magical moment when they encountered a strange culture or saw a place for the first time. They are tales to read while you're planning a trip, while you're on the road or while you're in an armchair, in front of a fire.

JURNEYS books catch the spirit of a place, illuminate a culture, recount a crazy adventure, or introduce a fascinating way of life. They always entertain, and always enrich the experience of travel.

ISLANDS IN THE CLOUDS
Travels in the Highlands of New Guinea
Isabella Tree

Isabella Tree's remarkable journey takes us to the heart of the remote and beautiful Highlands of Papua New Guinea and Irian Jaya – one of the most extraordinary and dangerous regions on earth. Funny and tragic by turns, *Islands in the Clouds* is her moving story of the Highland people and the changes transforming their world.

Isabella Tree, who lives in England, has worked as a freelance journalist on a variety of newspapers and magazines, including a stint as senior travel correspondent for the *Evening Standard*. A fellow of the Royal Geographical Society, she has also written a biography of the Victorian ornithologist John Gould.

'One of the most accomplished travel writers to appear on the horizon for many years . . . the dialogue is brilliant' – Eric Newby

---

SEAN & DAVID'S LONG DRIVE
Sean Condon

Sean Condon is young, urban and a connoisseur of hair wax. He can't drive, and he doesn't really travel well. So when Sean and his friend David set out to explore Australia in a 1966 Ford Falcon, the result is a decidedly offbeat look at life on the road. Over 14,000 death-defying kilometres, our heroes check out the re-runs on tv, get fabulously drunk, listen to Neil Young cassettes and wonder why they ever left home.

Sean Condon lives in Melbourne. He played drums in several mediocre bands until he found his way into advertising and an above-average band called Boilersuit. *Sean & David's Long Drive* is his first book.

'Funny, pithy, kitsch and surreal . . . This book will do for Australia what Chernobyl did for Kiev, but hey you'll laugh as the stereotypes go boom'
– Time Out

LONELY PLANET TRAVEL ATLASES

Lonely Planet has long been famous for the number and quality of its guidebook maps. Now we've gone one step further and in conjunction with Steinhart Katzir Publishers produced a handy companion series: Lonely Planet travel atlases – maps of a country produced in book form.

Unlike other maps, which look good but lead travellers astray, our travel atlases have been researched on the road by Lonely Planet's experienced team of writers. All details are carefully checked to ensure the atlas corresponds with the equivalent Lonely Planet guidebook.

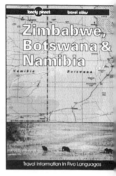

The handy atlas format means no holes, wrinkles, torn sections or constant folding and unfolding. These atlases can survive long periods on the road, unlike cumbersome fold-out maps. The comprehensive index ensures easy reference.

- full-colour throughout
- maps researched and checked by Lonely Planet authors
- place names correspond with Lonely Planet guidebooks
  – no confusing spelling differences
- legend and travelling information in English, French, German, Japanese and Spanish
- size: 230 x 160 mm

Available now:
Chile & Easter Island • Egypt • India & Bangladesh • Israel & the Palestinian Territories •Jordan, Syria & Lebanon • Kenya • Laos • Portugal • South Africa, Lesotho & Swaziland • Thailand • Turkey • Vietnam • Zimbabwe, Botswana & Namibia

---

LONELY PLANET TV SERIES & VIDEOS

Lonely Planet travel guides have been brought to life on television screens around the world. Like our guides, the programmes are based on the joy of independent travel, and look honestly at some of the most exciting, picturesque and frustrating places in the world. Each show is presented by one of three travellers from Australia, England or the USA and combines an innovative mixture of video, Super-8 film, atmospheric soundscapes and original music.

Videos of each episode – containing additional footage not shown on television – are available from good book and video shops, but the availability of individual videos varies with regional screening schedules.

Video destinations include: Alaska • American Rockies • Australia – The South-East • Baja California & the Copper Canyon • Brazil • Central Asia • Chile & Easter Island • Corsica, Sicily & Sardinia – The Mediterranean Islands • East Africa (Tanzania & Zanzibar) • Ecuador & the Galapagos Islands • Greenland & Iceland • Indonesia • Israel & the Sinai Desert • Jamaica • Japan • La Ruta Maya • Morocco • New York • North India • Pacific Islands (Fiji, Solomon Islands & Vanuatu) • South India • South West China • Turkey • Vietnam • West Africa • Zimbabwe, Botswana & Namibia

The Lonely Planet TV series is produced by:
Pilot Productions
The Old Studio
18 Middle Row
London W10 5AT UK

For video availability and ordering information contact your nearest Lonely Planet office.

Music from the TV series is available on CD & cassette.

PLANET TALK

Lonely Planet's FREE quarterly newsletter

e love hearing from you and think you'd like to hear from us.

*hen...*is the right time to see reindeer in Finland?
*here...*can you hear the best palm-wine music in Ghana?
*ow...*do you get from Asunción to Areguá by steam train?
*hat...*is the best way to see India?

or the answer to these and many other questions read PLANET TALK.

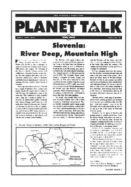

very issue is packed with up-to-date travel news and advice including:

a letter from Lonely Planet co-founders Tony and Maureen Wheeler
go behind the scenes on the road with a Lonely Planet author
feature article on an important and topical travel issue
a selection of recent letters from travellers
details on forthcoming Lonely Planet promotions
complete list of Lonely Planet products

join our mailing list contact any Lonely Planet office.

so available: Lonely Planet T-shirts. 100% heavyweight cotton.

LONELY PLANET ONLINE

Get the latest travel information before you leave or while you're on the road

hether you've just begun planning your next trip, or you're chasing down
ecific info on currency regulations or visa requirements, check out Lonely
anet Online for up-to-the minute travel information.

s well as travel profiles of your favourite destinations (including maps and
otos), you'll find current reports from our researchers and other travellers,
dates on health and visas, travel advisories, and discussion of the
ological and political issues you need to be aware of as you travel.

ere's also an online travellers' forum where you can share your experience
life on the road, meet travel companions and ask other travellers for their
commendations and advice. We also have plenty of links to other online
es useful to independent travellers.

d of course we have a complete and up-to-date list of all Lonely Planet
vel products including guides, phrasebooks, atlases, Journeys and videos
d a simple online ordering facility if you can't find the book you want
sewhere.

www.lonelyplanet.com
or
AOL keyword: lp

LONELY PLANET PRODUCTS

Lonely Planet is known worldwide for publishing practical, reliable and no-nonsense tra information in our guides and on our web site. The Lonely Planet list covers just about eve accessible part of the world. Currently there are nine series: *travel guides, shoestring guid walking guides, city guides, phrasebooks, audio packs, travel atlases, Journeys – a uniq collection of travel writing and Pisces Books - diving and snorkeling guides.*

EUROPE

Amsterdam • Austria • Baltic States phrasebook • Britain • Central Europe on a shoestring • Central Europe phrasebo Czech & Slovak Republics • Denmark • Dublin • Eastern Europe on a shoestring • Eastern Europe phrasebook • Esto Latvia & Lithuania • Finland • France • French phrasebook • Germany • German phrasebook • Greece • Greek phraseb • Hungary • Iceland, Greenland & the Faroe Islands • Ireland • Italian phrasebook • Italy • Lisbon • London• Mediterran Europe on a shoestring • Mediterranean Europe phrasebook • Paris • Poland • Portugal • Portugal travel atlas • Prag Romania & Moldova • Russia, Ukraine & Belarus • Russian phrasebook • Scandinavian & Baltic Europe on a shoestrin Scandinavian Europe phrasebook • Slovenia • Spain • Spanish phrasebook • St Petersburg • Switzerland •Trekking in Sp • Ukrainian phrasebook • Vienna • Walking in Britain • Walking in Switzerland • Western Europe on a shoestring • West Europe phrasebook

Travel Literature: The Olive Grove: Travels in Greece

NORTH AMERICA

Alaska • Backpacking in Alaska • Baja California • California & Nevada • Canada • Deep South• Florida • Hawaii • Honolulu • Los Angeles • Mexico • Miami • New England • New Orleans • New York City • New York, New Jersey & Pennsylvania • Pacific Northwest USA• Rocky Mountain States • San Francisco • Southwest USA • USA phrasebook • Washington, DC & the Capital Region

CENTRAL AMERICA & THE CARIBBEAN

• Bahamas and Turks & Caicos • Bermuda • Central America on a shoestring • Costa Rica • Cuba •Eastern Caribbean •Guatemala, Belize & Yucatán: La Ruta Maya • Jamaica

SOUTH AMERICA

Argentina, Uruguay & Paraguay • Bolivia • Brazil • Brazilian phrasebook • Buenos Aires • Chile & Easter Island • Chile & Easter Island travel atlas • Colombia Ecuador & the Galápagos Islands • Latin American Spanish phrasebook • Peru • Quechua phrasebook • Rio de Janeiro • South America on a shoestring • Trekking in the Patagonian Andes • Venezuela

Travel Literature: Full Circle: A South American Journey

ISLANDS OF THE INDIAN OCEAN

Madagascar & Comoros • Maldives• Mauritius, Réunion & Seychelles

AFRICA

Africa - the South • Africa on a shoestring • Arabic (Mor can) phrasebook • Cape Town • Central Africa • E Africa • Egypt • Egypt travel atlas• Ethiopian (Amha phrasebook • Kenya • Kenya travel atlas • Mala Mozambique & Zambia • Morocco • North Africa • So Africa, Lesotho & Swaziland • South Africa, Lesoth Swaziland travel atlas • Swahili phrasebook • Trekkin East Africa • West Africa • Zimbabwe, Botswana Namibia • Zimbabwe, Botswana & Namibia travel atla

Travel Literature: The Rainbird: A Central African Jo ney • Songs to an African Sunset: A Zimbabwean Story

MAIL ORDER

nely Planet products are distributed worldwide. They are also available by mail order from Lonely anet, so if you have difficulty finding a title please write to us. North American and South American sidents should write to Embarcadero West, 155 Filbert St, Suite 251, Oakland CA 94607, USA; ropean and African residents should write to 10a Spring Place, London NW5 3BH; and residents of er countries to PO Box 617, Hawthorn, Victoria 3122, Australia.

RTH-EAST ASIA

ijing • Cantonese phrasebook • China • Hong Kong • ng Kong, Macau & Guangzhou • Japan • Japanese rasebook • Japanese audio pack • Korea • Korean rasebook • Mandarin phrasebook • Mongolia • Mon-ian phrasebook • North-East Asia on a shoestring • oul • Taiwan • Tibet • Tibet phrasebook • Tokyo

avel Literature: Lost Japan

DDLE EAST & CENTRAL ASIA

ab Gulf States • Arabic (Egyptian) phrasebook • Central a • Central Asia phrasebook • Iran • Israel & the estinian Territories • Israel & the Palestinian Territories vel atlas • Istanbul • Jerusalem • Jordan & Syria • dan, Syria & Lebanon travel atlas • Lebanon • Middle st • Turkey • Turkish phrasebook • Turkey travel atlas • nen

vel Literature: The Gates of Damascus • Kingdom of Film Stars: Journey into Jordan

SO AVAILABLE:

vel with Children • Traveller's Tales

INDIAN SUBCONTINENT

Bangladesh • Bengali phrasebook • Delhi • Goa • Hindi/Urdu phrasebook • India • India & Bangladesh travel atlas • Indian Himalaya • Karakoram Highway • Nepal • Nepali phrasebook • Pakistan • Rajasthan • Sri Lanka • Sri Lanka phrasebook • Trekking in the Indian Himalaya • Trekking in the Karakoram & Hindukush • Trekking in the Nepal Himalaya

Travel Literature: In Rajasthan • Shopping for Buddhas

SOUTH-EAST ASIA

Bali & Lombok • Bangkok • Burmese phrasebook • Cambodia • Ho Chi Minh City • Indonesia • Indonesian phrasebook • Indonesian audio pack • Jakarta • Java • Laos • Lao phrasebook • Laos travel atlas • Malay phrasebook • Malaysia, Singapore & Brunei • Myanmar (Burma) • Philippines • Pilipino phrasebook • Singapore • South-East Asia on a shoestring • South-East Asia phrasebook • Thailand • Thailand's Islands & Beaches • Thailand travel atlas • Thai phrasebook • Thai audio pack • Thai Hill Tribes phrasebook • Vietnam • Vietnamese phrasebook • Vietnam travel atlas

AUSTRALIA & THE PACIFIC

Australia • Australian phrasebook • Bushwalking in Australia • Bushwalking in Papua New Guinea • Fiji • Fijian phrasebook • Islands of Australia's Great Barrier Reef • Melbourne • Micronesia • New Caledonia • New South Wales • New Zealand • Northern Territory • Outback Australia • Papua New Guinea • Papua New Guinea phrasebook • Queensland • Rarotonga & the Cook Islands • Samoa • Solomon Islands • South Australia • Sydney • Tahiti & French Polynesia • Tasmania • Tonga • Tramping in New Zealand • Vanuatu • Victoria • Western Australia

Travel Literature: Islands in the Clouds • Sean & David's Long Drive

ANTARCTICA

Antarctica

THE LONELY PLANET STORY

Lonely Planet published its first book in 1973 in response to the numerous 'How did you do it?' questions Maureen an Tony Wheeler were asked after driving, bussing, hitching, sailing and railing their way from England to Australia.

Written at a kitchen table and hand collated, trimmed and stapled, *Across Asia on the Cheap* became an instant loc bestseller, inspiring thoughts of another book.

Eighteen months in South-East Asia resulted in their second guide, *South-East Asia on a shoestring*, which they put togeth in a backstreet Chinese hotel in Singapore in 1975. The 'yellow bible', as it quickly became known to backpackers arou the world, soon became *the* guide to the region. It has sold well over half a million copies and is now in its 9th edition, s retaining its familiar yellow cover.

Today there are over 240 titles, including travel guides, walking guides, language kits & phrasebooks, travel atlases and tra literature. The company is the largest independent travel publisher in the world. Although Lonely Planet initially specialised guides to Asia, today there are few corners of the globe that have not been covered.

The emphasis continues to be on travel for independent travellers. Tony and Maureen still travel for several months of ea year and play an active part in the writing, updating and quality control of Lonely Planet's guides.

They have been joined by over 70 authors and 170 staff at our offices in Melbourne (Australia), Oakland (USA), Lond (UK) and Paris (France). Travellers themselves also make a valuable contribution to the guides through the feedback v receive in thousands of letters each year and on our web site.

The people at Lonely Planet strongly believe that travellers can make a positive contribution to the countries they visit, bc through their appreciation of the countries' culture, wildlife and natural features, and through the money they spend. addition, the company makes a direct contribution to the countries and regions it covers. Since 1986 a percentage of t income from each book has been donated to ventures such as famine relief in Africa; aid projects in India; agricultu projects in Central America; Greenpeace's efforts to halt French nuclear testing in the Pacific; and Amnesty Internationa

'I hope we send people out with the right attitude about travel. You realise when you travel that there are so ma different perspectives about the world, so we hope these books will make people more interested in what they se Guidebooks can't really guide people. All you can do is point them in the right direction.'

– Tony Whee

LONELY PLANET PUBLICATIONS

Australia
PO Box 617, Hawthorn 3122, Victoria
tel: (03) 9819 1877 fax: (03) 9819 6459
e-mail: talk2us@lonelyplanet.com.au

USA
Embarcadero West, 155 Filbert St, Suite 251,
Oakland, CA 94607
tel: (510) 893 8555 TOLL FREE: 800 275-8555
fax: (510) 893 8563
e-mail: info@lonelyplanet.com

UK
10a Spring Place,
London NW5 3BH
tel: (0171) 428 4800 fax: (0171) 428 4828
e-mail: go@lonelyplanet.co.uk

France:
71 bis rue du Cardinal Lemoine, 75005 Paris
tel: 1 44 32 06 20 fax: 1 46 34 72 55
e-mail: bip@lonelyplanet.fr

**World Wide Web: http://www.lonelyplanet.com
or *AOL keyword: lp***